Better Homes and Gardens®

CHRISTMAS COOKING
FROM THE HEART™

Gather Family & Friends

Elizabeth M. Burd
2013

Meredith® Consumer Marketing
Des Moines, Iowa

CHRISTMAS COOKING FROM THE HEART™

MEREDITH CORPORATION CONSUMER MARKETING
Vice President, Consumer Marketing: Janet Donnelly
Consumer Product Marketing Director: Heather Sorensen
Business Director: Ron Clingman
Consumer Marketing Product Manager: Janece Schwartzkopf
Senior Production Manager: Al Rodruck

WATERBURY PUBLICATIONS, INC.
Editorial Director: Lisa Kingsley
Creative Director: Ken Carlson
Associate Editor: Tricia Bergman
Associate Design Director: Doug Samuelson
Graphic Designer: Mindy Samuelson
Contributing Copy Editor: Terri Fredrickson
Contributing Proofreader: Gretchen Kauffman
Contributing Indexer: Elizabeth T. Parson

BETTER HOMES AND GARDENS® MAGAZINE
Editor in Chief: Gayle Goodson Butler
Art Director: Michael D. Belknap
Deputy Editor, Food and Entertaining: Nancy Wall Hopkins
Senior Food Editor: Richard Swearinger
Associate Food Editor: Erin Simpson
Editorial Assistant: Renee Irey

MEREDITH PUBLISHING GROUP
President: Tom Hardy

MEREDITH CORPORATION
President and Chief Executive Officer: Stephen M. Lacy

In Memoriam: E.T. Meredith III (1933–2003)

Test Kitchen

Our seal assures you that every recipe in *Christmas Cooking from the Heart*™ has been tested in the Better Homes and Gardens® Test Kitchen. This means that each recipe is practical and reliable, and meets our high standards of taste appeal. We guarantee your satisfaction with this book for as long as you own it.

All of us at Meredith® Consumer Marketing are dedicated to providing you with information and ideas to enhance your home. We welcome your comments and suggestions. Write to us at: Meredith Consumer Marketing, 1716 Locust St., Des Moines, IA 50309-3023. *Christmas Cooking from the Heart* is available by mail. To order editions from past years, call 800/627-5490.

Cover Photography:
Front cover: Dulce de Leche Cake (76), Cinna-Crunch Fudge (114), White Fruitcake Fudge (114), Chocolate Hazelnut Caramel Thumbprint Cookies (99), Pistachio-Cinnamon Brittle (120), Chocolate-Mint Checkerboard Cookies (102), Pistachio-Vanilla Bean Cookies (105), Peppermint Sandwich Crèmes (106), Raspberry-Almond Palmiers (105)

table of contents

WHITE CHOCOLATE AND
CRÈME DE MENTHE
SHORTBREAD, PAGE 95

BLACK-AND-WHITE
PRETZELS

gather family & friends

TRUE CELEBRATION ALWAYS SEEMS TO involve wonderful food that draws friends and family around the table to enjoy one another's company and the familiar dishes and flavors that make the holiday season so special. *Christmas Cooking from the Heart* is full of fresh takes on traditional foods for celebrating every special occasion from Thanksgiving through New Year's. Each year, the culinary experts in the Better Homes and Gardens® Test Kitchen come up with new ways to enjoy favorite holiday foods so you can plan an intimate Christmas Eve soup supper with the immediate family, serve a fabulous brunch for holiday house guests, or bake a batch of cookies for coworkers. The recipes you need to create a memorable holiday season are in this book, including helpful tips for planning, preparing, and serving meals during the busiest days of the year. Enjoying the season with family and friends is the greatest gift you can give yourself—and to those you love. Happy holidays!

BAKED HAM WITH
SAUTEED PEARS AND
APPLES

gather together

BETTER SHARED This is the main event—the holiday feast everyone looks forward to all year. Whether it's a cozy gathering for close family or a big party attended by a hungry crowd, you'll find in these pages the perfect appetizer (or two), main course, side dishes, and dessert for holiday occasions of every kind.

11

18

25

Honey-Glazed Pork Roast

Smoked paprika infuses this oven-roasted pork with an outdoorsy, barbecued flavor.

PREP **25 minutes**
ROAST **1 hour 10 minutes**
STAND **10 minutes** OVEN **350°F**
MAKES **8 servings**

2   to 3 teaspoons smoked paprika or paprika
2   teaspoons coarse kosher salt
1   3- to 5-pound bone-in pork roast, ribs removed and tied back on
    Fresh oregano sprigs
3   red and/or yellow sweet peppers, stemmed, seeded, and quartered
1   green pepper, stemmed, seeded, and quartered
1   tablespoon olive oil
    Salt and black pepper
⅓   cup honey
¼   cup lime juice
    Fresh oregano and/or thyme sprigs

1. Preheat oven to 350°F. In a small bowl combine paprika and coarse salt.
2. Place pork on a rack in a shallow roasting pan, bone side down. Rub paprika mixture all over pork, pressing in lightly. Add sprigs of fresh oregano and tie with kitchen string. Roast, uncovered, in the preheated oven for 20 to 30 minutes per pound (1 hour 10 minutes to 2 hours). When roast reaches 145°F internal temperature, remove and cover with foil. Let stand 10 minutes before serving.
3. Meanwhile, place sweet pepper pieces on a baking sheet. Drizzle peppers with 1 tablespoon oil and sprinkle lightly with salt and pepper; toss to coat. Spread peppers evenly on baking sheet. Place in oven with pork the last 40 to 45 minutes of roasting until peppers are tender and beginning to brown.
4. While roast stands, in a small saucepan combine honey and lime juice. Bring to boiling, stirring occasionally. Boil gently, uncovered, for 2 minutes. Remove from heat and cool slightly. Season with salt and pepper.
5. Slice pork and serve with peppers, honey glaze, and fresh herbs.
PER SERVING *282 cal, 14 g fat, 65 mg chol, 620 mg sodium, 15 g carb, 1 g fiber, 23 g pro.*

Baked Ham with Sautéed Pears and Apples

A little bit of red curry paste gives the glaze just a bit of spiciness—a perfect complement to the sweetness of the honey and sautéed fruit.

PREP **20 minutes** COOK **35 minutes**
ROAST **1 hour 30 minutes**
OVEN **325°F** MAKES **16 servings**

3   cups water
¾   cup sugar
⅓   cup honey
1   teaspoon red curry paste
1   5- to 6-pound cooked ham, rump half
3   tablespoons butter
4   ripe pears, cored and sliced
1   tablespoon grated fresh ginger
4   red cooking apples (such as Rome, Jonathan, or Braeburn), cored and sliced
    Fresh thyme sprigs (optional)

1. Preheat oven to 325°F. For glaze, in a large saucepan stir together the water, sugar, honey, and curry paste. Bring to boiling, stirring constantly to dissolve sugar. Boil gently, uncovered, for 25 to 30 minutes or until slightly thickened, stirring occasionally. Remove ½ cup of the glaze (set remaining glaze aside).
2. Place ham on the rack of a roasting pan. Roast, uncovered, for 1½ to 2¼ hours or until thermometer registers 140°F. Brush ham with reserved ½ cup glaze during the last 20 minutes of roasting.
3. For fruit, melt butter in a large skillet over medium-high heat. Add pears and ginger. Cook for 5 to 7 minutes or until pears begin to brown, gently stirring occasionally. Remove from skillet and keep warm. Add apples to skillet; cook for 5 to 7 minutes or until apples begin to brown, gently stirring occasionally. Combine apples with pears.
4. To serve, arrange fruit on platter. Slice ham and arrange on platter with fruit. Drizzle ham and fruit with remaining glaze. If desired, garnish with thyme sprigs.
PER SERVING *343 cal, 14 g fat, 82 mg chol, 930 mg sodium, 29 g carb, 2 g fiber, 28 g pro.*

Italian Sausage-Stuffed Beef Tenderloin

This sausage-and-Swiss chard-stuffed beef tenderloin is decadent, yes—and perfect for a celebratory holiday dinner.

PREP **40 minutes** ROAST **50 minutes**
STAND **35 minutes** OVEN **425°F**
MAKES **10 to 12 servings**

1   0.5-ounce package dried porcini mushrooms
2   tablespoons olive oil
2   onions, quartered and thinly sliced
8   ounces bulk mild Italian sausage
2   cloves garlic, minced
4   cups coarsely chopped Swiss chard
½   cup finely shredded Parmesan cheese (2 ounces)
½   teaspoon kosher salt
½   teaspoon dried Italian seasoning, crushed
¼   teaspoon cracked black pepper
1   pound center-cut beef tenderloin, trimmed of fat
1   tablespoon olive oil
1   to 2 teaspoons kosher salt
1   teaspoon cracked black pepper

1. Preheat oven to 425°F. Rinse dried mushrooms; place in a small bowl. Add enough boiling water to cover; let stand for 20 minutes. Drain; squeeze dry. Chop mushrooms; set aside.
2. In a large skillet heat the 2 tablespoons oil over medium heat. Add onions; cook and stir for 5 to 6 minutes or until golden. Add sausage, garlic, and mushrooms; cook until sausage is browned, using a wooden spoon to break up meat as it cooks. Add chard; cook and stir until wilted.
3. Spoon sausage mixture into a colander set in a bowl. Using a wooden spoon, press to remove excess liquid. Discard liquid.
4. Spoon sausage mixture into a medium bowl. Stir in Parmesan cheese, the ½ teaspoon salt, the Italian seasoning, and the ¼ teaspoon pepper.
5. Cut beef tenderloin in half horizontally, cutting to but not through the other side. Open tenderloin like a book. Spread the sausage mixture evenly over cut sides of the tenderloin. Bring up sides of tenderloin to enclose sausage mixture. Using 100%-cotton kitchen string, tie the tenderloin together at 3-inch intervals.
6. Place tenderloin on the rack of a roasting pan, placing the stuffing slit to one side. Brush tenderloin with the 1 tablespoon olive oil; sprinkle with the 1 teaspoon salt and the 1 teaspoon

pepper. Roast tenderloin to desired doneness. Allow 50 to 60 minutes for medium-rare (145°F) or 65 to 70 minutes for medium (160°F). Tent loosely with foil. Let stand at room temperature for 15 minutes before carving. Discard string. Thickly slice tenderloin; serve immediately.

PER SERVING *614 cal, 45 g fat, 138 mg chol, 652 mg sodium, 9 g carb, 1 g fiber, 42 g pro.*

Ginger-Orange-Glazed Turkey Breasts

These sweet-and-spicy glazed turkey breasts are perfect for families who fight over the white meat.

PREP **25 minutes** MARINATE **12 hours**
ROAST **45 minutes** STAND **5 minutes**
OVEN **350°F** MAKES **8 servings**

2   1½-pound skinless, boneless turkey breasts
2   cloves garlic, cut into 12 slivers total
1   to 2 fresh red chile peppers, cut into 12 pieces*
¼   cup orange juice
¼   cup olive oil
1   cup orange marmalade
½   cup finely chopped green onions (4)
½   cup orange juice
1   tablespoon grated fresh ginger
1   cloves garlic, minced
1   tablespoon orange liqueur
1   teaspoon kosher salt
1   teaspoon black pepper
    Sliced green onion, chopped chile peppers, and/or orange zest (optional)

1. Using a sharp paring knife, cut 12 slits into the top of each turkey breast. Tuck a garlic sliver or a chile pepper piece into slits, alternating garlic and chile pepper. Place turkey breasts side by side in a shallow glass baking dish.
2. In a small bowl combine the ¼ cup orange juice and the olive oil; pour over turkey. Cover; marinate in the refrigerator for at least 12 hours or up to 24 hours, turning occasionally.
3. For glaze, in a small saucepan combine marmalade, green onions, the ½ cup orange juice, the ginger, and minced garlic. Bring to boiling; reduce heat. Simmer, uncovered, for 5 minutes. Remove from heat; stir in orange liqueur.

4. Preheat oven to 350°F. Remove turkey breasts from marinade; discard marinade. Arrange turkey breasts on a rack in a large roasting pan. Spoon some of the glaze over turkey breasts. Sprinkle with salt and black pepper.
5. Roast for 45 to 50 minutes or until an instant-read thermometer inserted into the thickest part of each breast registers 160°F, spooning some of the remaining glaze over breasts every 15 minutes of roasting. Let stand for 5 minutes before slicing. If desired, garnish with additional sliced green onion, chopped chile peppers, and/or orange zest.
*Tip: Because chile peppers contain volatile oils that can burn your skin and eyes, avoid direct contact with them as much as possible. When working with chile peppers, wear plastic or rubber gloves. If your bare hands do touch the peppers, wash your hands and nails well with soap and warm water.

PER SERVING *369 cal, 8 g fat, 105 mg chol, 349 mg sodium, 31 g carb, 1 g fiber, 42 g pro.*

GINGER-ORANGE-GLAZED TURKEY BREASTS

Turkey Breast Stuffed with Sausage, Fennel, and Figs

Although beautiful and elegant, this stuffed turkey breast is simple enough to make for a casual gathering.

PREP 20 minutes
ROAST 1 hour 15 minutes
STAND 10 minutes OVEN 325°F
MAKES 8 to 10 servings

1   2- to 3-pound boneless turkey breast with skin*
½   teaspoon salt
½   teaspoon black pepper
8   ounces sweet Italian sausage (casings removed, if present)
½   cup thinly sliced green onions (4)
⅓   cup snipped dried figs
¾   teaspoon fennel seeds
¼   teaspoon salt
¼   teaspoon black pepper
1   tablespoon olive oil

1. Preheat oven to 325°F. Place turkey, skin side down, between two pieces of plastic wrap. Using the flat side of a meat mallet, pound lightly from the center to the edges into a square of even thickness. Remove plastic wrap. Sprinkle turkey evenly with the ½ teaspoon salt and the ½ teaspoon pepper.
2. For stuffing, in a medium skillet cook sausage until browned, using a wooden spoon to break up meat as it cooks. Drain off fat. In a medium bowl combine sausage, green onions, figs, and fennel seeds.
3. Spoon stuffing onto turkey. Roll up turkey and stuffing into a spiral. Tie at 2-inch intervals with 100%-cotton kitchen string. Sprinkle with the ¼ teaspoon salt and the ¼ teaspoon pepper.
4. Place turkey in a shallow roasting pan. Rub skin with the oil. Roast for 1¼ to 1¾ hours or until turkey is no longer pink (170°F) and an instant-read thermometer inserted into center of the stuffing registers 165°F.
5. Transfer turkey to a cutting board. Cover with foil; let stand for 10 minutes. Remove and discard string before slicing.
Tip: If you can't find boneless turkey breast with the skin on, purchase a 4- to 5-pound bone-in turkey breast and remove the bone (or ask your butcher to remove it for you).
PER SERVING *287 cal, 17 g fat, 87 mg chol, 472 mg sodium, 5 g carb, 1 g fiber, 27 g pro.*

Cream of Roasted Fennel Soup

Roasting the fennel and onion before pureeing them caramelizes their natural sugars and intensifies their flavors.

PREP 45 minutes ROAST 25 minutes
OVEN 375°F MAKES 8 servings

1   fennel bulb (1½ to 2 pounds)
1   cup coarsely chopped white onion (1 large)
1   tablespoon olive oil
½   teaspoon kosher salt
2   14.5-ounce cans reduced-sodium chicken broth
1   russet potato, peeled and cut into ½-inch cubes
1   cup half-and-half, light cream, or evaporated milk
2   tablespoons grapefruit juice
¾   teaspoon ground cumin
     Ground white pepper
     Kosher salt
1   tablespoon fennel seeds
     Croutons (optional)

1. Preheat oven to 375°F. Cut off and discard tough fennel stalks, reserving the feathery tops. Remove any wilted outer layers and cut a thin slice from base of bulb. Cut fennel bulb and tender stalks into ½-inch slices, removing core (if desired). Snip feathery tops; set aside.
2. In a 13×9×2-inch baking pan spread sliced fennel slices and onion in an even layer. Drizzle with oil; sprinkle with the ½ teaspoon salt. Roast about 25 minutes or just until vegetables are tender.
3. Transfer roasted fennel and onion to a large saucepan. Add broth and potato. Bring to boiling; reduce heat. Simmer, covered, about 10 minutes or until potato is tender. Cool slightly.
4. Place one-third of the fennel mixture in a blender or food processor. Cover and blend or process until smooth. Transfer to a bowl. Repeat two more times with the remaining fennel mixture. Return all of the fennel mixture to saucepan. Stir in half-and-half, grapefruit juice, and cumin. Heat through. Season to taste with white pepper and additional salt.
5. Meanwhile, in a small skillet cook fennel seeds over medium-high heat about 3 minutes or until lightly browned and fragrant, stirring frequently.
6. Garnish with fennel tops and toasted fennel seeds. If desired, serve with croutons.
PER SERVING *97 cal, 5 g fat, 11 mg chol, 416 mg sodium, 10 g carb, 2 g fiber, 3 g pro.*

TURKEY BREAST STUFFED WITH SAUSAGE, FENNEL, AND FIGS

Sweet Onion Soup with Porcini Mushrooms

Pancetta is salt-cured and spiced (but unsmoked) Italian bacon. It comes in very thin round slices. If you can't find it, you can substitute regular bacon.

PREP 30 minutes COOK 30 minutes
STAND 15 minutes MAKES 6 servings

1   ounce dried porcini mushrooms
2   cups boiling water
4   ounces pancetta
1   tablespoon butter or olive oil
1½ pounds sweet onions, such as Vidalia or Maui, sliced
4   cloves garlic, minced
1   tablespoon packed brown sugar
1   teaspoon salt
¼   cup Marsala wine
4   cups reduced-sodium beef broth
1   sprig fresh thyme
1   sprig fresh rosemary
1   bay leaf
1   recipe Toasted Cheese Bread

1. Place porcini mushrooms in a medium bowl. Pour the boiling water over mushrooms. Cover and let stand for 15 minutes. Meanwhile, in a 4-quart Dutch oven cook pancetta in hot butter over medium heat until lightly browned. Using a slotted spoon, remove pancetta; drain on paper towels, reserving drippings in Dutch oven. Chop pancetta.
2. Add sweet onions, garlic, brown sugar, and salt to the Dutch oven. Cook and stir over medium-low heat until golden, stirring occasionally.
3. Meanwhile, using a slotted spoon, remove porcini mushrooms from the liquid (do not discard liquid). Chop mushrooms; set aside. Reserve all but about ¼ cup of the mushroom liquid (discard the liquid at the bottom of the bowl, which may be gritty).
4. When the onions are golden, stir in mushrooms and Marsala wine. Cook until most of the liquid has evaporated. Add the reserved mushroom liquid, the beef broth, thyme, rosemary, and bay leaf. Bring to boiling; reduce heat. Simmer, uncovered, about 30 minutes. Discard thyme and rosemary sprigs and the bay leaf. Remove from heat; stir in pancetta. Serve over Toasted Cheese Bread.

Toasted Cheese Bread: Preheat broiler. Place twelve ½-inch slices baguette-style French bread on a baking sheet. Broil 4 to 5 inches from heat for 1 to 2 minutes or until toasted. Turn

CAULIFLOWER AND CARROT CUMIN SOUP

bread slices; sprinkle with 4 ounces Gruyère cheese, shredded (1 cup). Broil for 1 to 2 minutes more or until cheese is melted and browned.
PER SERVING *158 cal, 8 g fat, 18 mg chol, 1,118 mg sodium, 16 g carb, 2 g fiber, 6 g pro.*

Cauliflower and Carrot Cumin Soup

The fresh yellow color of this creamy soup brings a bit of sunshine to the holiday table.

PREP 25 minutes COOK 25 minutes
MAKES 6 servings

2   tablespoons olive oil
1   cup finely chopped onion (1 large)
2   garlic, minced
3   cups small cauliflower florets
1½   cups coarsely shredded fresh carrots (3 medium)
1   teaspoon ground cumin
2   14.5-ounce cans reduced-sodium chicken broth
1   cup half-and-half or light cream
1   tablespoon lime juice
     Salt
     Freshly ground black pepper

1. In a large saucepan heat oil over medium heat. Add onion and garlic; cook about 5 minutes or until onion is tender. Stir in cauliflower, carrots, and cumin. Add broth. Bring to boiling; reduce heat. Cover and simmer about 20 minutes or until cauliflower is very tender. Remove from heat; cool slightly. Using a slotted spoon, set aside 1½ cups of the vegetables.
2. Transfer half of the remaining mixture to a blender or food processor. Cover and blend or process until smooth. Transfer to a bowl. Repeat with the remaining broth mixture. Stir in the reserved 1½ cups vegetables, the half-and-half, and lime juice; heat through. Season to taste with salt and pepper.
PER SERVING *140 cal, 9 g fat, 15 mg chol, 466 mg sodium, 11 g carb, 3 g fiber, 5 g pro.*

Onion-Thyme Gravy

This recipe is perfect for those times when you'd like gravy for mashed potatoes but don't happen to be roasting a bird.

PREP **15 minutes** COOK **20 minutes**
MAKES **9 servings**

2   tablespoons butter
1   cup chopped onion (about 1 large)
3   shallots, chopped (about ⅔ cup)
1   teaspoon snipped fresh thyme or ¼ teaspoon dried thyme, crushed
2   tablespoons all-purpose flour
1   14.5-ounce can reduced-sodium chicken broth
1   tablespoon reduced-sodium soy sauce
1   tablespoon Worcestershire sauce
⅛   teaspoon salt
¼   teaspoon freshly ground black pepper

1. In a medium saucepan melt butter over medium-high heat. Add the onion, shallots, and thyme; cook, stirring occasionally, for 10 to 12 minutes or until vegetables are tender and browned. **2.** Stir in the all-purpose flour; cook and stir for 1 minute. Add the broth, soy sauce, and the Worcestershire sauce. Cook and stir until mixture comes to boiling; reduce heat to medium. Simmer, uncovered, for 8 to 9 minutes or until slightly thickened. Stir in the salt and pepper.
PER ¼ CUP *52 cal, 3 g fat, 7 mg chol, 244 mg sodium, 6 g carb, 0 g fiber, 1 g pro.*

Herb Gravy

Even for the most experienced cooks, good gravy can be an elusive endeavor. This herb-infused gravy is failproof. If you don't have enough pan juices, simply use additional chicken broth.

START TO FINISH **20 minutes**
MAKES **12 servings**

4   tablespoons unsalted butter
4   tablespoons all-purpose flour
2   teaspoons fresh thyme
1   teaspoon chopped fresh sage
1   cup reserved pan juices from cooked turkey
2   cups reduced-sodium chicken broth
    Sea salt and freshly ground pepper to taste

1. Melt butter in a skillet over medium-high heat until sizzling hot. Slowly stir in the flour, then reduce heat to medium. Cook about 2 minutes, stirring constantly, until flour is light brown. Stir in thyme and sage. Slowly whisk in pan juices from the turkey and the chicken broth; season with salt and pepper to taste. Cook and stir for 2 to 3 minutes, until liquid comes to boiling and begins to thicken.
PER ¼ CUP *54 cal, 4 g fat, 11 mg chol, 154 mg sodium, 3 g carb, 0 g fiber, 1 g pro.*

Pickled Beet and Sage Conserve

This earthy conserve is particularly good served with roast pork or beef.

PREP **20 minutes** COOK **40 minutes**
COOL **30 minutes** MAKES **16 servings**

2   16-ounce jars sliced or whole pickled beets
2   pears, cored, peeled, and coarsely chopped
½   cup sugar
2   tablespoons lemon juice
1   cup chopped walnuts, toasted (see tip, page 14)
2   tablespoons snipped fresh sage

1. Drain beets, reserving liquid from one of the jars (you should have ¾ cup liquid). Coarsely chop beets. In a large saucepan combine beets, pears, and the reserved liquid. Bring to boiling; reduce heat. Simmer, uncovered, about 10 minutes or until pears are soft, stirring occasionally. **2.** Stir sugar and lemon juice into beet mixture, stirring until sugar dissolves. Bring to boiling; reduce heat. Simmer, uncovered, about 30 minutes or until thickened, stirring often. Cool for 30 minutes. Stir in walnuts and sage before serving.
PER ¼ CUP *61 cal, 2 g fat, 0 mg chol, 75 mg sodium, 10 g carb, 1 g fiber, 1 g pro.*

Blackberry-Apple Relish

If you are using frozen blackberries, thaw them in a single layer on several layers of paper towels.

PREP **25 minutes** COOL **30 minutes**
MAKES **12 servings**

1   tablespoon vegetable oil
⅓   cup finely chopped shallots
2   apples, peeled, cored, and chopped (about 2½ cups)
½   cup packed brown sugar
¼   cup apple juice or apple cider
¼   teaspoon ground cinnamon
2   cups fresh or frozen blackberries, thawed

1. In a skillet heat oil over medium heat. Add shallots; cook and stir just until tender. Add apples, brown sugar, apple juice, and cinnamon; cook 5 minutes more or just until apples are tender and sugar is dissolved. Carefully stir in blackberries. Cool for 30 minutes.
PER ¼ CUP *82 cal, 1 g fat, 0 mg chol, 4 mg sodium, 18 g carb, 2 g fiber, 1 g pro.*

BLACKBERRY-APPLE RELISH

PICKLED BEET AND
SAGE CONSERVE

Cranberry Sauce with Lime and Ginger

For the best flavor, use pure maple syrup—it's worth the extra cost—in this contemporary cranberry sauce.

START TO FINISH 25 minutes
MAKES 12 servings

½ cup sugar
½ cup pure maple syrup or maple-flavor syrup
½ cup water
1½ teaspoons finely shredded lime peel
1 tablespoon lime juice
1 12-ounce package fresh cranberries
1 teaspoon grated fresh ginger
Thin lime wedges (optional)

1. In a heavy medium saucepan stir together sugar, maple syrup, the water, lime peel, and lime juice. Bring to boiling; reduce heat. Simmer, uncovered, about 3 minutes or until sugar is dissolved.
2. Stir in cranberries. Simmer, uncovered, for 5 minutes, stirring occasionally. Stir in ginger. Simmer, uncovered, about 6 minutes more or until berries have popped and mixture starts to thicken, stirring occasionally. Cool. If desired, garnish with lime wedges.
Make-Ahead Directions: Prepare as directed; cool. Transfer to an airtight container; cover. Chill for up to 3 days. Let stand at room temperature for 30 minutes before serving.
PER ¼ CUP *79 cal, 1 g fat, 0 mg chol, 2 mg sodium, 21 g carb, 1 g fiber, .1 g pro.*

Lemon-Walnut Green Beans

Simple and light, these lemony green beans tossed with crunchy walnuts add a fresh touch to a meal.

PREP 15 minutes COOK 10 minutes
MAKES 4 servings

12 ounces fresh green beans, trimmed
1 tablespoon vegetable oil spread
2 teaspoons finely shredded lemon peel
¼ teaspoon salt
2 tablespoons toasted walnuts, chopped*

1. Place a steamer basket in a large skillet with a tight-fitting lid. Add water to just below the basket. Bring water to boiling over medium-high heat. Place beans in steamer basket. Cover; steam for 8 to 10 minutes or until beans are crisp-tender. Lift steamer basket from skillet to remove the beans; set aside. Drain water from skillet.
2. In the same skillet add vegetable oil spread, lemon peel, and salt. Stir until melted and combined. Add beans to skillet. Toss to coat. Transfer to a serving dish. Sprinkle with walnuts.
*Tip: To toast nuts, seeds, or shredded coconut, place pieces in a single layer in a shallow baking pan. Bake in a 350°F oven for 5 to 10 minutes or until the pieces are golden brown, stirring frequently. Check the pieces frequently to make sure they aren't getting too dark. If they start to burn, they go quickly and generally can't be salvaged.
PER SERVING *72 cal, 5 g fat, 0 mg chol, 169 mg sodium, 7 g carb, 3 g fiber, 2 g pro.*

Loaded Creamed Corn with Tomato and Bacon

Just when you think it couldn't get any better, this cheesy, slow-cooked creamed corn gets a topping of more cheese, bacon, and fresh tomato.

PREP 25 minutes COOK 3 hours (low) or 1½ hours (high) STAND 5 minutes
MAKES 16 to 18 servings

4 12-ounce packages frozen whole kernel corn, thawed
1½ cups half-and-half or light cream
1 cup chopped onion (1 large)
½ cup freshly grated Parmesan cheese
¼ cup butter, cut up
1 teaspoon sugar
½ teaspoon salt
¼ teaspoon black pepper
5 thick slices bacon
¾ cup shredded Monterey Jack cheese with jalapeño peppers or Monterey Jack cheese (3 ounces)
½ cup chopped tomato (1 medium)
2 tablespoons snipped fresh parsley
1 teaspoon red wine vinegar
⅛ teaspoon sugar

1. In a blender combine the corn from 1 package and the half-and-half. Cover and blend until smooth. In a 3½- or 4-quart slow cooker combine blended

CRANBERRY SAUCE WITH LIME AND GINGER

corn mixture, the remaining corn, the onion, Parmesan cheese, butter, the 1 teaspoon sugar, the salt, and pepper.

2. Cover and cook on low-heat setting for 3 to 4 hours or on high-heat setting for 1½ to 2 hours.

3. In a skillet cook bacon over medium heat until crisp, turning once. Drain bacon on paper towels; cool. Cut bacon into 1-inch pieces.

4. Sprinkle Monterey Jack cheese and bacon over corn in slow cooker. Cover; let stand for about 5 minutes or until cheese is melted.

5. In a small bowl stir together tomato, parsley, vinegar, and the ⅛ teaspoon sugar. Before serving, spoon tomato mixture over corn in cooker.

PER SERVING *186 cal, 10 g fat, 27 mg chol, 258 mg sodium, 20 g carb, 2 g fiber, 7 g pro.*

Caramelized Brussels Sprouts with Lemon

Thanks to new cooking methods—such as pan roasting until they're golden brown and caramelized—Brussels sprouts are experiencing a renaissance.

PREP **15 minutes** COOK **6 minutes**
MAKES **6 servings**

¼   cup extra virgin olive oil
4   cups Brussels sprouts, rinsed, trimmed, and halved lengthwise (4 cups)
     Salt and freshly ground black pepper
2   tablespoons water
     Juice of half a lemon, about 1 tablespoon

1. In a very large nonstick skillet heat 3 tablespoons of the oil over medium heat. Arrange sprouts in a single layer, cut sides down. Drizzle with remaining olive oil and sprinkle with salt and pepper. Cover and cook for 3 minutes. Remove lid and sprinkle sprouts with the water. Cover and cook for 2 minutes more. Sprouts should just be beginning to caramelize and, when pierced with a fork, slightly tender.

2. Remove cover and increase heat slightly. When cut sides are well caramelized, toss sprouts in pan, drizzle with lemon juice, and sprinkle with more salt and pepper to taste.

PER SERVING *106 cal, 9 g fat, 0 mg chol, 209 mg sodium, 6 g carb, 2 g fiber, 2 g pro.*

CARAMELIZED BRUSSELS SPROUTS WITH LEMON

Layered Vegetable-Romano Torte

This eye-catching layered vegetable dish takes a little time to make but it is sure to impress—and it can be made up to 24 hours ahead.

PREP **1 hour** CHILL **12 hours**
STAND **1 hour** MAKES **12 servings**

- 3 tablespoons olive oil
- 4 medium zucchini, cut into ¼-inch slices (5 cups)
- 4 cups fresh baby spinach
- ¾ teaspoon sea salt
- ¾ teaspoon black pepper
- 1½ cups grated Romano cheese
- 1½ cups thinly sliced carrots (3 medium)
- 1 medium yellow squash, cut into ¼-inch slices
- 1 16-ounce jar roasted red sweet peppers, drained and sliced
  Snipped fresh parsley
- 1 recipe Greek Dressing or ⅔ cup bottled Greek or Caesar salad dressing

1. In a very large skillet heat 2 tablespoons of the olive oil over medium-high heat. Add zucchini; cook about 10 minutes or until tender, stirring occasionally. Stir in baby spinach. Cook and stir about 2 minutes or just until spinach wilts. Remove from heat. Sprinkle with ½ teaspoon of the sea salt and ½ teaspoon of the black pepper. Transfer half of the zucchini mixture to a bowl; set aside. Spoon the remaining zucchini mixture into an 8-inch springform pan, arranging in an even layer. Sprinkle with ½ cup of the Romano cheese. Set aside.
2. In the same skillet heat the remaining 1 tablespoon olive oil over medium heat. Add carrots; cook and stir for 2 minutes. Stir in yellow squash. Cook for 8 to 10 minutes more or until carrots and squash are tender, stirring occasionally. Remove from heat. Sprinkle with the remaining ¼ teaspoon sea salt and the remaining ¼ teaspoon black pepper. Add mixture in an even layer to the 8-inch springform pan. Sprinkle with another ½ cup of the Romano cheese.
3. Arrange roasted red peppers in an even layer over the carrots and squash. Sprinkle with the remaining ½ cup Romano cheese. Spoon the reserved zucchini mixture evenly over the top.
4. Top springform pan with a sheet of waxed paper or parchment paper. Place an 8-inch round cake pan on top of the waxed paper and weight down with unopened heavy cans or jars. Place the torte in a 15×10×1-inch baking pan. Chill for at least 12 hours or up to 24 hours.
5. To serve, remove cans or jars and cake pan. Carefully drain any excess juice from the torte. Carefully remove the sides of the springform pan. Place torte on a serving plate. Let stand for 1 hour to allow torte to come to room temperature. Sprinkle with parsley. Drizzle each serving with some of the Greek Dressing.

Greek Dressing: In a screw-top jar combine ⅓ cup olive oil; 3 tablespoons red wine vinegar; 2 tablespoons lemon juice; 1 tablespoon snipped fresh oregano; 1 small clove garlic, minced; ½ teaspoon salt; and ¼ teaspoon black pepper. Cover and shake well. Serve immediately. Makes ⅔ cup.

PER SERVING *156 cal, 12 g fat, 10 mg chol, 350 mg sodium, 7 g carb, 2 g fiber, 5 g pro.*

Cauliflower-Fontina Gratin

This creamy, cheesy gratin is lovely served with a simple beef tenderloin roast and a crisp green salad.

PREP **30 minutes** BAKE **25 minutes**
STAND **30 minutes** OVEN **375°F**
MAKES **12 servings**

- 6 cups cauliflower florets (2 small heads)
- ¼ cup butter
- ¼ cup all-purpose flour
- 2 cups half-and-half, or light cream
- ½ cup milk
- ¾ cup shredded Fontina cheese (3 ounces)
- 1 tablespoon snipped fresh thyme or 1 teaspoon dried thyme, crushed
- ½ teaspoon salt
- ¼ teaspoon black pepper
- ⅔ cup soft bread crumbs
- 2 tablespoons olive oil

1. Preheat oven to 375°F. Grease a 2-quart square baking dish; set aside. In a Dutch oven cook cauliflower in boiling lightly salted water about 5 minutes or just until tender; drain. Transfer to a bowl of ice water to stop cooking. Drain again; set aside.
2. In a medium saucepan melt butter over medium-low heat. Stir in flour. Cook and stir for 1 minute. Stir in half-and-half and the ½ cup milk. Cook and stir over medium heat until thickened

LAYERED VEGETABLE-ROMANO TORTE

ROASTED BEETS WITH ORANGES AND BLUE CHEESE

SAUTÉED CABBAGE WITH BACON

and bubbly. Cook and stir for 1 minute more. Remove from heat. Stir in Fontina cheese, the 1 tablespoon fresh thyme, the salt, and pepper.

3. Spread about 1 cup of the sauce evenly in the bottom of the prepared dish. Arrange cauliflower florets in an even layer in the baking dish. Spread the remaining sauce over the cauliflower.

4. Sprinkle gratin evenly with bread crumbs; drizzle evenly with olive oil. Bake for 25 to 30 minutes or until lightly browned and bubbly.

PER SERVING *167 cal, 13 g fat, 34 mg chol, 234 mg sodium, 8 g carb, 1 g fiber, 5 g pro.*

Roasted Beets with Oranges and Blue Cheese

This simple side is a fabulous combination of earthy beets and sweet oranges—with a bit of salty tang from the blue cheese.

PREP **15 minutes** ROAST **40 minutes**
OVEN **425°F** MAKES **4 servings**

12 ounces trimmed small red and/or yellow beets, peeled and quartered
2 teaspoons canola oil

⅛ teaspoon salt
⅛ teaspoon black pepper
1 Cara Cara or other navel orange, peeled, seeded, sectioned, and chopped
2 tablespoons crumbled blue cheese or feta cheese

1. Preheat oven to 425°F. In a 2-quart baking dish combine beets, oil, salt, and pepper. Toss to coat. Cover and roast for 20 minutes. Uncover and stir beets. Roast, uncovered, about 20 minutes more or until beets are tender.

2. Transfer beets to a serving platter. Sprinkle evenly with chopped orange and cheese.

PER SERVING *75 cal, 4 g fat, 3 mg chol, 176 mg sodium, 9 g carb, 2 g fiber, 2 g pro.*

Sautéed Cabbage with Bacon

Try this humble but tasty dish with roast pork.

START TO FINISH **20 minutes**
MAKES **4 servings**

2 slices turkey bacon or regular bacon, chopped
4 cups thinly sliced green cabbage

1 red sweet pepper, cut into bite-size strips
1 onion, halved and thinly sliced
2 tablespoons water
2 tablespoons light mayonnaise
1 tablespoon course-ground mustard
1 tablespoon cider vinegar
¼ teaspoon caraway seeds, crushed
⅛ teaspoon celery seeds

1. In a large nonstick skillet cook bacon over medium heat for 5 minutes or until cooked through, stirring occasionally. Remove bacon from skillet and set aside. Add cabbage, sweet pepper, onion, and the water to skillet. Cover and cook over medium heat for 5 minutes or until vegetables are just tender, stirring occasionally.

2. In a small bowl combine mayonnaise, mustard, vinegar, caraway seeds, and celery seeds. Add to cabbage mixture in skillet. Toss until well coated. Sprinkle with cooked bacon and serve warm.

PER SERVING *82 cal, 4 g fat, 10 mg chol, 255 mg sodium, 8 g carb, 3 g fiber, 2 g pro.*

Chardonnay Glazed Carrots

Verjus is a bit like vinegar—though it's not as strong—and is used to heighten flavor in the same way. Look for it in gourmet markets.

PREP **15 minutes** COOK **25 minutes**
MAKES **8 servings**

2 pounds assorted carrots
1 cup Chardonnay verjus or ¾ cup white grape juice plus ¼ cup white wine vinegar
½ cup honey
2 tablespoons unsalted butter
1 teaspoon kosher salt
2 cinnamon sticks
2 bay leaves
2 tablespoons sliced chives

1. Peel large carrots. Slice carrots lengthwise and/or crosswise. Heat a large skillet over medium-high heat. Add verjus, honey, butter, salt, cinnamon sticks, and bay leaves. Bring to boiling, stirring to combine. Add carrots; return to boiling. Reduce heat to medium.

Cook, uncovered, 25 minutes, stirring often, until carrots are tender and glaze thickens.

2. Remove from heat. Remove and discard cinnamon stick and bay leaves. Sprinkle with chives.

PER SERVING *156 cal, 3 g fat, 8 mg chol, 314 mg sodium, 28 g carb, 3 g fiber, 1 g pro.*

Bacon-Topped Green Bean Casserole

While many takes on this classic American dish pop up on tables all across the country this time of year, there are few as elegant and downright delicious as this version made with wild mushrooms, cream, and bacon.

PREP **40 minutes** BAKE **30 minutes**
OVEN **375°F** MAKES **8 servings**

1½ pounds fresh green beans, trimmed
1 cup boiling water
½ ounce dried wild mushrooms, such as morel, chanterelle, oyster, and/or porcini mushrooms
7 to 8 slices bacon (8 ounces), cut into small pieces

12 ounces cremini mushrooms, sliced
2 cloves garlic, minced
3 tablespoons butter
3 tablespoons all-purpose flour
2 cups half-and-half or light cream
2 teaspoons snipped fresh rosemary or ½ teaspoon dried rosemary, crushed
1 teaspoon salt
½ teaspoon black pepper

1. Preheat oven to 375°F. In an extra-large skillet cook beans in boiling lightly salted water about 3 minutes or until crisp-tender; drain. Transfer to a bowl of ice water to stop cooking. Drain again; set aside. Meanwhile, in a small bowl pour the 1 cup boiling water over the dried mushrooms. Cover and let stand for 15 minutes.

2. In the same extra-large skillet cook bacon until crisp. Using a slotted spoon, transfer bacon to a small bowl lined with a paper towel; crumble bacon. Reserve about 1 tablespoon of the bacon drippings in skillet; discard the remaining drippings. Cook cremini mushrooms in the reserved drippings over medium-high heat until lightly browned, stirring occasionally. Stir in garlic. Cook and stir for 1 minute more. Remove from heat. Stir in green beans.

3. Meanwhile, use a fork to remove the dried mushrooms from the water (do not discard liquid). Chop the mushrooms; add to green bean mixture.

4. For sauce, in a medium saucepan melt butter over medium heat. Stir in flour. Cook and stir for 1 minute. Stir in all but about 2 tablespoons of the mushroom liquid (discard the liquid at the bottom of the bowl, which may be gritty). Stir in half-and-half. Cook and stir over medium heat until thickened and bubbly. Cook and stir for 1 minute more. Remove from heat. Stir in rosemary, salt, and pepper.

5. Stir the sauce into the bean mixture. Spoon into a 2-quart square baking dish. Bake for 25 to 30 minutes or until bubbly. Top with bacon. Bake for 5 minutes more.

PER SERVING *334 cal, 24 g fat, 67 mg chol, 1,045 mg sodium, 14 g carb, 3 g fiber, 16 g pro.*

CHARDONNAY GLAZED CARROTS

BACON-TOPPED
GREEN BEAN
CASSEROLE

Creamy Brie-Topped Potatoes

Few things are as tantalizing as creamy potatoes topped with gooey, melty, toasty cheese. Serve this dish alongside a holiday ham or beef roast.

PREP **45 minutes** BAKE **40 minutes**
OVEN **350°F** MAKES **12 servings**

3   pounds Yukon gold potatoes (about 9 medium)
½   teaspoon salt
¼   teaspoon black pepper
5   slices thick-sliced bacon, chopped
1   large onion, thinly sliced
2   cloves garlic, minced
⅓   cup dry white wine
2   teaspoons snipped fresh thyme
¼   cup chicken broth
¼   cup whipping cream
2   8-ounce rounds Brie cheese
    Fresh thyme sprigs (optional)

1. Preheat oven to 350°F. Grease a 2-quart gratin dish or rectangular baking dish; set aside. In a covered Dutch oven cook potatoes in enough simmering salted water to cover for 25 minutes; drain. Rinse with cold water; drain again. Slice potatoes about ¼ inch thick. Sprinkle with salt and pepper. Place half of the potatoes in the bottom of the prepared dish.
2. Meanwhile, in a large skillet cook bacon over medium heat for 1 minute. Add onion and garlic; cook and stir about 5 minutes or until bacon is crisp and onion is tender. Drain off fat. Carefully add wine to bacon mixture.

Simmer, uncovered, until wine is almost evaporated. Stir in the snipped thyme.
3. Spoon bacon mixture over potatoes in dish. Top with the remaining potatoes. Pour broth and cream over potato mixture. Cut Brie crosswise into ¼-inch-thick rectangles and layer on top of potato mixture.
4. Bake about 40 minutes or until potatoes are tender and cheese is lightly browned. If desired, garnish with fresh thyme sprigs.

PER SERVING *267 cal, 15 g fat, 49 mg chol, 468 mg sodium, 22 g carb, 3 g fiber, 12 g pro.*

Butternut Squash-Wild Rice Casserole

Wild rice adds a nutty taste and crunchy texture to this autumnal vegetable side.

PREP 30 minutes ROAST 20 minutes
BAKE 45 minutes OVEN 425°F/350°F
MAKES 10 to 12 servings

1   pound butternut squash, peeled, seeded, and cut into ½-inch cubes
1   to 2 tablespoons olive oil
2   6-ounce packages long grain and wild rice mix
¾   cup chopped onions
¾   cup chopped celery
¾   cup chopped carrots
⅓   cup butter
2   10.5-ounce cans condensed chicken with white and wild rice soup or cream of chicken soup
1   8-ounce carton sour cream
⅔   cup dry white wine or chicken broth
¼   cup snipped fresh basil or 2 teaspoons dried basil, crushed
1½ cups finely shredded Parmesan cheese (6 ounces)

1. Preheat oven to 425°F. In a large bowl toss squash with oil to coat; spread into a 15×10×1-inch baking pan. Roast about 20 minutes or until lightly browned and tender, stirring twice. Reduce oven temperature to 350°F.
2. Meanwhile, prepare rice mix according to package directions; set aside. In a large skillet cook onions, celery, and carrots in hot butter over medium heat until tender. Stir in soup, sour cream, wine, and basil. Stir in cooked rice mix, roasted squash, and ¾ cup of the Parmesan cheese.
3. Transfer rice mixture to a 2½- to 3-quart casserole. Sprinkle with the remaining ¾ cup Parmesan cheese. Bake for 45 to 50 minutes or until heated through.
PER SERVING *357 cal, 16 g fat, 39 mg chol, 1,136 mg sodium, 42 g carb, 3 g fiber, 11 g pro.*

Easy Pommes Anna-Style Casserole

Pommes Anna is a traditional French dish featuring paper-thin slices of potato layered and cooked in a generous amount of butter. This slow-cooker version simplifies the process.

PREP 25 minutes
COOK 5½ hours (low)
MAKES 12 servings

3   pounds Yukon gold potatoes (about 9 medium)
1   teaspoon kosher salt or salt
½   teaspoon coarsely ground black pepper
¾   cup chopped green onions (6)
6   slices bacon, crisp-cooked and crumbled
3   cloves garlic, minced
⅔   cup melted butter
    Sliced green onions

1. Scrub or peel *potatoes. Using a mandoline, slice potatoes about ⅛ inch thick. Layer half the potatoes in the bottom of a 3½- to 4-quart slow cooker. Sprinkle with half of the salt and half of the pepper. Sprinkle with half of the chopped green onions, half of the bacon, and half of the garlic. Repeat layers. Drizzle evenly with butter.
2. Cover and cook on low-heat setting for 5½ to 6 hours or until potatoes are tender when pierced with a fork. Loosen edges with a spatula. Garnish with the sliced green onions.
***Tip:** For a more golden dish, make sure to peel the potatoes before cooking.
PER SERVING *203 cal, 12 g fat, 32 mg chol, 334 mg sodium, 21 g carb, 3 g fiber, 4 g pro.*

Fresh Pea Risotto

Because this dish requires some stirring and pot-watching, serve it with something simple, such as ham.

START TO FINISH 35 minutes
MAKES 6 servings

8   cups chicken broth
2   tablespoons butter
2   shallots, thinly sliced
1   garlic, minced
½   teaspoon fennel seeds, crushed
2   cups arborio rice
1½ cups shelled fresh peas or frozen peas
½   cup finely shredded Parmesan or Asiago cheese
2   ounces prosciutto, cut into thin strips
½   teaspoon finely shredded lemon peel
⅛   teaspoon black pepper
2   tablespoons sliced almonds, toasted

1. In a large saucepan bring broth to boiling; reduce heat. Cover; keep warm.
2. In a Dutch oven melt butter over medium heat. Add shallots, garlic, and fennel seeds; cook 4 minutes or until tender. Stir in rice. Cook and stir for 2 to 3 minutes or until rice begins to brown.
3. Slowly add 1 cup of the chicken broth to the rice mixture, stirring constantly. Continue to cook and stir over medium heat until liquid is absorbed. Add another cup of the broth to the rice mixture, stirring constantly. Continue to cook and stir until the liquid is absorbed. Add 2 more cups of broth, 1 cup at a time, stirring constantly until the liquid is absorbed. Stir in fresh peas (if using). Add remaining broth, 1 cup at a time, stirring constantly until the broth has been absorbed (about 15 to 20 minutes).
4. Stir in frozen peas (if using), cheese, prosciutto, lemon peel, and pepper. Top servings with almonds.
PER SERVING *308 cal, 10 g fat, 19 mg chol, 1,616 mg sodium, 43 g carb, 2 g fiber, 12 g pro.*

FRESH PEA RISOTTO

Savory Pear-Hazelnut Bake

Roasted vegetable dishes are a dime a dozen—try a roasted fruit dish for a change of pace.

PREP 20 minutes BAKE 27 minutes
OVEN 375°F MAKES 6 servings

4   just-ripe green- and red-skin pears, quartered, cored, and cut into ½-inch slices
2   tablespoons lemon juice
1   tablespoon snipped fresh rosemary
¼   cup finely shredded Parmesan cheese (1 ounce)
¼   cup toasted hazelnuts,* chopped

1. Preheat oven to 375°F. In a 1½- to 2-quart shallow gratin dish combine pear slices, lemon juice, and rosemary; toss to coat. Spread in an even layer in the dish. Cover and bake for 25 to 30 minutes or until fruit is just tender.
2. Sprinkle with cheese. Bake, uncovered, 2 to 3 minutes more or until cheese is melted. Sprinkle with toasted hazelnuts. Serve warm.
*Tip: To toast hazelnuts, preheat oven to 350°F. Place nuts in a shallow baking pan. Bake about 10 minutes or until toasted. Cool nuts slightly. Place the warm nuts on a clean kitchen towel. Rub the nuts with the towel to remove the loose skins.
PER SERVING *115 cal, 4 g fat, 2 mg chol, 58 mg sodium, 19 g carb, 4 g fiber, 3 g pro.*

Romaine and Radicchio Salad

With bright green romaine and deep red radicchio, this simple salad adds a bit of Christmas color to the holiday table.

START TO FINISH 20 minutes
MAKES 8 to 10 servings

10 cups torn romaine or mixed salad greens
2   cups torn radicchio
⅓   cup olive oil
¼   cup white wine vinegar
4   anchovy fillets, drained and finely chopped
¼   teaspoon salt
½   teaspoon freshly ground black pepper
1   cup finely shredded Parmesan cheese

1. In a large bowl combine romaine and radicchio.
2. For the dressing, in a medium bowl whisk together oil, vinegar, anchovies, salt, and pepper until thoroughly combined. Drizzle dressing over romaine mixture. Add Parmesan cheese; toss gently to coat. Serve immediately.
PER SERVING *155 cal, 13 g fat, 10 mg chol, 350 mg sodium, 4 g carb, 7 g pro.*

Citrus Salad

Be sure to get off as much of the white pith—the membrane right under the citrus peel—as you can. It's bitter and not pleasant to eat. It can be lightly scraped with a paring knife.

START TO FINISH 20 minutes
MAKES 6 to 8 servings

3   oranges
1   tablespoon Dijon mustard
1   tablespoon snipped fresh tarragon
¼   cup olive oil
2   heads Bibb lettuce, torn
1   pink grapefruit, peeled and thinly sliced
2   clementines, peeled and separated into segments
½   cup unsweetened flaked coconut, toasted (see tip, page 14)

1. For the dressing, squeeze juice from 1 orange and transfer to a small bowl. Whisk in mustard, tarragon, and the oil. Peel and slice remaining oranges.
2. Toss lettuce with dressing; gently toss in citrus slices and segments. Arrange on platter. Top with toasted coconut.
PER SERVING *211 cal, 15 g fat, 0 mg chol, 67 mg sodium, 19 g carb, 5 g fiber, 3 g pro.*

Beet, Carrot, and Apple Salad

Because the beets bleed their bright color on everything they touch, be sure to toss the salad right before serving.

START TO FINISH 45 minutes
MAKES 8 servings

    Zest and juice of 1 orange
    Zest and juice of 1 lime
2   tablespoons sherry vinegar
¾   cup extra virgin olive oil
    Sea salt and freshly ground black pepper
1   pound beets, peeled and cut into matchsticks
2   carrots, peeled and cut into matchsticks
1   Granny Smith apple, cored, peeled, and cut into matchsticks
1   turnip, peeled and cut into matchsticks
1   bunch fresh parsley, stems removed

1. In a large bowl combine the orange zest and juice, lime zest and juice, and vinegar. Slowly whisk in the olive oil,

SAVORY PEAR-HAZELNUT BAKE

PERSIMMON, BLOOD ORANGE, AND POMEGRANATE SALAD

then season with salt and pepper to taste.

2. In the same bowl layer beets, carrots, apple, and turnip. Season with additional salt and pepper to taste. Toss salad right before serving, then top with parsley leaves.

PER SERVING *118 cal, 10 g fat, 0 mg chol, 87 mg sodium, 7 g carb, 2 g fiber, 1 g pro.*

Persimmon, Blood Orange, and Pomegranate Salad

This brightly hued salad takes full advantage of produce that is at its peak during fall and winter.

START TO FINISH **50 minutes**
MAKES **6 servings**

1   pomegranate
2   large ripe Fuyu persimmons, mangoes, or papayas
5   cups mesclun, arugula, baby arugula, or mixed salad greens
6   tablespoons thinly sliced green onions (3)

1   recipe Pine Nut-Persimmon Vinaigrette
4   medium blood and/or navel oranges, peeled and thinly sliced

1. Score an X into the top of the pomegranate. Break apart into quarters. Working in a bowl of cool water, immerse each quarter; use your fingers to loosen the seeds from the white membrane. Discard peel and membrane. Drain the seeds; set aside.
2. Cut each persimmon in half; remove core. Slice into ¼- to ½-inch-thick slices.
3. In a large bowl combine mesclun and green onions. Drizzle ½ cup of the Pine Nut-Persimmon Vinaigrette over musclun; toss to coat.
4. To serve, arrange mesclun mixture on 6 chilled salad plates. Arrange persimmons and oranges on top of greens, tucking a few in and under leaves. Sprinkle with pomegranate seeds. Pass the remaining Pine Nut-Persimmon Vinaigrette.

Pine Nut-Persimmon Vinaigrette:
Remove the core from 1 large ripe Fuyu persimmon; cut in half. Scoop out pulp (you should have about ⅓ cup), discarding skin. Place pulp in a blender or food processor. Cover and blend or process until smooth. Add ⅓ cup olive oil; ¼ cup red or white wine vinegar; 3 tablespoons toasted pine nuts; 1½ teaspoons finely shredded blood orange peel or orange peel; 2 tablespoons blood orange juice or orange juice; 1 tablespoon honey; ½ of a large shallot, cut up; ½ teaspoon Dijon mustard; dash ground cinnamon or ground allspice; and dash freshly ground black pepper. Cover and blend or process until smooth.

PER SERVING *238 cal, 15 g fat, 0 mg chol, 18 mg sodium, 26 g carb, 3 g fiber, 2 g pro.*

OLIVE BREAD STUFFING
WITH FENNEL AND
MUSHROOMS

Olive Bread Stuffing with Fennel and Mushrooms

One way to add flavor and interest to stuffing is to start with interesting bread.

PREP 1 hour BAKE 1 hour
OVEN 375°F MAKES 12 servings

3   tablespoons butter
3   tablespoons olive oil
1   pound trimmed fennel bulbs, cored and diced (about 2 bulbs)
3   cups chopped onions (3 large)
¼   cup chopped green onions, white parts only (about 5 onions)
1   teaspoon salt
½   teaspoon freshly ground black pepper
12   ounces cremini mushrooms, quartered
4   ounces shiitake mushrooms, stemmed and quartered
15   cups stale artisanal olive bread cut into 1-inch cubes

1   cup freshly grated Parmesan cheese
¼   cup oil-pack dried tomatoes, drained and chopped
1   cup reduced-sodium chicken broth
1   tablespoon snipped fresh tarragon
1   tablespoon snipped fresh thyme
1   tablespoon snipped fresh basil

1. Preheat oven to 375°F. In a large skillet heat butter and olive oil over medium-high heat until foamy. Stir in fennel, onions, and green onions. Sprinkle with salt and pepper. Cook and stir about 6 minutes or until vegetables are soft. Add mushrooms; cook and stir about 4 minutes or until mushrooms are slightly soft.
2. Transfer mixture to a large bowl. Stir in bread cubes, ¾ cup of the Parmesan cheese, and the dried tomatoes.
3. Grease a 3-quart rectangular baking dish. Transfer bread mixture to prepared dish. Drizzle with broth. Carefully stir in tarragon, thyme, and basil. Bake,

covered, for 40 minutes. Sprinkle with the remaining ¼ cup Parmesan cheese. Bake, uncovered, for 20 to 25 minutes more or until hot in center (165°F).
PER SERVING *265 cal, 10 g fat, 13 mg chol, 694 mg sodium, 36 g carb, 3 g fiber, 10 g pro.*

Roasted Chestnut Stuffing

You may not roast them over an open fire, but the chestnuts add a traditional touch to this savory herbed stuffing.

PREP 40 minutes BAKE 40 minutes
ROAST 15 minutes OVEN 400°F/350°F
MAKES 12 servings

¼   cup butter
1   cup chopped celery (2 stalks)
½   cup chopped onion (1 medium)
½   cup chopped carrot (1 medium)
1   tablespoon snipped fresh parsley (optional)
½   teaspoon poultry seasoning
¼   teaspoon black pepper
8   cups dried white bread cubes
1   recipe Roasted Chestnuts or one 15-ounce can chestnuts, drained and coarsely chopped
1   to 1⅓ cups chicken broth
¼   cup chicken broth (optional)

1. Preheat oven to 350°F. In a large skillet melt butter over medium heat. Add celery, onion, and carrot; cook for 7 to 10 minutes or until tender, stirring occasionally. Remove from heat; stir in parsley (if desired), poultry seasoning, and pepper.
2. In a very large bowl combine celery mixture, bread cubes, and Roasted Chestnuts. Drizzle with enough of the 1 to 1⅓ cups broth to moisten, tossing lightly to combine. Place stuffing in a 2-quart casserole.
3. If desired, drizzle stuffing with an additional ¼ cup chicken broth to moisten. Bake, covered, for 40 to 50 minutes or until hot in center (165°F).
Roasted Chestnuts: Preheat oven to 400°F. With a knife, cut an X into the shells of 2 pounds fresh chestnuts. Spread chestnuts on a large baking sheet. Roast for 15 minutes; cool. Peel and coarsely chop.
PER SERVING *250 cal, 6 g fat, 10 mg chol, 347 mg sodium, 44 g carb, 5 g fiber, 4 g pro.*

Sweet Potato Spoon Bread

Spoon bread made with cornmeal is an old-fashioned favorite. Sweet potatoes give this version sweetness and a beautiful golden hue.

PREP 25 minutes
BAKE 1 hour 10 minutes
STAND 10 minutes OVEN 400°F/350°F
MAKES 8 servings

4   tablespoons (½ stick) unsalted butter, melted
2   sweet potatoes (about 1 pound)
2½ cups milk
1   tablespoon fresh thyme
1   tablespoon light brown sugar
2   teaspoons coarse sea salt
½   teaspoon freshly ground black pepper
1   cup finely ground white or yellow cornmeal
2   teaspoons baking powder
4   eggs, separated

1. Preheat oven to 400°F. Generously grease a 2-quart soufflé or casserole dish with about 1 tablespoon of the butter; set aside.
2. Wrap potatoes in foil. Bake for 45 to 55 minutes, until soft to the touch. Remove from oven; discard foil. When cool enough to handle, remove and discard peels. In a bowl mash potatoes.
3. Reduce oven temperature to 350°F. In a large saucepan bring milk, thyme, brown sugar, salt, and pepper to a low boil over medium heat. In a slow, steady stream, whisk cornmeal into milk mixture. Cook, whisking constantly, for 4 to 5 minutes, until mixture is thick and pulls away from bottom of pan. Remove from heat; cool slightly. Add potatoes, egg yolks, remaining 3 tablespoons butter, and baking powder to cornmeal mixture; stir to thoroughly combine.
4. In a large mixing bowl beat egg whites with electric mixer until soft peaks form. Leaving obvious swirls of egg white, gently fold egg whites into the potato-cornmeal mixture. Spoon batter into prepared dish.
5. Bake for 35 to 40 minutes, until internal temperature reaches 165°F. Edges will be firm and the center a bit soft. Remove from oven. Let stand for 10 minutes. Serve warm.

PER SERVING *234 cal, 10 g fat, 127 mg chol, 576 mg sodium, 28 g carb, 1 g fiber, 8 g pro.*

FIGGY BRIE ROLLS

Figgy Brie Rolls

These whole wheat rolls have a surprise inside—a gooey filling of melted Brie and dried figs.

PREP 25 minutes   RISE 1 hour
BAKE 20 minutes   COOL 5 minutes
OVEN 350°F   MAKES 12 rolls

⅓   cup finely chopped dried figs
1   teaspoon snipped fresh sage
1   teaspoon honey
1   16-ounce loaf frozen wheat bread
    dough, thawed
2   ounces Brie cheese, cut into ½-inch
    pieces
1   egg white
1   tablespoon water
    Small fresh sage leaves

1. Line a 9×9×2-inch baking pan with foil. Grease foil; set aside. For filling, in a small bowl combine figs, snipped sage, and honey; set aside.
2. Cut dough into 12 equal portions. Shape dough portions into balls. Working with 1 dough ball at a time, flatten it to a 3-inch circle. Top with a rounded teaspoon of the filling and a few pieces of the cheese. Fold dough over filling; pinch edges to seal. Place rolls, seam sides down, in the prepared baking pan. Cover and let rise until double in size (1 to 1¼ hours).
3. Preheat oven to 350°F. In a small bowl whisk together egg white and the water; brush lightly over rolls. Gently press small sage leaves onto tops of rolls; brush again with egg white mixture.
4. Bake about 20 minutes or until golden. Cool in pan on a wire rack for 5 minutes. Serve warm.
PER ROLL *127 cal, 3 g fat, 5 mg chol, 245 mg sodium, 21 g carb, 2 g fiber, 6 g pro.*

Herbed Boule

Boule means "ball" in French. It refers to the shape of this savory bread.

PREP 40 minutes
RISE 1 hour 5 minutes
STAND 10 minutes   BAKE 22 minutes
OVEN 450°F   MAKES 24 servings

5½   to 6 cups all-purpose flour
2   packages active dry yeast
2   teaspoons salt
2   cups warm water (120°F to 130°F)
2   tablespoons snipped fresh thyme,
    snipped fresh sage, and/or snipped
    fresh rosemary

Cornmeal
1 egg white, lightly beaten
1 tablespoon water
2 cups ice cubes

1. In a large bowl stir together 2 cups of the flour, the yeast, and salt. Add the 2 cups warm water to the flour mixture. Beat with an electric mixer on low to medium for 30 seconds, scraping sides of bowl constantly. Beat on high for 3 minutes. Using a wooden spoon, stir in thyme and as much of the remaining flour as you can.
2. Turn dough out onto a lightly floured surface. Knead in enough of the remaining flour to make a stiff dough that is smooth and elastic (8 to 10 minutes total). Shape dough into a ball. Place in a lightly greased bowl, turning once to grease surface. Cover; let rise in a warm place until double in size (about 40 to 45 minutes).*
3. Punch dough down. Turn dough out onto a lightly floured surface. Divide dough in half. Cover; let rest for 10 minutes. Meanwhile, lightly grease a baking sheet; sprinkle with cornmeal.
4. Shape each dough portion into a 6-inch round loaf. Transfer the dough rounds to the prepared baking sheet. Cover; let rise in a warm place until nearly double in size (25 to 30 minutes).
5. Adjust one oven rack to the lowest position and another oven rack to the lower-middle position. Set a shallow baking pan on the bottom rack. Preheat the oven to 450°F. Using a sharp knife, make an X in the top of each loaf. In a small bowl combine egg white and the 1 tablespoon water; brush tops of loaves. Place baking sheet with dough rounds on the lower-middle rack. Place ice cubes in the shallow baking pan (as they melt, they will create steam and help the dough rise and take on a crisp crust). Bake for 22 to 25 minutes or until the loaves sound hollow when tapped. If necessary, cover baking pan with foil after 15 minutes to prevent overbrowning.
*Tip: Because this dough rises faster than many other yeast breads, watch the rising time carefully.
PER SERVING *110 cal, 0 g fat, 0 mg chol, 198 mg sodium, 23 g carb, 1 g fiber, 3 g pro.*

Buttermilk-Sage Dinner Rolls

Buttermilk gives breads a pleasant tang and a super-soft texture.

PREP 45 minutes RISE 1 hour
BAKE 15 minutes OVEN 375°F
MAKES 24 rolls

8 tablespoons (1 stick) unsalted butter, cut in cubes
10 fresh sage leaves, chopped
3 tablespoons sugar
1½ cups well-shaken buttermilk
1 tablespoon plus 1 teaspoon active dry yeast (from two ¼-ounce envelopes)
½ cup warm water (105°F to 115°F)
4½ cups all-purpose flour
2 teaspoons kosher salt
½ teaspoon baking soda
2 tablespoons unsalted butter, melted

1. Lightly grease twenty-four 2½-inch muffin cups; set aside.
2. In a saucepan combine butter, sage, and 2 tablespoons of the sugar over medium-high heat; stir just until butter is melted. Stir in buttermilk and heat just until warmed; do not let mixture come to a boil. Remove from heat; cool to room temperature.
3. In a bowl combine the yeast and remaining 1 tablespoon sugar. Stir in the warm water; set aside in a warm place for 5 minutes, until yeast froths and doubles in size. Add the yeast mixture to the buttermilk mixture; stir to combine.
4. In a another large bowl stir together the flour, salt, and baking soda. Add the buttermilk-yeast mixture and stir to combine, forming a sticky dough. Loosely cover the bowl with a clean cloth; let stand in a warm place about 30 minutes, until dough has risen slightly. (At this point, the dough can be refrigerated in an airtight container up to 1 day. Before proceeding with recipe, remove from refrigerator and let rest for 15 to 20 minutes.)
5. Preheat oven to 375°F. Turn out dough onto a lightly floured surface. Knead several times, until dough is easy to work with. Pinch off pieces of dough and form into 1-inch balls. To shape cloverleaf rolls, place three 1-inch balls in each muffin cup. Loosely cover with a clean cloth and let rise in a warm place for 30 to 45 minutes or until doubled in size.
6. Uncover rolls, brush lightly with melted butter, then bake about 15 minutes, until golden brown. Remove from oven. Serve warm.
PER ROLL *142 cal, 5 g fat, 13 mg chol, 205 mg sodium, 20 g carb, 1 g fiber, 3 g pro.*

HERBED BOULE

MARINATED
SHRIMP SCAMPI

nibbles & sips

SUMPTUOUS SNACKS Little morsels loaded with big flavors are the perfect solution to holiday entertaining. Their portability means guests can mix and mingle while enjoying cheesy pastries, dips, spreads, and spiced nuts. Make one or two nibbles as a prelude to dinner—or set out an appetizer buffet and make it dinner.

30

36

38

Rich Norwegian Meatballs

Freshly grated nutmeg and (surprise!) strong coffee give these savory meatballs their Nordic flavor.

PREP 40 minutes COOK 24 minutes
CHILL 2 hours MAKES 72 meatballs

1½	cups soft bread crumbs
½	cup half-and-half or light cream
¼	cup strong coffee
2	eggs, lightly beaten
1	medium onion, finely chopped
¼	cup finely snipped fresh parsley
1	teaspoon salt
1	teaspoon freshly grated nutmeg
¼	teaspoon black pepper
1	pound lean ground beef
½	pound uncooked ground turkey breast and/or lean ground pork
¼	cup butter
¼	cup all-purpose flour
1	cup beef broth
1	cup strong coffee
1	teaspoon freshly grated nutmeg
½	teaspoon salt

1. In a large bowl combine bread crumbs, half-and-half, and the ¼ cup coffee. Let stand until mixture is evenly moist.
2. Add eggs, onion, parsley, the 1 teaspoon salt, 1 teaspoon nutmeg, and the pepper. Add beef and turkey. Mix well. Cover and chill for 2 hours. With moistened hands, shape mixture into 72 meatballs.
3. In a very large skillet melt 2 tablespoons of the butter over medium heat. Cook half of the meatballs in hot butter about 12 minutes or until done (instant-read thermometer reads 165°F), carefully turning to brown evenly. With a slotted spoon, remove meatballs from skillet. Add remaining butter to skillet and repeat with remaining meatballs. Remove meatballs from skillet.
4. Stir flour into pan drippings until smooth. Add broth, the 1 cup coffee, 1 teaspoon nutmeg, and the ½ teaspoon salt. Cook and stir over medium heat until thickened and bubbly.
5. Return all meatballs to skillet; heat through, gently stirring occasionally.
*Note: The internal color of a meatball is not a reliable doneness indicator. A beef and turkey meatball cooked to 165°F is safe, regardless of color. To measure the doneness of a meatball, insert an instant-read thermometer into the center of the meatball.
PER MEATBALL *30 cal, 2 g fat, 14 mg chol, 80 mg sodium, 1 g carb, 0 g fiber, 2 g pro.*

Marinated Shrimp Scampi

These garlic-and-lemon infused shrimp are equally good served warm or at room temperature.

PREP 35 minutes MARINATE 1 hour
BROIL 4 minutes MAKES 10 servings

¼	cup olive oil
¼	cup dry white wine
6	cloves garlic, minced
2	teaspoons finely shredded lemon peel
½	teaspoon salt
½	teaspoon crushed red pepper
2	pounds fresh or frozen extra-jumbo shrimp in shells (32 to 40)
2	tablespoons fresh parsley
	Lemon wedges

1. For marinade, in a small bowl combine olive oil, wine, garlic, lemon peel, salt, and crushed red pepper.
2. Thaw shrimp, if frozen. Peel and devein shrimp, leaving tails intact. Rinse shrimp; pat dry with paper towels. Place shrimp in a large resealable plastic bag set in a shallow bowl. Pour marinade over shrimp. Seal bag; turn to coat shrimp. Marinate in the refrigerator for 1 hour.
3. Preheat broiler. Remove shrimp from marinade, reserving marinade. Arrange shrimp on the unheated rack of a broiler pan. Broil 4 to 5 inches from heat for 2 minutes. Turn shrimp over and brush with reserved marinade; discard any remaining marinade. Broil for 2 to 4 minutes or until shrimp are opaque.
4. Mound shrimp on a serving platter; sprinkle with parsley. Serve with lemon wedges.
PER SERVING *126 cal, 4 g fat, 138 mg chol, 193 mg sodium, 2 g carb, 1 g fiber, 19 g pro.*

Greek Stuffed Meatballs

Kasseri is the cheese that is traditionally used in saganaki, the famous "flaming cheese" appetizer served in many Greek restaurants.

PREP 40 minutes BAKE 25 minutes
COOK: 3 hours (low) or 1½ hours (high) OVEN 350°F
MAKES 42 meatballs

2	eggs, lightly beaten
1	cup seasoned fine dry bread crumbs
¼	cup finely chopped pimiento-stuffed green olives
¼	cup finely chopped black olives
¼	cup snipped fresh parsley
4	cloves garlic, minced
1	teaspoon salt
¼	teaspoon black pepper
1	pound lean ground beef
1	pound ground lamb
6	ounces kasseri or feta cheese, cut into ½-inch cubes
1	recipe Greek Tomato Sauce

1. Preheat oven to 350°F. In a large bowl combine eggs, bread crumbs, green olives, black olives, parsley, garlic, salt, and pepper. Add beef and lamb; mix until thoroughly combined.
2. Shape some of the meat mixture into a ball around each cheese cube, being sure to completely enclose the cheese. Arrange meatballs in a single layer in a 15×10×1-inch baking pan. Bake for 25 minutes. Drain well.
3. Place meatballs in a 4- to 5-quart slow cooker. Pour Greek Tomato Sauce over meatballs in cooker; gently toss to coat.
4. Cover and cook on low-heat setting for 3 to 4 hours or on high-heat setting for 1½ to 2 hours. Serve immediately or keep warm, covered, on warm-heat setting or low-heat setting for up to 2 hours. Serve with toothpicks.
Greek Tomato Sauce: In a medium saucepan heat 1 tablespoon olive oil over medium heat. Cook ½ cup chopped onion and 1 clove garlic, minced, in hot oil until tender. Stir in 8 ounces canned tomato sauce; ¼ cup dry red wine or beef broth; 1 teaspoon dried oregano, crushed; and ½ teaspoon ground cinnamon. Cook until heated through.
PER MEATBALL *104 cal, 7 g fat, 30 mg chol, 448 mg sodium, 5 g carb, 1 g fiber, 6 g pro.*

GREEK-STUFFED
MEATBALLS

MINI GRUYÈRE PUFFS

Mini Gruyère Puffs

These little bites of cheese pastry are the perfect nibble with a glass of wine.

PREP **15 minutes** COOL **5 minutes**
BAKE **20 minutes** STAND **3 minutes**
OVEN **450°F/375°F** MAKES **20 servings**

½ cup water
¼ cup butter
½ teaspoon dried basil, crushed
¼ teaspoon garlic salt
    Dash cayenne pepper
½ cup all-purpose flour
2 eggs
½ cup shredded Gruyère cheese or Swiss cheese (2 ounces)
2 tablespoons grated Parmesan cheese
    Grated Gruyère cheese or Swiss cheese

1. Preheat oven to 450°F. Grease a baking sheet; set aside. In a small saucepan combine the water, butter, basil, garlic salt, and cayenne pepper. Bring to boiling over medium heat, stirring to melt butter. Immediately add flour all at once, stirring vigorously. Cook and stir until mixture forms a ball that doesn't separate. Remove from heat. Cool for 5 minutes.
2. Add eggs, one at a time, to mixture in saucepan, beating with a spoon after each addition until smooth. Stir in shredded Gruyère cheese. Drop dough by rounded teaspoons about 2 inches apart onto the prepared baking sheet.* Sprinkle with Parmesan cheese.

3. Bake for 10 minutes. Reduce oven temperature to 375°F. Bake for 10 to 12 minutes or until puffed and golden. Turn off oven. Let puffs stand in oven for 3 minutes. Sprinkle lightly with grated Gruyère cheese. Transfer puffs to a wire rack; cool completely.
*Tip:** If you prefer to pipe the dough, fit a pastry bag with a ½-inch open star tip.
PER SERVING *53 cal, 4 g fat, 31 mg chol, 76 mg sodium, 2 g carb, 0 g fiber, 2 g pro.*

Olive-Cherry Bruschetta

A tapenade of dried tart cherries and piquant green olives on tangy goat cheese gives these appetizer toasts a pleasing sweet-salty flavor.

PREP **45 minutes** BAKE **5 minutes**
OVEN **425°F** MAKES **32 servings**

32 ¾-inch-thick slices rustic baguette-style sourdough bread (16 ounces)
6 tablespoons olive oil
    Salt and black pepper
1 cup pimiento-stuffed Spanish Manzanilla olives, sliced
½ cup kalamata pitted olives, chopped
½ cup dried tart cherries, snipped
¼ cup bottled whole hot cherry peppers, seeded and chopped
1 large shallot, quartered and thinly sliced
1 tablespoon snipped fresh basil
1 teaspoon finely shredded lime peel
2 teaspoons fresh lime juice
6 ounces goat cheese (chèvre)
2 ounces very thinly sliced prosciutto, cut into 32 pieces
2 tablespoons snipped fresh chives

1. Preheat oven to 425°F. Place baguette slices on a very large baking sheet. Brush slices with 4 tablespoons of the oil, then season lightly with salt and black pepper. Toast bread on middle rack of oven about 5 minutes, until crisp and light brown, turning once. Remove from oven; set aside.
2. For olive-cherry tapenade, in a medium bowl stir together the remaining 2 tablespoons olive oil, olives, cherries, peppers, shallot, basil, lime peel, and lime juice.
3. Spread goat cheese on toast slices. Top with prosciutto and olive-cherry tapenade; sprinkle with snipped chives.
PER SERVING *104 cal, 5 g fat, 4 mg chol, 294 mg sodium, 11 g carb, 1 g fiber, 3 g pro.*

Herb-Dijon Marinated Veggies

This mix of marinated vegetables presents a perfect opportunity to use the appetizer forks, if you have them. If not, they're not a bad investment.

PREP **20 minutes**
MARINATE **30 minutes**
MAKES **6 to 8 servings**

3 tablespoons dry white wine, such as Pinot Grigio or Sauvignon Blanc
2 tablespoons snipped fresh basil
1 tablespoon snipped fresh parsley
1 tablespoon olive oil
2 teaspoons snipped fresh thyme or oregano or ½ teaspoon dried thyme or oregano, crushed
2 teaspoons Dijon mustard
1 cloves garlic, minced
¼ teaspoon salt
1½ cups fresh small cremini mushrooms
1 cup grape or cherry tomatoes
1 cup yellow and/or orange sweet pepper strips
1 zucchini, quartered lengthwise and cut into 1-inch pieces (about 1 cup)

1. In a large bowl whisk together wine, basil, parsley, oil, thyme, mustard, garlic, and salt. Add mushrooms, tomatoes, sweet pepper, and zucchini; toss to coat.
2. Cover vegetables and marinate at room temperature for 30 to 60 minutes, stirring occasionally. Using a slotted spoon, transfer vegetables to a serving bowl.
PER SERVING *52 cal, 3 g fat, 0 mg chol, 143 mg sodium, 5 g carb, 1 g fiber, 2 g pro.*

OLIVE-CHERRY BRUSCHETTA

Salami Crostini

Be sure to get soft salami for this rich spread. Hard salami—which is air-dried during the curing process—won't mince well in the food processor.

PREP **20 minutes**   BAKE **8 minutes**
OVEN **400°F**   MAKES **24 servings**

1   recipe Crostini
4   ounces soft Italian salami (such as Genoa or Toscano)
¼   cup ricotta cheese
4   teaspoons spicy brown mustard or smoky mustard
1   tablespoon coarsely snipped fresh chives
     Milk (optional)

1. Prepare crostini. Cut salami into large chunks. Place in a food processor; cover and process until finely chopped. Add cheese, mustard, and chives; cover and process until nearly smooth.
2. Transfer salami mixture to a small serving bowl. If necessary, stir in enough milk to reach spreading consistency. Serve with crostini.
Crostini: Preheat oven to 400°F. Cut one 8-ounce loaf baguette-style French bread into ½-inch diagonal slices. Arrange bread slices on a large baking sheet. Lightly brush one side of bread slices with olive oil. Bake in the preheated oven about 8 minutes or until lightly browned, turning once. Cool.

PER SERVING *61 cal, 3 g fat, 6 mg chol, 163 mg sodium, 5 g carb, 0 g fiber, 2 g pro.*

Antipasto Platter with Tomato Chutney

Antipasto platters give you a lot of leeway in choosing the elements that comprise it. Shoot for a balance of colors and textures.

PREP 30 minutes COOK 30 minutes
COOL 20 minutes MAKES 10 servings

- 2 pounds roma tomatoes, seeded and coarsely chopped*
- 1 onion, finely chopped
- 2 cloves garlic, minced
- ½ cup red wine vinegar
- 1 tablespoon sugar
- ½ teaspoon salt
- ½ teaspoon paprika
- ⅛ teaspoon cayenne pepper
- 1 tablespoon snipped fresh basil
  Antipasto ingredients such as olive-oil-packed tuna sprinkled with capers and caper berries; pickled peppers; blanched asparagus and broccoli; paper-thin slices prosciutto; and/or whole grain crackers or breads

1. In a medium saucepan combine tomatoes, onion, garlic, vinegar, sugar, salt, paprika, and cayenne pepper. Bring to boiling; reduce heat. Simmer, uncovered, for 30 minutes or until mixture is thickened and saucelike, stirring occasionally.
2. Remove from heat; cool about 20 minutes. Serve warm sprinkled with basil and with desired antipasto ingredients. Store any remaining chutney in refrigerator. Bring to room temperature before serving.
***Tip** If desired, omit roma tomatoes and use one 28-ounce can whole plum tomatoes, drained and cut up. This will yield less chutney (1½ cups).
PER SERVING 29 cal, 0 g fat, 0 mg chol, 122 mg sodium, 6 g carb, 1 g fiber, 1 g pro.

Honey and Black Bean Dip

This hot bean dip served on tortilla chips will disappear in a flash.

PREP 30 minutes BAKE 25 minutes
OVEN 375°F MAKES 12 servings

- 7½ to 8 ounces uncooked Mexican chorizo sausage (casings removed if present)
- 1 carrot, finely chopped
- ½ cup finely chopped onion (1 medium)
- ½ cup chopped red sweet pepper (1 small)
- 2 cloves garlic, minced
- 1 tablespoon honey
- 1 15-ounce can black beans, rinsed and drained
- 1 cup shredded Monterey Jack cheese (4 ounces)
  Shredded Monterey Jack cheese (optional)
  Snipped fresh cilantro (optional)
  Tortilla chips

1. Preheat oven to 375°F. Heat a large skillet over medium-high heat. Add chorizo to the skillet. Cook about 5 minutes or until golden brown, using a wooden spoon to break up meat as it cooks. Using a slotted spoon, transfer meat to a bowl. Reserve 2 teaspoons of the drippings in the skillet; discard remaining drippings. Add carrot and onion to skillet. Cook and stir over medium heat for 8 to 10 minutes or until soft. Add sweet pepper and garlic. Cook and stir for 2 minutes more. Remove from heat. Stir in honey. Let cool.
2. In a medium bowl use a potato masher to mash the beans slightly. Stir in cheese, cooled chorizo, and cooked vegetables. Transfer to a shallow 1-quart baking dish.
3. Bake, covered, for 15 minutes. Uncover. If desired, top with additional shredded cheese. Bake about 10 minutes more or until heated through. If desired, sprinkle with snipped fresh cilantro. Serve with tortilla chips.
PER SERVING 162 cal, 10 g fat, 24 mg chol, 400 mg sodium, 11 g carb, 3 g fiber, 10 g pro.

Eggplant Dip

The flavor of this chunky dip is similar to *baba ghanoush*—the Middle Eastern eggplant puree.

PREP 45 minutes ROAST 40 minutes
STAND 30 minutes OVEN 400°F
MAKES 40 servings

- 4 pounds eggplants or 4 pounds baby eggplants (about 12)
- 4 bulbs garlic
- 1 cup olive oil
- 4 teaspoons salt
- 3 cups coarsely chopped red sweet peppers (4 medium)
- ⅔ cup lemon juice
- ½ cup snipped fresh parsley
- ¼ cup snipped fresh oregano
  Fresh oregano leaves (optional)
  Toasted baguette-style French bread, sliced or flatbread, broken into pieces

1. Preheat oven to 400°F. Wash eggplants; trim and cut into ½- to 1-inch pieces. Divide eggplant between two 15×10×1-inch baking pans or shallow roasting pans. Using a sharp knife, cut off the top ½ inch from garlic bulbs to expose individual cloves. Leaving garlic bulbs whole, remove any loose, papery outer layers. Place garlic bulbs on a 12-inch square of heavy foil; drizzle with 1 tablespoon of the olive oil. Wrap foil up around the garlic bulbs to completely enclose.
2. Drizzle ¼ cup of the remaining olive oil over eggplant in each pan and sprinkle half of the salt over eggplant in each pan; toss to coat. Place eggplant and garlic packet in oven, placing pans on separate oven racks. Roast for 20 minutes, stirring once. Add half of the sweet peppers to each pan with eggplant; stir to combine. Roast about 20 minutes more or until vegetables are tender, stirring once. Remove pans and garlic from oven and cool.
3. Transfer eggplant and peppers to a very large glass or nonreactive bowl. Squeeze garlic pulp from individual cloves into a small bowl; using the back of a spoon, mash garlic pulp. Add the remaining olive oil and the lemon juice to garlic; whisk to combine. Add garlic mixture, parsley, and snipped oregano to eggplant mixture; toss to combine.
4. If desired, garnish with oregano leaves. Serve with bread.
PER SERVING 67 cal, 6 g fat, 0 mg chol, 235 mg sodium, 4 g carb, 2 g fiber, 1 g pro.

HONEY AND BLACK BEAN DIP

CREAMY FENNEL AND LEEK DIP

1 teaspoon peppercorn melange, cracked
8 ounces feta cheese, cubed

1. In a small bowl combine olive oil, herbs, lemon juice, garlic, and cracked peppercorns. Stir until well mixed. Add cheese cubes; toss very gently to coat. Divide between 2 clean half-pint jars with tight-fitting lids.
2. Seal jars; chill for at least 3 days or up to 5 days.
3. Let stand at room temperature for 30 minutes before serving.
PER SERVING *107 cal, 9 g fat, 25 mg chol, 317 mg sodium, 2 g carb, 0 g fiber, 4 g pro.*

Onion and Garlic Macadamia Nuts
These spiced, buttery-tasting nuts are truly a Christmas treat.

PREP **10 minutes** COOK **5 minutes**
MAKES **12 servings**

3 tablespoons olive oil
1 tablespoon dried parsley flakes
1 tablespoon onion salt
1½ teaspoons sugar
1½ teaspoons lemon juice
¾ teaspoon garlic powder
3 cups macadamia nuts (about 14 ounces)

1. In a large skillet heat oil over medium heat for 1 to 2 minutes or until hot. Carefully add parsley, onion salt, sugar, lemon juice, and garlic powder, stirring until combined. Add macadamia nuts.
2. Cook and stir for 5 minutes. Drain nuts on paper towels; cool.
PER SERVING *274 cal, 29 g fat, 0 mg chol, 402 mg sodium, 5 g carb, 3 g fiber, 3 g pro.*

Creamy Fennel and Leek Dip
Clean the leeks by swirling the slices in a bowl of water, then patting them dry. Their layers can harbor sand and grit.

PREP **20 minutes** COOK **10 minutes**
BAKE **20 minutes** OVEN **350°F**
MAKES **12 servings**

2 ounces pancetta, finely chopped
1 tablespoon olive oil
2 fennel bulbs, halved lengthwise, cored, and thinly sliced
2 leeks, thinly sliced
½ cup mayonnaise or salad dressing
½ cup sour cream
1 cup grated Asiago cheese
¼ cup whipping cream
½ teaspoon salt
½ teaspoon crushed red pepper
Baguette-style French bread, torn

1. Preheat oven to 350°F. In a large skillet cook pancetta in olive oil over medium heat until golden brown. Add fennel and leeks; cook about 10 minutes or until tender and just starting to brown, stirring occasionally. Remove from heat; let cool.

2. In a medium bowl combine mayonnaise, sour cream, ¾ cup of the Asiago cheese, the whipping cream, salt, and crushed red pepper. Stir in the cooled fennel mixture. Transfer to a 9-inch pie plate or a 1-quart shallow baking dish or individual-size baking dishes. Sprinkle with the remaining ¼ cup Asiago cheese.
3. Bake about 20 minutes or until bubbly around edges. Serve with torn bread.
PER SERVING *188 cal, 17 g fat, 29 mg chol, 370 mg sodium, 6 g carb, 1 g fiber, 4 g pro.*

Marinated Feta
The pepper blend called for in this recipe includes a trio of white, black, and pink peppercorns.

PREP **15 minutes** CHILL **3 days**
STAND **30 minutes** MAKES **8 servings**

2 tablespoons olive oil
2 tablespoons snipped assorted fresh herbs, such as oregano, basil, thyme, and/or parsley
1 tablespoon lemon juice
2 garlic, minced

MARINATED FETA

ONION AND GARLIC
MACADAMIA NUTS

Gorgonzola-Thyme Stuffed Olives

An olive bar—found at specialty markets and some grocery stores—is a great place to buy the olives.

START TO FINISH 25 minutes
MAKES 40 servings

3   ounces Gorgonzola cheese, crumbled
2   ounces cream cheese, softened
2   teaspoons snipped fresh thyme
½   teaspoon black pepper
40 whole pitted green olives

1. In a medium bowl beat Gorgonzola cheese and cream cheese with an electric mixer on medium until creamy. Stir in thyme and pepper.
2. Spoon cheese mixture into a pastry bag fitting with a small plain round tip. Pipe the cheese mixture into each olive.
PER SERVING *19 cal, 2 g fat, 3 mg chol, 100 mg sodium, 0 g carb, 0 g fiber, 1 g pro.*

Confetti Peanut Butter Munchies

Kids will go crazy for this crunchy, sweet-salty snack dusted with a snowy coating of powdered sugar.

PREP 25 minutes STAND 1 hour
MAKES 22 servings

7   cups crispy corn and rice cereal
2   cups pretzel sticks or nuggets
1   cup semisweet chocolate pieces
½   cup peanut butter
¼   cup butter
1   teaspoon vanilla
2   cups powdered sugar
½   cup dried mango, coarsely chopped
½   cup dried pineapple, coarsely chopped
¼   cup dried cranberries
¼   cup golden raisins

1. In an extra-large bowl combine cereal and pretzels; set aside. In a small saucepan combine chocolate pieces, peanut butter, and butter. Cook and stir over medium-low heat until melted. Remove from heat. Stir in vanilla. Pour chocolate mixture over cereal mixture; toss gently to coat.
2. Place powdered sugar in a large resealable plastic bag. Add cereal mixture; seal bag and shake to coat. Spread cereal mixture on a sheet of waxed paper and let stand about 1 hour or until set.
3. In a large bowl combine cereal mixture, mango, pineapple, cranberries, and raisins.
PER SERVING *212 cal, 8 g fat, 6 mg chol, 199 mg sodium, 36 g carb, 1 g fiber, 3 g pro.*

Mulled Cranberry Punch

This warm punch is made in a slow cooker, so it can stay warm for the duration of the party.

PREP 15 minutes COOK 4 hours (low) or 2 hours (high) MAKES 12 servings

1   orange
8   sticks cinnamon, broken
8   whole cloves
4   whole allspice
1   32-ounce bottle cranberry juice
1   11.5-ounce can frozen white grape-raspberry juice concentrate
4   cups water

1. Use a vegetable peeler to remove several 2- to 3-inch-long sections of orange peel from the orange, avoiding the white pith underneath. Juice the orange.
2. For a spice bag, cut a 6-inch square from a double thickness of 100%-cotton cheesecloth. Place orange peel, cinnamon, cloves, and allspice in the center of the square. Bring the corners together and tie closed with 100%-cotton kitchen string.
3. In a 3½- to 4-quart slow cooker combine cranberry juice, juice concentrate, the water, orange juice, and spice bag.
4. Cook, covered, on low-heat setting for 4 to 6 hours or on high-heat setting for 2 to 3 hours. Remove spice bag and discard. Serve immediately or keep warm on low-heat setting for up to 2 hours.
PER SERVING *114 cal, 0 g fat, 0 mg chol, 7 mg sodium, 29 g carb, 1 g fiber, 0 g pro.*

GORGONZOLA-THYME
STUFFED OLIVES

CONFETTI PEANUT
BUTTER MUNCHIES

Creamy Berry Citrus Punch

The "creamy" element in this sweet punch is provided by a pint each of orange and raspberry sherbets.

START TO FINISH **15 minutes**
MAKES **16 servings**

2   cups refrigerated limeade
2   cups white cranberry juice
1   pint orange sherbet
1   pint raspberry sherbet
1   2-liter bottle lemon-lime carbonated beverage, chilled
    Kumquat slices, lime slices, lemon slices, and/or fresh or frozen cranberries

1. In a punch bowl or very large pitcher stir together limeade and cranberry juice. Cover and chill until ready to serve.

2. Just before serving, top with scoops of orange and raspberry sherbets. Slowly pour carbonated beverage down the side of the bowl. Stir gently to muddle. Add desired fruit.

PER SERVING *133 cal, 0 g fat, 0 mg chol, 52 mg sodium, 33 g carb, 1 g fiber, 0 g pro.*

Honey-Mulled Apple Cider

This classic holiday drink warms the body and soul—and makes the house smell wonderful too.

PREP **10 minutes**
COOK **5 hours (low) or 2½ hours (high)**
MAKES **10 servings**

6   sticks cinnamon, broken
1   teaspoon whole allspice
1   teaspoon whole cloves

10 cups pasteurized apple cider or apple juice (2½ quarts)
⅓   cup honey or packed light brown sugar
    Cinnamon sticks (optional)

1. For spice bag, place broken stick cinnamon, allspice, and cloves on a square of 100%-cotton cheesecloth. Bring up corners and tie closed with clean kitchen string.
2. In a 3½- to 5-quart slow cooker combine spice bag, apple cider, and honey.
3. Cover and cook on low-heat setting for 5 to 6 hours or on high-heat setting for 2½ to 3 hours. Remove and discard spice bag. Ladle cider into mugs. If desired, serve with cinnamon sticks for stirring.

PER SERVING *150 cal, 0 g fat, 0 mg chol, 8 mg sodium, 38 g carb, 0 g fiber, 0 g pro.*

MASCARPONE-STUFFED
FRENCH TOAST WITH SALTED
CARAMEL-BANANA SAUCE

delicious morning meals

RISE & SHINE This time of year, you need no excuse to skip the usual oatmeal and wheat toast and indulge in something a little more luxurious. Rouse sleepyheads from their beds with a cheesy sausage strata, biscuits and gravy, homemade fruit and cheese pastries, or chocolate pancakes.

42

45

54

Poblano-Chorizo Strata

Bolillo rolls are the Mexican version of the baguette. While their shape is oval—not long and thin—their interior is soft and exterior is crisp.

PREP 40 minutes CHILL 2 hours
BAKE 1 hour STAND 10 minutes
OVEN 325°F MAKES 10 to 12 servings

- ½ pound uncooked chorizo sausage
- 2 onions, thinly sliced
- 2 fresh poblano chile peppers, seeded and thinly sliced (see tip, page 9)
- 1 red sweet pepper, thinly sliced
- 8 cups 1-inch cubes Mexican bolillo rolls or crusty Italian bread
- 6 eggs, lightly beaten
- 2½ cups milk
- 1 teaspoon Mexican oregano or regular oregano, crushed
- ½ teaspoon paprika
- ½ cup queso fresco, crumbled Snipped fresh cilantro (optional)

1. In a large skillet cook chorizo over medium heat until browned. Using a slotted spoon, transfer chorizo to a bowl, reserving 1 tablespoon drippings in skillet. Add onions to drippings in skillet; cook and stir over medium heat about 10 minutes or until tender. Stir in chile peppers and sweet pepper; cook about 5 minutes or just until peppers are tender. Remove from heat. Stir in chorizo.
2. Lightly grease a 3-quart rectangular or oval baking dish. Spread half of the bread cubes in the prepared dish. Spoon half of the chorizo mixture over. Repeat layers.
3. In a large bowl whisk together eggs,

milk, oregano, and paprika. Pour evenly over layers in baking dish. Cover with foil. Chill for at least 2 hours or up to 24 hours.
4. Preheat oven to 325°F. Bake, covered, for 30 minutes. Uncover. Bake for 30 to 45 minutes more or until an instant-read thermometer inserted in the center registers 170°F. Sprinkle with cheese for the last 5 minutes of baking. Let stand for 10 minutes before serving. If desired, sprinkle with cilantro.

PER SERVING 257 cal, 14 g fat, 156 mg chol, 412 mg sodium, 17 g carb, 1 g fiber, 15 g pro.

Four-Cheese Zucchini Strata

Four words: provolone, cheddar, blue, and Parmesan. Need we say more?

PREP 35 minutes CHILL 2 hours
BAKE 45 minutes STAND 10 minutes
OVEN 325°F MAKES 8 to 10 servings

- 2 tablespoons olive oil
- 4 zucchini, halved lengthwise and cut into ¼-inch slices (about 5 cups) Butter
- 8 cups bite-size pieces Italian flatbread with garlic (focaccia)
- 1 cup shredded provolone cheese (4 ounces)
- 1 cup shredded white cheddar cheese (4 ounces)
- ½ cup crumbled blue cheese (2 ounces)
- ½ cup grated Parmesan cheese (2 ounces)
- 7 eggs, lightly beaten
- 2 cups milk
- 2 tablespoons snipped fresh parsley
- ½ teaspoon salt
- ½ teaspoon black pepper

1. In a very large skillet heat olive oil over medium-high heat. Gradually add zucchini slices. Cook until zucchini is lightly browned, stirring occasionally. Remove from heat. Meanwhile, lightly butter a 3-quart rectangular or oval baking dish. Place half of the torn bread in the prepared dish. Arrange half of the zucchini over the bread. Sprinkle half of each cheese over the zucchini. Repeat layers.
2. In a large bowl whisk together eggs, milk, parsley, salt, and pepper. Pour evenly over layers in baking dish. Cover with plastic wrap. Chill for least 2 hours or up to 24 hours.

3. Preheat oven to 325°F. Remove plastic wrap. Bake for 45 to 50 minutes or until center is set and an instant-read thermometer inserted in the center registers 170°F. Let stand for 10 minutes before serving.

PER SERVING 347 cal, 23 g fat, 228 mg chol, 742 mg sodium, 16 g carb, 1 g fiber, 22 g pro.

Greek-Style Frittata

This simple and savory egg dish also makes a lovely, casual supper during the busy holiday season. Just add a green salad and some bread.

PREP 15 minutes BAKE 10 minutes
OVEN 425°F MAKES 4 servings

- ½ cup dried tomato slices (not oil-packed)
- ½ cup boiling water
- 8 eggs
- ½ cup roasted red peppers, drained and chopped
- ½ cup purchased Italian olive antipasto marinated in garlic and herbs
- 1 teaspoon dried oregano, crushed or 2 teaspoons fresh oregano
- 1 tablespoon olive oil
- 2 ounces feta cheese, crumbled Freshly ground black pepper Fresh oregano (optional) Feta cheese, crumbled (optional)

1. Preheat oven to 425°F. In a small bowl combine tomato slices and ½ cup the boiling water; set aside for 5 minutes. Drain tomatoes, reserving liquid.
2. Meanwhile in a large bowl whisk eggs; stir in roasted peppers. Lightly drain and chop the antipasto mixture; add to eggs. Whisk in oregano and the reserved liquid from the tomato soaking step.
3. In a large oven-going skillet heat oil over medium heat. Pour egg mixture into the hot skillet. Stir in feta; top with tomatoes and place in oven. Bake 10 to 13 minutes or until set.
4. Remove from oven; cool several minutes on wire rack before serving. Top with black pepper. If desired, sprinkle with oregano and feta cheese.

PER SERVING 252 cal, 18 g fat, 436 mg chol, 668 mg sodium, 7 g carb, 1 g fiber, 16 g pro.

POBLANO-CHORIZO STRATA

GREEK-STYLE FRITTATA

43

Breakfast Lasagna Rolls

Creamy lasagna for breakfast will certainly get sleepyheads out of bed!

PREP **30 minutes** BAKE **35 minutes**
OVEN **350°F** MAKES **8 servings**

- 8   dried whole-grain lasagna noodles
  Nonstick cooking spray
- 8   eggs or 2 cups refrigerated or frozen egg product, thawed
- 2   teaspoons snipped fresh dill weed or ½ teaspoon dried dill weed
  Salt
- 2   teaspoons olive oil
- 4   cups fresh spinach
- 4   ounces reduced-sodium thinly sliced cooked ham
- ½   cup bottled roasted red sweet peppers, drained and cut into strips
- 1½   cups sliced fresh mushrooms
- 4   green onions, thinly sliced (½ cup)
- 1   12-ounce can evaporated fat-free milk
- 2   tablespoons flour
- 1   tablespoon Dijon mustard
- ¼   teaspoon black pepper
- 1   cup shredded reduced-fat cheddar cheese (4 ounces)
  Paprika

1. Preheat oven to 350°F. Cook lasagna noodles according to package directions. Drain; rinse with cold water. Drain again. Place noodles in a single layer on a sheet of foil; set aside. Lightly coat a 2-quart rectangular baking dish with cooking spray; set aside.

2. Using a whisk, in a medium bowl beat together eggs, dill weed, and salt. In a large nonstick skillet heat 1 teaspoon of the oil over medium heat; pour in egg mixture. Cook over medium heat, without stirring, until eggs begin to set on the bottom and around edges. With a spatula, lift and fold the partially cooked eggs so the uncooked portions flows underneath. Continue cooking over medium heat for 2 to 3 minutes or until eggs are cooked through but still glossy and moist. Remove from heat; set aside. Gently stir spinach into mixture in skillet. Cover and let stand about 3 minutes or until spinach is wilted.

3. Top each lasagna noodle with ham, cutting slices to fit noodles. Divide the egg mixture evenly over ham. Top with sweet pepper strips. Starting from a short end, roll up each noodle. Place the lasagna rolls, seam sides down, in the prepared baking dish; set aside.

4. For the sauce, in a large skillet heat the remaining 1 teaspoon oil over medium-high heat. Add mushrooms and green onions; cook and stir about 3 minutes or until tender. In a medium bowl stir together ¼ cup of the evaporated milk and the flour until smooth; stir in the remaining evaporated milk, the mustard, and black pepper. Stir the milk mixture into the mushroom mixture in skillet. Cook and stir until slightly thickened and bubbly. Remove from heat. Stir in the cheese until melted. Pour sauce over the lasagna rolls.

5. Cover and bake about 35 minutes or until heated through. To serve, sprinkle with paprika.

PER SERVING *287 cal, 11 g fat, 229 mg chol, 437 mg sodium, 26 g carb, 4 g fiber, 22 g pro.*

Ham and Cheese Slab Pies

Flaky pastry envelops layers of ham, cream cheese, Gruyère, and red onion in this very special breakfast treat.

PREP 30 minutes BAKE 25 minutes
OVEN 400°F MAKES 12 to 16 wedges

2　3-ounce packages cream cheese, softened
2　tablespoons honey mustard
1　17.3-ounce package frozen puff pastry sheets, thawed (2 sheets)
6　ounces thinly sliced Black Forest ham
½　of a medium red onion, thinly sliced
6　ounces thinly sliced Gruyère, Swiss, or cheddar cheese
1　egg
1　tablespoon water

1. Preheat oven to 400°F. Line 2 large baking sheets with parchment paper; set aside. In a small bowl stir together cream cheese and mustard. On a lightly floured surface roll each sheet of thawed puff pastry into a 15×12-inch rectangle. Transfer each pastry sheet to a prepared baking sheet; spread half of each pastry lengthwise with cream cheese mixture, leaving a ½-inch border around outside edges.
2. Add individual layers of ham, onion, and Gruyère cheese over cream cheese layer, leaving a ½-inch border around outside edges. In a small bowl whisk together egg and the water. Brush some of the egg mixture on the uncovered edges of the pastries. Fold uncovered portion of each pastry rectangle up and over filling. Use a fork to seal edges together. Brush tops with egg mixture. Cut decorative slits in top of each pastry for steam to escape.
3. Bake about 25 minutes or until pastries are golden on both the top and bottom. If top browns more quickly than the bottom, cover with foil. Slide pies and parchment paper onto wire racks; cool slightly. To serve, cut crosswise into wedges.
PER WEDGE *360 cal, 26 g fat, 56 mg chol, 361 mg sodium, 21 g carb, 1 g fiber, 11 g pro.*

Caramelized Onion and Potato Breakfast Casserole

Be sure to cook the onions for the full 20 minutes over low heat to draw out their sweetness.

PREP 45 minutes BAKE 45 minutes
STAND 15 minutes OVEN 350°F
MAKES 8 servings

4　cups sliced golden potatoes, cut ⅛ to ¼ inch thick (about 1½ pounds)
1　tablespoon olive oil
2　ounces pancetta, chopped
3　cups thinly sliced sweet onions, such as Vidalia or Maui Butter
6　eggs lightly beaten
½　cup milk
1　cup shredded Gruyère cheese or Swiss cheese
1　teaspoon salt
1　teaspoon snipped fresh rosemary
½　teaspoon black pepper

1. Preheat oven to 350°F. In a large saucepan cook potatoes, covered, in boiling lightly salted water about 5 minutes or until slightly tender but still firm. Drain; set aside. In a large skillet heat olive oil over medium-high heat. Add pancetta; cook until lightly browned. Using a slotted spoon, remove pancetta, reserving drippings in skillet. Set pancetta aside. Add onions to skillet. Cook and stir over medium-low heat about 20 minutes or until lightly browned and very tender. Remove from heat. Carefully stir potatoes and pancetta into onions in skillet.
2. Butter a 2-quart rectangular baking dish. Spread potato mixture into dish. In a medium bowl whisk together eggs and milk. Add cheese, salt, rosemary, and pepper; stir. Pour over potato mixture.
3. Bake, uncovered, for 45 to 50 minutes or until golden and a knife inserted in the center comes out clean. Let stand for 15 minutes before serving.
PER SERVING *250 cal, 13 g fat, 180 mg chol, 535 mg sodium, 22 g carb, 3 g fiber, 13 g pro.*

HAM AND CHEESE
SLAB PIES

Sugared Bacon-Wrapped Sausages

You might consider making a double batch of these. Their sweet-salty flavor is addictive.

PREP 30 minutes BAKE 1 hour
OVEN 300°F MAKES 24 sausages

  Nonstick cooking spray
24 small cooked smoked sausage links
8 slices bacon or applewood-smoked bacon, each slice cut crosswise into thirds
⅓ cup packed brown sugar
½ teaspoon Chinese five-spice powder or apple pie spice

1. Preheat oven to 300°F. Line a 15×10×1-inch baking pan with foil; lightly coat with cooking spray. Set aside.
2. Wrap each sausage link with a bacon piece, overlapping the bacon piece at the end. Press the end of the bacon piece to seal or secure it with a wooden toothpick.
3. In a large resealable plastic bag combine brown sugar and five-spice powder. Add several bacon-wrapped sausages to bag; seal. Shake bag gently to coat sausages with brown sugar mixture; place sausages in prepared pan. Repeat with remaining bacon-wrapped sausages and brown sugar mixture.

4. Bake for 1 hour or until the bacon browns. Serve immediately.
To Make Ahead: Prepare as directed through Step 2, except do not preheat oven or line baking pan. Cover and chill for up to 24 hours. To serve, preheat oven to 300°F. Line baking pan as directed. Continue as directed in Step 3.
PER SAUSAGE *54 cal, 4 g fat, 8 mg chol, 133 mg sodium, 3 g carb, 0 g fiber, 2 g pro.*

AGED-CHEDDAR BISCUITS
WITH PEPPERED
HAM GRAVY

PEACH-PROSCIUTTO
CORNMEAL MUFFINS

Aged-Cheddar Biscuits with Peppered Ham Gravy

You can use white or yellow cheddar in these tender biscuits.

PREP 30 minutes   BAKE 14 minutes
OVEN 400°F   MAKES 10 servings

4 cups all-purpose flour
2 tablespoons baking powder
1 teaspoon salt
¾ cup butter
1½ cups shredded aged sharp cheddar cheese (6 ounces)
1½ cups milk
   Milk
1 recipe Peppered Ham Gravy

1. Preheat oven to 400°F. Line a large baking sheet with parchment paper; set aside. In a bowl combine flour, baking powder, and salt. Using a pastry blender, cut in butter until mixture resembles coarse crumbs. Add cheese; mix well. Make a well in the center of the flour mixture. Add the 1½ cups milk all at once. Using a fork, stir until moistened.
2. Turn dough out onto a lightly floured surface. Knead dough by folding and gently pressing it just until dough holds together. Pat or lightly roll dough until ¾ inch thick. Cut dough with a floured 2- to 2½-inch round cutter; reroll scraps as necessary.
3. Place dough rounds 1 inch apart on prepared baking sheet. Brush tops with additional milk. Bake for 14 to 16 minutes or until golden. Transfer biscuits to a wire rack.
4. Split biscuits and place on serving plates. Top with Peppered Ham Gravy.
Peppered Ham Gravy: In a large skillet heat 3 tablespoons olive oil over medium heat. Add 3½ cups cubed ham and 1 cup chopped onion (1 large). Cook until ham is browned and onion is tender, stirring occasionally. Stir ¼ cup all-purpose flour into ham mixture. Cook and stir over medium heat for 1 minute. Gradually whisk in 3 cups milk. Cook and stir until thickened and bubbly. Cook and stir for 1 minute more. Stir in 1 teaspoon cracked black pepper and ½ teaspoon dried sage, crushed. If desired, stir in 2 tablespoons snipped fresh parsley.
PER SERVING *562 cal, 30 g fat, 90 mg chol, 1,318 mg sodium, 50 g carb, 2 g fiber, 22 g pro.*

Peach-Prosciutto Cornmeal Muffins

Substitute cooked and crumbled bacon for the prosciutto if you like.

PREP 25 minutes   BAKE 14 minutes
OVEN 400°F   MAKES 12 servings

1 cup yellow cornmeal
¾ cup all-purpose flour
3 tablespoons sugar
2½ teaspoons baking powder
¼ teaspoon salt
¾ cup half-and-half or light cream
2 eggs
¼ cup butter, melted and cooled
1 cup chopped fresh or frozen unsweetened peaches
4 ounces thinly sliced prosciutto, chopped

1. Preheat oven to 400°F. Grease twelve 2½-inch muffin cups; set aside. In a medium bowl stir together cornmeal, flour, sugar, baking powder, and salt.
2. In a medium bowl whisk together half-and-half, eggs, and melted butter. Stir in peaches and prosciutto. Add peach mixture to cornmeal mixture; stir just until combined. Divide batter among prepared muffin cups.
3. Bake 14 minutes or until edges are golden.
PER SERVING *184 cal, 9 g fat, 51 mg chol, 337 mg sodium, 20 g carb, 1 g fiber, 6 g pro.*

Cranberry-Buttermilk Muffins

For the pretty effect shown here, line the muffin cups with squares of parchment paper.

PREP **20 minutes** BAKE **15 minutes**
COOL **10 minutes** OVEN **400°F**
MAKES **12 muffins**

1   cup fresh cranberries
2   tablespoons sugar
2   cups all-purpose flour
⅓   to ½ cup sugar
4   teaspoons baking powder
1   teaspoon finely shredded orange peel
½   teaspoon salt
1   egg, lightly beaten
¾   cup buttermilk
¼   cup butter, melted
    Coarse sugar

1. Preheat oven to 400°F. Grease twelve 2½-inch muffin cups or line with paper bake cups. In a medium mixing bowl toss cranberries with 2 tablespoons sugar; set aside.
2. In a large bowl combine flour, ⅓ to ½ cup sugar, the baking powder, orange peel, and salt; stir well. In a small bowl combine egg, buttermilk, and butter. Make a well in center of flour mixture; add egg mixture and cranberries. Stir just until moistened. Spoon into prepared muffin cups. Sprinkle tops with coarse sugar.
3. Bake muffins about 15 minutes or until golden and a toothpick inserted comes out clean. Cool slightly on a wire rack. Serve warm.

PER MUFFIN *163 cal, 5 g fat, 29 mg chol, 306 mg sodium, 27 g carb, 1 g fiber, 3 g pro.*

Cinnamon Scones with Fruitcakey Ribbon

Even those who aren't fans of fruitcake will love these tender scones with a filling of dried cranberries, dried currants, and candied orange peel soaked in brandy.

PREP **40 minutes** STAND **30 minutes**
BAKE **35 minutes** COOL **10 minutes**
OVEN **375°F** MAKES **12 scones**

½   cup chopped dried cranberries
¼   cup dried currants
2   tablespoons chopped candied orange peel
¼   cup brandy or orange juice
3   tablespoons butter, softened
½   cup packed dark brown sugar
1   tablespoon ground cinnamon
1   tablespoon all-purpose flour
1   cup quick-cooking oats
2   cups all-purpose flour
⅓   cup granulated sugar
½   teaspoon salt
½   cup butter, cut up
2   eggs
⅓   cup sour cream
¼   cup milk
1   teaspoon vanilla
1   egg white
1   tablespoon water
1   recipe Cinnamon Sugar

1. In a small saucepan combine cranberries, currants, orange peel, and brandy. Bring just to boiling over medium-high heat. Remove from heat, cover saucepan, and let stand for 30 minutes.
2. Drain and discard excess brandy from fruit mixture; set fruit aside. In a small bowl combine the 3 tablespoons butter, brown sugar, cinnamon, and the 1 tablespoon flour; mix well. Add reserved fruit; toss to combine. Set aside.
3. Preheat oven to 375°F. Lightly grease a 9×1½-inch round baking pan; set aside.
4. In a large bowl stir together oats, the 2 cups flour, the granulated sugar, and salt. Using a pastry blender, cut the ½ cup butter into flour mixture until mixture is the texture of cornmeal. Make a well in the center.
5. In a small bowl whisk together eggs, sour cream, milk, and vanilla. Add sour cream mixture all at once to flour mixture. Using a fork, stir just until moistened. Turn dough out onto a lightly floured surface. Knead dough by folding and gently pressing it for three to four turns. Divide dough in half.
6. Pat half of dough evenly in prepared pan. Spread reserved fruit mixture evenly over dough. On a lightly floured sheet of waxed paper pat second half dough into a 9-inch circle. Cut into 12 wedges. Using waxed paper, carefully invert cut circle on top of fruit mixture; remove waxed paper. Press gently on edges to seal layers together. In a small bowl whisk together egg white and the water; brush over dough. Sprinkle with Cinnamon Sugar.
7. Bake for 35 to 40 minutes or until golden brown. Cool in pan on wire rack for 10 minutes. Invert scones onto a large plate, then invert scones again onto a serving plate. Serve warm.

Cinnamon Sugar: In a small bowl stir together 2 teaspoons granulated sugar and ¼ teaspoon ground cinnamon.

PER SCONES *326 cal, 13 g fat, 66 mg chol, 198 mg sodium, 45 g carb, 2 g fiber, 5 g pro.*

CRANBERRY-BUTTERMILK MUFFINS

Chocolate Pancakes

Use either natural or Dutch-process cocoa powder for these very special pancakes. Both work equally well.

PREP 15 minutes COOK 4 minutes
OVEN 200°F MAKES 18 pancakes

1⅔ cups all-purpose flour
⅓   cup unsweetened cocoa powder
¼   cup sugar
1   teaspoon baking soda
¼   teaspoon salt
1   egg, lightly beaten
2¼ cups buttermilk or sour milk*
3   tablespoons vegetable oil
1   teaspoon vanilla

½   cup miniature semisweet chocolate pieces, snipped dried cherries, or toasted chopped walnuts (optional)
    Whipped cream
    Fresh raspberries or sliced strawberries (optional)

1. Preheat oven to 200°F. In a large bowl combine flour, cocoa powder, sugar, baking soda, and salt. In another bowl combine egg, buttermilk, oil, and vanilla. Stir buttermilk mixture into flour mixture until slightly lumpy. If desired, stir in chocolate pieces.
2. Heat a lightly greased griddle or heavy skillet over medium heat until a few drops of water dance across the surface.

Reduce heat to medium-low. For each pancake, pour ¼ cup batter onto griddle. Cook for 2 to 3 minutes per side or until lightly browned; turn pancakes when tops are bubbly and edges are slightly dry. Keep pancakes warm in oven. To serve, top with whipped cream. If desired, top with fresh berries.
*Tip: To make 2¼ cups sour milk, place 7 teaspoons vinegar in a glass measuring cup. Add enough milk to make 2¼ cups total liquid; stir. Let stand for 5 minutes before using.

PER PANCAKE *119 cal, 6 g fat, 23 mg chol, 142 mg sodium, 14 g carb, 1 g fiber, 3 g pro.*

DANISH FRUIT AND
CHEESE PASTRIES

Danish Fruit and Cheese Pastries

Sure, you can buy Danish pastries from your local bakery, but making your own is so much more satisfying.

PREP **45 minutes** RISE **30 minutes**
BAKE **15 minutes** OVEN **350°F**
MAKES **24 servings**

2	16-ounce loaves frozen sweet roll dough, thawed
1	3-ounce package cream cheese, softened
1	egg yolk
2	tablespoons sugar
1	tablespoon all-purpose flour
¼	teaspoon vanilla
¼	teaspoon almond extract or finely shredded orange peel
¼	cup desired flavor jam, preserves, canned pie filling, or fruit curd
1	recipe Lemon Curd Icing (optional)

1. Line two large baking sheets with parchment paper; set aside.

2. To shape spiral pastries, on a lightly floured surface roll 1 loaf of dough into a 12-inch square. Cut square into twelve 12×1-inch strips. With one end of a strip in each hand, twist ends in opposite directions three or four times. Coil the strip into a spiral round, tucking the outside end underneath. Repeat with remaining strips, placing 2 inches apart on baking sheets. Repeat with the remaining loaf of sweet roll dough. Cover and let rise in a warm place until nearly double in size (30 to 45 minutes). Meanwhile, in a small bowl combine cream cheese, egg yolk, sugar, flour, vanilla, and almond extract. Beat with an electric mixer on medium until well mixed and smooth. Preheat oven to 350°F. Spoon a rounded measuring teaspoon of the cream cheese mixture into the center of each coil.

3. Bake 15 to 18 minutes or until golden. Cool pastries slightly on a wire rack. Top the center of each pastry coil with ½ teaspoon jam. If desired, drizzle with Lemon Curd Icing. Serve warm or at room temperature.

PER SERVING *137 cal, 4 g fat, 34 mg chol, 81 mg sodium, 22 g carb, 1 g fiber, 3 g pro.*

Lemon Curd Icing: In a bowl combine ¾ cup powdered sugar, 1 tablespoon lemon curd, ¼ teaspoon vanilla, and, if desired, ⅛ teaspoon almond extract. Stir in 1 tablespoon milk. If necessary, add additional milk, 1 teaspoon at a time, to reach drizzling consistency.

Turnovers: On a lightly floured surface roll one loaf of dough into a 12×9-inch rectangle. Cut rectangle into twelve 3-inch squares. Place a rounded measuring teaspoon of cream cheese mixture into the center of each square. Top each with ½ teaspoon jam. Fold each pastry square diagonally in half.

Using the tines of a fork, seal edges. With fork, poke a few holes in the top of each triangle. Place on prepared baking sheets. Cover and let rise in a warm place until nearly double in size (30 to 45 minutes). Repeat with the remaining loaf of sweet roll dough, remaining cream cheese mixture, and remaining jam. Bake as directed in Step 3. If desired, drizzle with Lemon Curd Icing. Serve warm or at room temperature.

Envelopes: On a lightly floured surface roll one loaf of dough into a 12×9-inch rectangle. Cut rectangle into twelve 3-inch squares. Place a rounded measuring teaspoon of cream cheese mixture into the center of each square. Top each with ½ teaspoon jam. Fold points to the center, forming an envelope. Pinch points together in the center to seal. (If necessary to seal, lightly moisten points with water.) Cover and let rise in a warm place until nearly double in size (30 to 45 minutes). Repeat with the remaining loaf of sweet roll dough, remaining cream cheese mixture, and remaining jam. Bake as directed in Step 3. If desired, drizzle with Lemon Curd Icing. Serve warm or at room temperature.

Overnight Blueberry Coffee Cake

Do the prep work the night before and just pop it in the oven in the morning—easier than pie!

PREP 25 minutes CHILL 8 hours
BAKE 35 minutes OVEN 350°F
MAKES 12 servings

      Nonstick cooking spray
1   cup whole wheat pastry flour
¾   cup yellow cornmeal
⅓   cup granulated sugar
1½   teaspoons ground cinnamon
1   teaspoon baking soda
½   teaspoon ground ginger
1   cup plain fat-free Greek yogurt
¾   cup refrigerated or frozen egg
      product, thawed, or 3 eggs, lightly
      beaten
⅓   cup canola oil
¼   cup unsweetened applesauce
1   tablespoon butter flavoring
2   cups frozen blueberries
2   tablespoons packed dark brown
      sugar
      Frozen light whipped dessert
      topping, thawed (optional)
      Ground ginger (optional)

1. Lightly coat a 2-quart rectangular baking dish with nonstick cooking spray; set aside. In a large bowl stir together pastry flour, cornmeal, granulated sugar, 1 teaspoon of the cinnamon, the baking soda, the ½ teaspoon ginger, and ¼ teaspoon salt.
2. In a medium bowl whisk together yogurt, egg, oil, applesauce, and butter flavoring until well mixed. Add egg mixture to the flour mixture; stir just until combined. Spread half of the batter into the prepared dish.
3. Sprinkle with 1 cup of the frozen blueberries. Top with the remaining batter; spread evenly. Cover and chill in the refrigerator for 8 to 24 hours.
4. Allow the coffee cake to stand at room temperature while the oven preheats to 350°F. In a small bowl toss together the remaining 1 cup frozen blueberries, the brown sugar, and the remaining ½ teaspoon cinnamon; sprinkle on top of the batter. Bake, uncovered, about 35 minutes or until a toothpick inserted near the center comes out clean. Serve warm. If desired, serve with whipped topping and sprinkle with additional ginger.
PER SERVING *175 cal, 7 g fat, 0 mg chol, 195 mg sodium, 25 g carb, 2 g fiber, 5 g pro.*

Pineapple Upside-Down Coffee Cake

A classic American dessert gets a morning makeover.

PREP 25 minutes BAKE 35 minutes
OVEN 350°F MAKES 12 servings

½   cup butter (1 stick)
1   cup packed brown sugar
12   canned pineapple rings in juice*
2   cups all-purpose flour
2   teaspoons baking powder
½   teaspoon salt
½   teaspoon ground nutmeg
½   cup butter, softened (1 stick)
½   cup granulated sugar
½   cup packed brown sugar
2   eggs
½   cup milk
1   teaspoon vanilla
      Vanilla Greek yogurt or sweetened
      whipped cream (optional)
1   tablespoon packed brown sugar
      (optional)
12   maraschino cherries (optional)

1. Preheat oven to 350° F. Butter the bottom and sides of a 13×9×2-inch baking pan. Line bottom of pan with parchment paper; set pan aside. For topping, melt ½ cup butter in a medium saucepan over low heat. Stir in 1 cup brown sugar. Bring mixture to boiling over medium heat, stirring frequently. Pour into prepared pan. Drain pineapple rings, reserving ½ cup juice. Fit rings tightly into bottom of pan.
2. In a medium bowl whisk together flour, baking powder, salt, and nutmeg. In a large bowl beat softened butter, granulated sugar, and ½ cup brown sugar with an electric mixer on medium for 2 minutes, scraping sides of bowl occasionally. Add eggs; beat until combined. Beat in half the flour mixture. Pour in reserved ½ cup pineapple juice and the milk; beat until combined. Beat in remaining flour mixture and vanilla.
3. Spread batter carefully over pineapple slices in pan. Bake for 35 to 40 minutes or until toothpick inserted in center comes out clean. Cool cake in pan on a wire rack 10 minutes. Place a baking sheet over cake; carefully invert. If any pineapple sticks to pan, gently replace on cake top.
4. Meanwhile, in a small bowl stir together the yogurt and 1 tablespoon brown sugar. Serve cake warm topped with yogurt mixture and maraschino cherries.
*Tip: You will need to purchase one 20-ounce can of pineapple slices and one 8-ounce can of pineapple slices for the 12 slices. There will be a few slices of leftover pineapple.
PER SERVING *396 cal, 17 g fat, 77 mg chol, 290 mg sodium, 60 g carb, 1 g fiber, 4 g pro.*

ALMOND CARAMEL
CINNAMON ROLLS

Mascarpone-Stuffed French Toast with Salted Caramel-Banana Sauce

Decadent and absolutely divine, this stuffed French toast cloaked in caramel sauce may be the best meal you have the whole holiday season.

PREP 20 minutes CHILL 2 hours
BAKE 1 hour OVEN 375°F
MAKES 6 servings

12 slices Texas toast
1   8-ounce package cream cheese, softened
½   cup mascarpone cheese (4 ounces)
½   cup chopped pecans or macadamia nuts, toasted
2   tablespoons packed brown sugar
1   teaspoon ground cinnamon
¼   teaspoon salt
6   eggs, lightly beaten
3   cups milk
¼   teaspoon salt
1   recipe Salted Caramel-Banana Sauce

1. Arrange half of the bread slices in a single layer in a 3-quart rectangular baking dish. In a small bowl combine cream cheese, mascarpone cheese, pecans, brown sugar, cinnamon, and salt. Spread cheese mixture evenly over bread in baking dish. Top with the remaining bread slices to make six stacks.
2. In a medium bowl whisk together eggs, milk, and salt. Pour egg mixture evenly over bread stacks, covering all of the tops. Cover with plastic wrap. Chill for at least 2 hours or up to 24 hours.
3. Preheat oven to 375°F. Line a 15×10×1-inch baking pan with parchment paper. Arrange bread stacks in the prepared pan. Bake about 1 hour or until golden, turning stacks every 15 minutes. Serve warm with Salted Caramel-Banana Sauce.

Salted Caramel-Banana Sauce: In a heavy medium saucepan stir together ¾ cup packed brown sugar, ½ cup whipping cream, ½ cup butter, and 2 tablespoons light-color corn syrup. Bring to boiling over medium-high heat, whisking occasionally; reduce heat to medium. Boil gently for 3 minutes more. Remove from heat. Stir in 1 teaspoon vanilla and ½ teaspoon sea salt. Pour into a small bowl. Cool to room temperature. Stir in 1 banana, thinly sliced.

PER SERVING *965 cal, 61 g fat, 355 mg chol, 1,107 mg sodium, 90 g carb, 4 g fiber, 24 g pro.*

Almond Caramel Cinnamon Rolls

Have plenty of napkins on hand when you serve these fabulously sticky buns.

PREP 45 minutes STAND 5 minutes
RISE 1 hour BAKE 25 minutes
COOL 5 minutes OVEN 350°F
MAKES 15 rolls

1   cup warm water (105°F to 115°F)
½   cup granulated sugar
1   package active dry yeast
2   to 2¼ cups all-purpose flour
1   cup whole wheat flour
¼   cup refrigerated or frozen egg product, thawed
2   tablespoons canola oil
1   teaspoon salt
⅔   cup packed brown sugar
⅓   cup butter, melted
¼   cup hot water
1   tablespoon ground cinnamon
½   cup sliced almonds, toasted if desired (see tip, page 14)

1. In a large bowl combine the 1 cup warm water, ¼ cup of the granulated sugar, and the yeast. Let stand for 5 minutes. Stir in 2 cups of the all-purpose flour, the whole wheat flour, egg, oil, and salt.
2. On a lightly floured surface knead in enough of the remaining all-purpose flour to make a moderately soft dough that is smooth and elastic (3 to 5 minutes total). Lightly coat a large bowl with nonstick cooking spray. Place dough in bowl; turn to coat dough surface. Cover; let rise in a warm place until double in size (about 1 hour).
3. Meanwhile, for caramel sauce, in a small bowl stir together brown sugar, 4 tablespoons of the melted butter, and the ¼ cup hot water. Lightly coat a 3-quart rectangular baking dish with nonstick cooking spray. Add caramel sauce, spreading evenly in the dish.
4. To make rolls, roll dough into a 17×12-inch rectangle. Brush dough with the remaining 1½ tablespoons melted butter. Sprinkle with remaining ¼ cup granulated sugar and the cinnamon. Sprinkle with sliced almonds. Starting from a long side, tightly roll up dough into a spiral; pinch seam to seal. Cut spiral crosswise into 12 even slices.
5. Arrange slices over caramel sauce in baking dish. Cover and let rise in a warm place until double in size (30 minutes to 1 hour).
6. Preheat oven to 350°F. Bake, uncovered, about 25 minutes or until golden brown.
7. Let cool in baking dish on wire rack for 5 minutes. Invert onto a serving platter; remove baking dish.

PER ROLL *194 cal, 6 g fat, 7 mg chol, 185 mg sodium, 31 g carb, 2 g fiber, 4 g pro.*

MASCARPONE-STUFFED FRENCH TOAST WITH SALTED CARAMEL-BANANA SAUCE

Lemon Breakfast Parfaits

Amid all of the holiday indulgence, this fruit-and-yogurt breakfast parfait offers a refreshing change of pace.

PREP **20 minutes** STAND **5 minutes**
COOL **30 minutes** MAKES **6 servings**

- ¾ cup fat-free milk
  Dash salt
- ⅓ cup couscous
- ½ cup lemon low-fat yogurt
- ½ cup low-fat sour cream
- 1 tablespoon honey
- ¼ teaspoon finely shredded lemon peel
- 3 cups assorted fruit, such as sliced strawberries, kiwifruit, nectarine, blueberries, and/or raspberries
  Chopped crystallized ginger (optional)
  Fresh mint (optional)

1. In a medium saucepan bring the milk and salt to boiling; stir in the couscous. Simmer, covered, for 1 minute. Remove from heat; let stand for 5 minutes. Stir with a fork until fluffy. Cool.

2. In a small bowl combine the yogurt, sour cream, honey, and lemon peel; stir into the couscous. In another bowl combine desired fruit.

3. To serve, divide half of the fruit mixture among 6 parfait glasses. Spoon couscous mixture over fruit; top with remaining fruit. If desired, garnish with chopped crystallized ginger and mint.

PER SERVING *127 cal, 2 g fat, 6 mg chol, 70 mg sodium, 22 g carb, 2 g fiber, 5 g pro.*

Chocolate Lover's Granola

Packaged prettily, this makes a lovely hostess gift.

PREP **20 minutes** BAKE **30 minutes**
OVEN **300°F** MAKES **14 servings**

- 2 cups regular rolled oats
- 1 cup sliced or slivered almonds, coarsely chopped, or chopped walnuts
- ½ cup flaked coconut (optional)
- ½ cup dry-roasted sunflower kernels
- ¼ cup toasted wheat germ
- ¼ cup flaxseed meal
- ½ cup honey
- 2 tablespoons vegetable oil
- 2 ounces bittersweet chocolate
- 1 cup white chocolate baking pieces
- 1 cup semisweet chocolate pieces

1. Preheat oven to 300°F. Grease a 15×10×1-inch baking pan; set aside. In a large bowl combine oats, nuts, coconut (if desired), sunflower kernels, wheat germ, and flaxseed meal. In a small saucepan combine the honey, oil, and chocolate; heat over low heat until chocolate is melted. Stir into oat mixture. Spread evenly into pan.

2. Bake for 30 to 35 minutes or until light brown, stirring after 20 minutes. Spread on a large piece of foil; cool completely. Before serving, stir in 1 cup white chocolate baking pieces and 1 cup semisweet chocolate pieces.

PER SERVING *198 cal, 10 g fat, 0 mg chol, 2 mg sodium, 24 g carb, 4 g fiber, 6 g pro.*

LEMON BREAKFAST PARFAITS

CHOCOLATE LOVER'S GRANOLA

Iced Caramel-Cream Coffee

Turn your kitchen into a specialty coffee shop with this caramel-and-cream java.

START TO FINISH 5 minutes
MAKES 2 servings

2 cups cold strong brewed coffee
2 tablespoons no-sugar-added French vanilla-flavor instant breakfast mix
2 tablespoons sugar-free caramel ice cream topping
  Ice cubes
2 tablespoons frozen light whipped dessert topping, thawed
2 teaspoons sugar-free caramel ice cream topping
  Coarsely crushed chocolate-covered coffee beans (optional)

1. In a blender combine coffee, instant breakfast mix, and 2 tablespoons ice cream topping. Cover and blend until smooth. Pour over ice in 2 glasses. Top with dessert topping and drizzle with 2 teaspoons ice cream topping. If desired, sprinkle with coarsely crushed coffee beans.

PER SERVING *87 cal, 1 g fat, 1 mg chol, 62 mg sodium, 20 g carb, 1 g fiber, 2 g pro.*

CRISPY SPIRALS

savory & sweet breads

LOVELY LOAVES The aroma of bread baking in the oven fills the house with a sense of comfort and coziness. Whether it's a fruited quick bread, bacon-studded scones, or gooey orange sweet rolls, these Christmas breads make any meal special.

61

66

71

CARROT BREAD WITH CREAM CHEESE ICING

Lemon-Poppy Seed Bread

This classic quick bread makes a lovely accompaniment to a cup of coffee or tea.

PREP **20 minutes** BAKE **50 minutes**
STAND **10 minutes + overnight**
COOL **10 minutes** OVEN **350°F**
MAKES **1 loaf (16 slices)**

1¾ cups all-purpose flour
¾ cup sugar
2 teaspoons baking powder
¼ teaspoon salt
1 egg, lightly beaten
1 cup milk
¼ cup vegetable oil or butter, melted
2 teaspoons finely shredded lemon peel
1 tablespoon lemon juice
1 tablespoon poppy seeds
2 tablespoons lemon juice (optional)
1 tablespoon sugar (optional)

1. Preheat oven to 350°F. Grease the bottom and ½ inch up the sides of an 8×4×2-inch loaf pan; set aside. In a medium bowl stir together flour, the ¾ cup sugar, the baking powder, and salt. Make a well in center of flour mixture; set aside.
2. In another medium bowl combine egg, milk, oil, lemon peel, and the 1 tablespoon lemon juice. Add egg mixture all at once to flour mixture. Stir just until moistened (batter should be lumpy). Stir in poppy seeds. Spoon batter into the prepared pan, spreading evenly.
3. Bake for 50 to 55 minutes or until a wooden toothpick inserted near the center comes out clean. If desired, in a bowl stir together the 2 tablespoons lemon juice and 1 tablespoon sugar; brush over top of the hot loaf. Cool in pan on a wire rack for 10 minutes. Remove from pan; cool completely on rack. Wrap and store overnight before slicing.
PER SLICE *147 cal, 6 g fat, 14 mg chol, 98 mg sodium, 20 g carb, 1 g fiber, 3 g pro.*

Carrot Bread with Cream Cheese Icing

All of the delicious, sweet, and nicely spiced flavors of carrot cake show up in this moist bread.

PREP **20 minutes** BAKE **55 minutes**
COOL **10 minutes** STAND **overnight**
OVEN **350°F** MAKES **1 loaf (16 slices)**

2 cups all-purpose flour
⅔ cup packed brown sugar
2 teaspoons baking powder
1 teaspoon ground cinnamon
½ teaspoon ground cardamom or nutmeg
¼ teaspoon baking soda
¼ teaspoon salt
2 cups shredded carrot
2 beaten eggs
⅔ cup milk
⅓ cup canola oil
1 recipe Cream Cheese Icing

1. Preheat oven to 350°F. Grease the bottom and ½ inch up the sides of an 8×4×2-inch loaf pan; set aside.
2. In a bowl stir together flour, sugar, baking powder, cinnamon, cardamom, baking soda, and salt. In another bowl combine carrot, eggs, milk, and oil; add to dry ingredients, stirring just until moistened.
3. Spoon batter into prepared pan. Bake for 55 to 60 minutes or until a toothpick inserted near the center comes out clean. Cool in pan 10 minutes; remove and cool completely on wire rack. Wrap and store overnight. Drizzle with Cream Cheese Icing before slicing.
Cream Cheese Icing: Whisk together 1 ounce (2 tablespoons) cream cheese, ¾ cup powdered sugar, ½ teaspoon vanilla (optional) and 3 to 4 teaspoons milk until smooth and glazelike.
PER SLICE *205 cal, 7 g fat, 33 mg chol, 148 mg sodium, 32 g carb, 1 g fiber, 3 g pro.*

Slightly Caffeinated Banana Bread

Freshly ground coffee goes right into the batter.

PREP 20 minutes BAKE 1 hour
COOL 10 minutes
OVEN 350°F MAKES 1 loaf (14 slices)

2   cups all-purpose flour
1   to 2 teaspoons freshly ground
    coffee beans
½   teaspoon baking soda
½   teaspoon salt
1   egg, lightly beaten
1   cup granulated sugar
1   cup mashed ripe bananas
    (3 medium)
⅓   cup butter, melted
3   tablespoons milk
1   teaspoon vanilla
2   tablespoons turbinado raw sugar

1. Preheat oven to 350°F. Grease and flour bottom and ½ inch up the sides of an 8×4×2-inch loaf pan; set aside. In a large bowl combine flour, coffee, baking soda, and salt. Make a well in center of flour mixture; set aside.
2. In a medium bowl combine egg, granulated sugar, bananas, melted butter, milk, and vanilla. Add egg mixture all at once to flour mixture. Stir just until moistened. Spoon batter into prepared pan. Sprinkle with raw sugar.
3. Bake for 60 to 70 minutes or until a wooden toothpick inserted near center comes out clean (if necessary, cover loosely with foil the last 15 minutes of baking to prevent overbrowning).
4. Cool in pan on a wire rack for 10 minutes. Remove from pan. Cool completely on rack. Wrap; store overnight before slicing.
PER SLICE *184 cal, 5 g fat, 27 mg chol, 166 mg sodium, 33 g carb, 1 g fiber, 3 g pro.*

Crispy Spirals

Starting with prepared puff pastry makes these pastries a cinch.

PREP 25 minutes BAKE 20 minutes
OVEN 375°F MAKES 6 spirals

1   frozen puff pastry sheet (½ of a
    17.3-ounce package), thawed
1   egg yolk
1   tablespoon water
2   tablespoons sugar
1   teaspoon ground cinnamon
3   to 4 tablespoons orange marmalade
    or apple jelly, melted

1. Preheat oven to 375°F. Line a large baking sheet with parchment paper; set aside. On a lightly floured surface, unfold puff pastry sheet. If necessary, use a rolling pin to flatten and smooth the pastry. In a small bowl whisk together egg yolk and the water. In another small bowl stir together sugar and cinnamon. Brush pastry with egg mixture. Sprinkle with cinnamon-sugar.
2. Cut the pastry into 12 equal strips. Place 2 strips together at one end; pinch ends together to make one long strip. Repeat with remaining strips to make six long strips. Twist each long strip several times. On the prepared baking sheet wrap the twisted strips into slightly loose single-layer spirals. Brush the ends of the strips lightly with some of the egg yolk mixture. Pinch ends to seal. Space spirals 2 inches apart on the baking sheet.
3. Bake for 20 to 22 minutes or until puffed and light brown. Transfer pastries to a wire rack and cool completely. Brush cooled pastries with melted jelly.
PER SPIRAL *232 cal, 13 g fat, 35 mg chol, 157 mg sodium, 26 g carb, 0 g fiber, 2 g pro.*

SLIGHTLY CAFFEINATED BANANA BREAD

Ginger Blueberry Muffins

Cake flour gives these gingery muffins an especially silky, tender texture.

PREP 30 minutes BAKE 15 minutes
COOL 5 minutes OVEN 375°F
MAKES 24 muffins

1¾ cups fresh blueberries
1⅔ cups cake flour
1¼ cups bread flour
2   teaspoons baking powder
1   teaspoon ground ginger
¾   teaspoon salt
½   teaspoon baking soda
⅓   cup honey
3   tablespoons molasses
1   tablespoon grated fresh ginger
⅔   cup butter, softened
⅔   cup packed brown sugar
2   eggs
½   cup buttermilk
    Powdered sugar

1. Arrange blueberries in a single layer in a 15×10×1-inch baking pan. Freeze for 30 minutes or until berries are firm.
2. Preheat oven to 375°F. Grease twenty-four 2½-inch muffin cups or line with paper bake cups; set aside. In a large bowl combine cake flour, bread flour, baking powder, ginger, salt, and baking soda; set aside. In a small bowl combine the honey, molasses, and fresh ginger.
3. In a large mixing bowl beat butter and brown sugar with an electric mixer on medium until light and fluffy. Add the eggs, one at time, beating after each addition just until combined. Add the honey mixture, beating on low until just combined. Alternately add the flour mixture and buttermilk, beating on low until just combined after each addition. Fold in blueberries. Spoon batter into prepared muffin cups, filling each two-thirds full.
4. Bake for 15 to 17 minutes or until golden and a wooden toothpick inserted near the center comes out clean. Cool in muffin cups on a wire rack for 5 minutes. Remove from muffin cups; serve warm sprinkled with powdered sugar.
PER MUFFIN *167 cal, 6 g fat, 31 mg chol, 180 mg sodium, 27 g carb, 1 g fiber, 2 g pro.*

Chocolate-Glazed Ginger-Pumpkin Muffins

A garnish of sparkling crystallized ginger adds warmth to these chocolate-topped muffins.

PREP 20 minutes BAKE 18 minutes
STAND 30 minutes OVEN 400°F
MAKES 16 muffins

2   cups all-purpose flour
⅔   cup packed brown sugar
⅓   cup granulated sugar
2   teaspoons baking powder
1   teaspoon ground cinnamon
½   teaspoon ground ginger
¼   teaspoon salt
¾   cup canned pumpkin
½   cup butter, melted
½   cup buttermilk
2   eggs
1   recipe Chocolate Glaze
1   to 2 tablespoons finely chopped crystallized ginger

1. Preheat oven to 400°F. Line sixteen 2½-inch muffin cups with paper bake cups; set aside. In a medium bowl stir together flour, brown sugar, granulated sugar, baking powder, cinnamon, ground ginger, and salt. Make a well in the center of the flour mixture; set aside.
2. In a small bowl stir together the pumpkin, melted butter, buttermilk, and eggs. Add egg mixture all at once to flour mixture. Stir just until moistened (batter should be lumpy). Spoon batter evenly into prepared muffin cups.
3. Bake for 18 to 20 minutes or until a wooden toothpick inserted in the centers of muffins comes out clean. Remove muffins from muffin cups; cool completely on a wire rack.
4. Spoon some of the Chocolate Glaze on top of the muffins. Place dipped muffins upright on the wire rack. Sprinkle tops of muffins with chopped crystallized ginger. Let stand for 30 minutes or until glaze sets.
Chocolate Glaze: In a small saucepan combine 4 ounces chopped bittersweet chocolate and ¼ cup butter, cut up. Cook and stir over very low heat until melted and smooth and slightly thickened. Stir in 1 tablespoon light-color corn syrup. Let glaze cool slightly.
PER MUFFIN *240 cal, 12 g fat, 50 mg chol, 165 mg sodium, 31 g carb, 2 g fiber, 4 g pro.*

Curried Squash Muffins

These sweet and spicy muffins (if you add the optional cayenne) are great for breakfast or dinner.

PREP 25 minutes BAKE 20 minutes
COOL 5 minutes OVEN 350°F
MAKES 16 muffins

1   cup all-purpose flour
½   cup white whole wheat flour
2   teaspoons baking powder
2   teaspoons ground cinnamon
1   teaspoon curry powder
½   teaspoon salt
½   teaspoon cayenne pepper (optional)
½   cup butter, softened
½   cup packed brown sugar
1   cup mashed roasted butternut squash or 1 cup frozen cooked winter squash, thawed
¼   cup finely chopped crystallized ginger
1   egg
1   teaspoon vanilla
⅓   cup milk
    Powdered sugar (optional)

1. Preheat oven to 350°F. Line sixteen 2½-inch muffin cups with paper bake cups; set aside. In a medium bowl combine all-purpose flour, white whole wheat flour, baking powder, cinnamon, curry powder, salt, and cayenne pepper (if using); set aside.
2. In a large bowl beat butter with an electric mixer on medium to high for 30 seconds. Add brown sugar; beat until combined. Add squash, ginger, egg, and vanilla; beat until combined. Alternately add the flour mixture and milk to squash mixture, beating on low after each addition just until combined.
3. Spoon batter into prepared muffin cups, filling each about two-thirds full.
4. Bake about 20 minutes or until muffin tops spring back when lightly touched. Cool in muffin cups on a wire rack for 5 minutes. Remove from muffin cups. If desired, sprinkle lightly with powdered sugar. Serve warm.
PER MUFFIN *141 cal, 6 g fat, 28 mg chol, 171 mg sodium, 20 g carb, 1 g fiber, 2 g pro.*

APRICOT AND
CHÈVRE MUFFINS

Apricot and Chèvre Muffins

Goat cheese adds a subtle tang to these muffins. Try them at dinner with roast lamb or ham.

PREP **30 minutes** BAKE **15 minutes**
COOL **5 minutes** OVEN **400°F**
MAKES **15 muffins**

2   cups all-purpose flour
1   tablespoon baking powder
½   teaspoon salt
4   tablespoons butter
⅓   cup finely chopped shallots
1   cup snipped dried apricots
2   tablespoons honey
¼   cup semisoft goat cheese (chèvre)
      (2 ounces)
¼   cup packed brown sugar
2   eggs
¾   cup fat-free half-and-half
1   tablespoon snipped fresh thyme
      Honey (optional)

1. Preheat oven to 400°F. Line fifteen 2½-inch muffin cups with paper bake cups; set aside. In a medium bowl combine flour, baking powder, and salt. In a large skillet melt 2 tablespoons of the butter over medium heat. Add shallots; cook and stir until tender. Stir in dried apricots and the 2 tablespoons honey; set aside.
2. In a large bowl combine the remaining 2 tablespoons butter and the goat cheese. Beat with an electric mixer on medium to high for 30 seconds. Add brown sugar; beat until combined. Beat in eggs until combined. Alternately add flour mixture and half-and-half to brown sugar mixture, beating after each addition just until combined. Stir in apricot mixture and thyme. Spoon batter into the prepared muffin cups, filling each about two-thirds full.
3. Bake for 15 to 17 minutes or until tops spring back when lightly touched. Cool in muffin cups on a wire rack for 5 minutes. Remove from muffin cups. Serve warm. If desired, serve with additional honey.
PER MUFFIN *166 cal, 5 g fat, 39 mg chol, 216 mg sodium, 26 g carb, 1 g fiber, 4 g pro.*

Pesto and Cheese Shortbread Spirals

These savory, buttery spirals make a delicious appetizer or accompaniment to a simple salad or soup supper.

PREP **30 minutes** CHILL **1 hour**
BAKE **11 minutes** COOL **20 minutes**
OVEN **375°F** MAKES **40 spirals**

⅓   cup butter, softened
½   cup Asiago cheese, finely shredded
      (2 ounces)
1   cup all-purpose flour
1   to 2 tablespoons cold water
3   tablespoons butter, softened
⅓   cup purchased dried-tomato pesto
1   cup all-purpose flour

1. In a medium mixing bowl beat the ⅓ cup butter with an electric mixer on medium for 30 seconds. Beat in cheese until combined. Beat in as much of the 1 cup flour as you can with the mixer. Using a wooden spoon, stir in any remaining flour. If necessary, add the cold water and gently knead dough until it holds together. Between two sheets of waxed paper, roll dough into a 10×12-inch rectangle. Set aside.
2. In another medium mixing bowl beat the 3 tablespoons butter with an electric mixer on medium for 30 seconds. Beat in pesto until combined. Beat in as much of the 1 cup flour as you can with the mixer. Using a wooden spoon, stir in any remaining flour. If necessary, gently knead dough until it holds together. Between two sheets of waxed paper, roll dough into a 10×12-inch rectangle.
3. Remove top sheets of waxed paper. Invert the pesto dough rectangle on top of the cheese dough rectangle, lining up the edges of the two rectangles. Remove top layer of waxed paper. Roll up dough into a spiral, starting from a long side and using bottom layer of waxed paper to help lift and roll dough. Discard waxed paper. Pinch edges to seal. Wrap dough roll in plastic wrap. Chill roll for 1 to 2 hours or until very firm.
4. Preheat oven to 375°F. Line large baking sheets with parchment paper. Unwrap roll. Cut roll crosswise into ¼-inch-thick slices. Place slices 1 inch apart on the prepared baking sheets.
5. Bake for 11 to 13 minutes or until edges are firm and just starting to brown. Transfer to a wire rack; cool.
PER SPIRAL *58 cal, 4 g fat, 8 mg chol, 48 mg sodium, 5 g carb., 0 g fiber, 1 g pro.*

Spicy Pepper Jack and Sausage Scones

Serve these with scrambled eggs for breakfast.

PREP 25 minutes   BAKE 15 minutes
OVEN 400°F   MAKES 12 scones

12 ounces bulk pork sausage
3¼ cups all-purpose flour
½ cup sugar
2½ teaspoons baking powder
¼ teaspoon salt
¾ cup butter, cut up
6 ounces Monterey Jack cheese with jalapeño peppers, shredded (1½ cups)
1¼ cups buttermilk

1. Preheat oven to 400°F. In a large skillet cook sausage over medium heat until browned, breaking meat into small pieces with a wooden spoon. Drain fat and set sausage aside.
2. In a very large bowl combine flour, sugar, baking powder, and salt. Using a pastry blender, cut in butter until mixture resembles coarse crumbs. Stir in cheese and sausage. Make a well in the center of the flour mixture. Add 1 cup of the buttermilk all at once to flour mixture. Using a fork, stir just until mixture is moistened.
3. Turn dough out onto a lightly floured surface. Knead dough by folding and gently pressing it for 10 to 12 strokes or just until dough holds together. Pat or lightly roll dough into a 9-inch circle. Cut dough into 12 or 16 wedges using a pizza cutter or floured knife.
4. Arrange wedges 1 inch apart on an ungreased baking sheet. Brush with some of the remaining buttermilk. Bake for 15 to 18 minutes or until golden brown. Serve warm.
PER SCONE *421 cal, 24 g total fat, 74 mg chol, 633 mg sodium, 36 g carb, 1 g fiber, 13 g pro.*

Cranberry Scones

For the most tender texture and rich flavor, be sure to use real butter.

PREP 30 minutes   BAKE 30 minutes
FREEZE 20 minutes
OVEN 375°F   MAKES 8 scones

3½ cups all-purpose flour
1 cup sugar
4 teaspoons baking powder
1 teaspoon salt
1 tablespoon finely shredded lemon or orange peel
1 cup butter
1 cup cranberries
¾ cup whole milk
¼ cup sour cream
1 recipe Powdered Sugar Icing (optional)
   Finely shredded lemon peel (optional)

1. In a large bowl combine flour, sugar, baking powder, salt, and lemon peel. Using a pastry blender or two knives, cut in butter until mixture resembles coarse crumbs. Stir in cranberries. Make a well in center of flour mixture.
2. In a small bowl combine milk and sour cream. Add to flour mixture. Stir just until moistened. Do not overmix.
3. Turn dough out onto a lightly floured surface. Quickly knead dough about 6 to 8 strokes or until nearly smooth. Place dough on an ungreased baking sheet. Using a lightly floured rolling pin or floured hands, roll or pat into a 10-inch circle that is ¾ inch thick. Cover and freeze for 20 minutes or until dough is firm enough to cut; cut into 8 wedges, but do not separate wedges.
4. Bake for 30 minutes or until lightly browned. Cool slightly; if desired, drizzle with Powdered Sugar Icing and sprinkle with lemon peel.
PER SCONE *533 cal, 26 g fat, 66 mg chol, 651 mg sodium, 71 g carb, 2 g fiber, 7 g pro.*

Powdered Sugar Icing: In a medium bowl combine 1 cup powdered sugar and enough milk (3 to 4 teaspoons) to make drizzling consistency.

PESTO AND CHEESE SHORTBREAD SPIRALS

Bacon and Dried Tomato Scones

Try these herbed scones with your favorite cheddar cheese soup.

PREP 25 minutes   BAKE 12 minutes
OVEN 400°F   MAKES 16 scones

¾ cup dried tomatoes (not oil-packed)
2½ cups all-purpose flour
1   tablespoon baking powder
1   teaspoon dried basil, crushed
1   teaspoon dried oregano, crushed
¼   teaspoon garlic salt
¾   cup butter, cut up
8   slices bacon, crisp-cooked, drained, and crumbled
¼   cup sour cream
2   eggs, lightly beaten
2   tablespoons milk

½ cup shredded mozzarella cheese
    Crisp-cooked bacon, crumbled (optional)

1. Preheat oven to 400°F. Place tomatoes in a bowl. Add enough boiling water to cover. Let stand 5 minutes. Drain well; chop tomatoes.
2. In large bowl combine flour, baking powder, basil, oregano, and garlic salt. Cut in butter until mixture resembles coarse crumbs. Stir in chopped tomatoes and bacon. Make a well in center of flour mixture; set aside. In small bowl combine sour cream, eggs, and milk; add all at once to flour mixture. Stir with a fork just until moistened. Turn dough out onto a lightly floured surface. Knead dough gently 10 to 12 strokes or until dough holds together. Divide in half. Pat or lightly roll each dough half to a 7-inch circle. Cut each circle into 8 wedges.
3. Place wedges 2 inches apart on a very large ungreased baking sheet. Bake for 5 minutes. Sprinkle tops of scones with cheese. Bake 7 to 8 minutes more or until tops are lightly browned. Serve warm. Top with additional crumbled bacon.

PER SCONE *202 cal, 13 g fat, 57 mg chol, 326 mg sodium, 17 g carb, 1 g fiber, 6 g pro.*

Chile-Cheddar Casserole Bread

Try serving this bread in place of the usual corn bread with a big pot of chili.

PREP 20 minutes RISE 1 hour
BAKE 45 minutes STAND 10 minutes
COOL 20 minutes OVEN 350°F
MAKES 8 to 12 servings

¼ cup warm hot-style vegetable juice (105°F to 115°F)
1 package active dry yeast
1 cup sour cream
¼ cup finely chopped onion
2 eggs
2 tablespoons sugar
1 teaspoon salt
½ teaspoon ancho chile powder
2½ cups all-purpose flour
1⅓ cups finely shredded sharp cheddar cheese (about 5 ounces)
1 4-ounce can fire-roasted diced green chiles, undrained
Sliced green onion (optional)

1. In a large mixing bowl combine vegetable juice and yeast; let stand until mixture is foamy. Add sour cream, onion, eggs, sugar, salt, ancho chile powder, and 1 cup of the flour. Beat with an electric mixer on medium for 2 minutes. Using a wooden spoon, stir in the remaining 1½ cups flour, 1 cup of the cheese, and the green chiles until a soft, sticky dough forms.
2. Transfer dough to a greased 2-quart oval or rectangular baking dish. Cover; let rise in a warm place until double in size (1 to 1½ hours).
3. Preheat oven to 350°F. Bake for 40 minutes; remove from oven and sprinkle with remaining cheese. Return to oven; bake for 5 minutes more. Let dish stand on a wire rack for 10 minutes. Remove bread from dish. Let cool on wire rack for 20 minutes before serving. If desired, garnish with sliced green onion and additional chile powder.
PER SERVING *203 cal, 8 g fat, 57 mg chol, 340 mg sodium, 24 g carb, 1 g fiber, 8 g pro.*

Potato-Bacon Casserole Bread with Caramelized Onions

This no-knead bread nearly bakes itself.

PREP 30 minutes RISE 40 minutes
BAKE 45 minutes COOL 10 minutes
OVEN 375°F MAKES 8 to 12 servings

6 slices bacon, chopped
½ cup chopped onion (1 medium)
Cornmeal
1 cup warm milk (105°F to 115°F)
1 package active dry yeast
⅓ cup butter, melted
1 egg
1 teaspoon salt
3 cups all-purpose flour
1 cup mashed potatoes, at room temperature

1. In a large skillet cook bacon over medium heat until crisp. Using a slotted spoon, transfer bacon to paper towels to drain.
2. Transfer 2 tablespoons of bacon drippings in skillet to a small bowl. Drain and discard all but 2 tablespoons of the remaining drippings from skillet. Cook onion in hot drippings in skillet over medium heat about 6 minutes or until dark brown. Remove from heat; set aside.
3. Brush the reserved bacon drippings over the bottom and sides of a 2-quart square baking dish. Sprinkle bottom and sides of dish generously with cornmeal. Set aside.
4. In a large mixing bowl combine warm milk and yeast; let stand until mixture is foamy. Add butter, egg, salt, and 1 cup of the flour. Beat with an electric mixer on medium for 2 minutes, scraping sides of bowl occasionally. Using a wooden spoon, stir in the remaining 2 cups flour, the mashed potatoes, bacon, and onion until a soft, sticky dough forms.
5. Transfer dough to the prepared baking dish. Cover; let rise in a warm place until double in size (about 40 minutes).
6. Preheat oven to 375°F. Bake for 45 to 50 minutes or until loaf is golden brown. Cool in dish on a wire rack for 10 minutes. Remove bread from dish. Serve warm or cool completely on a wire rack.
PER SERVING *391 cal, 19 g fat, 62 mg chol, 596 mg sodium, 45 g carb, 2 g fiber, 10 g pro.*

Cheesy Breadsticks

Jazz up frozen bread dough with cheese, fennel seeds, and ham to make these homey breadsticks.

PREP 30 minutes RISE 30 minutes
BAKE 20 minutes OVEN 350°F
MAKES 12 breadsticks

1 16-ounce loaf frozen bread dough
1 teaspoon fennel seeds, crushed
½ cup shredded cheddar, Swiss, or Monterey Jack cheese (2 ounces)
2 to 3 ounces thinly sliced smoked ham
1 egg

1. Thaw frozen bread dough according to package directions.
2. On a lightly floured surface, roll dough into a 12×10-inch rectangle. Sprinkle with crushed fennel seeds and lightly press seeds into the dough. Sprinkle the bottom half of the rectangle with the cheese; top with the smoked ham. Fold dough lengthwise over cheese and ham; seal edges. Using a pizza cutter, cut dough crosswise into twelve 1-inch strips. Twist strips and place on parchment-lined baking sheet. Cover and let rise in a warm place until double in size (about 30 minutes).
3. Preheat oven to 350°F. In a small bowl whisk together 1 egg and 1 tablespoon water. Brush breadsticks with egg mixture. Bake for 20 to 25 minutes or until crisp and lightly golden.
PER BREADSTICK *129 cal, 4 g total fat, 25 mg chol, 275 mg sodium, 18 g carb, 0 g fiber, 5 g pro.*

POTATO-BACON CASSEROLE BREAD WITH CARAMELIZED ONIONS

Brandied Blue Cheese Bread

An herbed blue cheese butter melts between slices of a crusty baguette as it warms in the oven. Irresistible!

PREP **10 minutes** BAKE **10 minutes**
OVEN **350°F** MAKES **12 slices**

- 1   12- to 16-ounce baguette-style French bread
- ½   cup butter, softened
- ½   of a 4-ounce package crumbled blue cheese (½ cup)
- 1   tablespoon snipped fresh chives
- 1   tablespoon brandy (optional)
- ⅛   teaspoon cayenne pepper

1. Preheat oven to 350°F. Use a serrated knife to cut bread crosswise into 1-inch slices, cutting to but not through the bottom crust.
2. In a small bowl stir together butter, cheese, chives, brandy (if desired), and cayenne pepper. Spread mixture between slices of bread. Wrap loaf in foil.
3. Bake for 10 to 15 minutes or until bread is heated through and cheese is melted.

PER SLICE *166 cal, 10 g fat, 24 mg chol, 305 mg sodium, 16 g carb, 1 g fiber, 5 g pro.*

Orange-Honey Sweet Rolls

White whole wheat flour gives baked goods the same silky, light texture as white flour—but with more fiber.

PREP **45 minutes**
RISE **1 hour + 30 minutes**
BAKE **25 minutes** COOL **1 minute**
STAND **10 minutes** OVEN **350°F**
MAKES **15 rolls**

- 2   packages active dry yeast
- 1¼   cups warm water (110°F to 115°F)
- ½   cup nonfat dry milk powder
- ⅓   cup butter, softened
- ⅓   cup honey
- 2   eggs, lightly beaten
- 2   tablespoons toasted wheat germ
- 1   teaspoon salt
- 3   cups white whole wheat flour or all-purpose flour
- 2   cups bread flour
- 1   cup golden raisins
- ¼   cup butter, softened
- ¼   cup honey
- 2   teaspoons finely shredded orange peel
- 1   recipe Orange Icing

1. In a large mixing bowl dissolve the yeast in the warm water; let stand for 5 minutes. Add dry milk, the ⅓ cup butter, ⅓ cup honey, eggs, wheat germ, and salt. Beat with an electric mixer on low for 30 seconds, scraping bowl. Add 2 cups of the white whole wheat flour. Beat on low to medium for 30 seconds. Beat on high for 3 minutes. Using a wooden spoon, stir in remaining white whole wheat flour and as much of the bread flour as you can.
2. Turn dough out onto a lightly floured surface. Knead in enough of the remaining bread flour to make a moderately soft dough that is smooth and elastic (about 6 minutes). Shape dough into a ball.
3. Place dough in a lightly greased bowl; turn once to coat the top. Cover loosely with plastic wrap and a clean kitchen towel; let rise in a warm place until double in size (about 1 hour).
4. Punch dough down. Turn out onto a lightly floured surface. Cover; let rest for 10 minutes. Meanwhile, lightly grease a 13×9×2-inch baking pan; set aside.
5. For the filling, in a small bowl cover raisins with cold water; let stand for 5 minutes and drain well. In a medium bowl whisk together the ¼ cup butter, ¼ cup honey, and orange peel until creamy and well combined.
6. Roll dough into an 18×15-inch rectangle. Spread the butter mixture to within ½ inch of the edges. Sprinkle with raisins. Roll up rectangle, starting from a long side. Seal seams. Slice roll into 15 pieces. Place, cut sides down, in pan.
7. Cover loosely with plastic wrap, leaving room for rolls to rise. Let dough rise in a warm place until nearly double (about 30 minutes).
8. Preheat oven to 350°F. Remove plastic wrap. Bake about 25 minutes or until lightly browned. Remove from oven. Cool for 1 minute. Carefully invert rolls onto a wire rack. Cool slightly. Invert again onto a serving platter. Drizzle with Orange Icing.

Orange Icing: In a small bow combine 1 cup powdered sugar and 1 teaspoon finely shredded orange peel. Stir in enough orange juice (1 to 2 tablespoons) to reach drizzling consistency.

PER ROLL *346 cal, 8 g fat, 48 mg chol, 241 mg sodium, 61 g carb, 4 g fiber, 9 g pro.*

ORANGE-HONEY
SWEET ROLLS

Pumpkin Crescent Rolls with Honey Butter

Slightly sweet but not overly so, these flaky, golden-hued rolls are delicious with fall and winter soups.

PREP 45 minutes
RISE 1 hour + 30 minutes
BAKE 15 minutes OVEN 375°F
MAKES 36 rolls

5½ to 6 cups all-purpose flour
1   package active dry yeast
1   cup canned pumpkin
1   cup water
½   cup nonfat dry milk powder
6   tablespoons butter
⅓   cup packed brown sugar
2   tablespoons honey
1   teaspoon salt
½   teaspoon ground cinnamon
2   eggs
1   cup whole wheat flour
1   recipe Honey Butter
2   tablespoons butter, melted

1. In a large mixing bowl stir together 2 cups of the all-purpose flour and the yeast; set aside.
2. In a medium saucepan heat and stir pumpkin, the water, milk powder, the 6 tablespoons butter, the brown sugar, honey, salt, and cinnamon over medium heat until warm (120°F to 130°F) and butter just melts. Add pumpkin mixture and eggs to flour mixture. Beat with an electric mixer on low for 30 seconds, scraping sides of bowl constantly. Beat on high for 3 minutes. Using a wooden spoon, stir in the whole wheat flour and as much of the remaining all-purpose flour as you can.
3. Turn dough out onto a lightly floured surface. Knead in enough of the remaining flour to make a moderately soft dough that is smooth and elastic (3 to 5 minutes total). Shape dough into a ball. Place in a lightly greased bowl, turning once to grease surface of dough. Cover; let rise in a warm place until double in size (1 hour).
4. Punch dough down. Turn dough out onto a lightly floured surface. Divide into thirds. Cover dough; let rest for 10 minutes. Meanwhile, lightly grease three baking sheets or line them with parchment paper; set aside.
5. On the lightly floured surface roll each dough portion into a 12-inch circle. Spread with Honey Butter. Cut each dough circle into 12 wedges. To shape rolls, begin at wide end of each wedge and loosely roll toward the point. Place, point sides down, 2 to 3 inches apart on prepared baking sheets. Cover; let rise in a warm place until nearly double in size (about 30 minutes).
6. Preheat oven to 375°F. Uncover and bake rolls, one or two sheets at a time, about 15 minutes or until golden, rotating baking sheets halfway through baking if necessary. (Cover and chill remaining baking sheet[s] until ready to bake.) Brush tops of rolls with melted butter. Serve warm.

Honey Butter: In a small mixing bowl beat ¼ cup softened butter and 2 tablespoons honey with an electric mixer on low until light and fluffy.

PER ROLL *140 cal, 4 g fat, 22 mg chol, 103 mg sodium, 22 g carb, 1 g fiber, 3 g pro.*

PUMPKIN CRESCENT ROLLS WITH HONEY BUTTER

Creamy Caramel Crunch Rolls

The crunch in these luscious, gooey breakfast breads comes from honey-roasted peanuts.

PREP 35 minutes   RISE 45 minutes
BAKE 40 minutes   COOL 5 minutes
OVEN 350°F   MAKES 16 rolls

1   cup packed brown sugar
½   cup butter, cut up
¼   cup whipping cream
½   teaspoon salt
1   tablespoon vanilla
2   16-ounce loaves frozen sweet roll dough, thawed
⅓   cup peanut butter
½   cup packed brown sugar
1   teaspoon ground cinnamon
½   cup chopped honey-roasted peanuts

1. Lightly grease a 13×9×2-inch baking pan; set aside. For caramel mixture, in a small saucepan combine the 1 cup brown sugar, the butter, whipping cream, and salt. Cook and stir over medium heat until sugar dissolves. Remove from heat. Stir in vanilla. Pour into baking pan.

2. On a lightly floured surface, roll each loaf of thawed dough to an 18×6-inch rectangle. Spread each dough rectangle with half of the peanut butter, spreading to within ½ inch of edges. In a small bowl combine the ½ cup brown sugar and the cinnamon. Stir in nuts. Sprinkle half of the nut mixture over each dough rectangle. Starting from a long side, roll up each rectangle into a spiral; pinch dough to seal seams. Cut each spiral into eight even slices. Place slices, cut sides down, on top of caramel mixture. Cover and let rise in a warm place until nearly double in size (45 to 60 minutes).

3. Preheat oven to 350°F. Bake about 40 minutes or until tops of rolls are golden and edges of rolls are browned. If necessary to prevent overbrowning, cover top with foil after 30 minutes of baking. Cool in pan on a wire rack for 5 minutes. Invert onto a serving platter. Serve warm.

PER ROLL *355 cal, 13 g fat, 32 mg chol, 451 mg sodium, 51 g carb, 2 g fiber, 8 g pro.*

Spicy Apricot and Sausage Braid

Use clean kitchen shears to finely snip the apricots in a small bowl.

PREP **1 hour** RISE **1 hour**
CHILL **2 hours** STAND **30 minutes**
BAKE **20 minutes** OVEN **350°F**
MAKES **1 loaf (16 slices)**

4   ounces andouille sausage, finely chopped
½   cup finely chopped dried apricots
½   to 1 teaspoon crushed red pepper
½   cup snipped fresh cilantro
2   tablespoons honey
3   cups all-purpose flour
1   package active dry yeast
1   teaspoon kosher salt
⅔   cup warm water (105°F to 115°F)
2   eggs, lightly beaten
¼   cup olive oil
1   egg, lightly beaten
1   teaspoon water

1. In a large nonstick skillet cook sausage over medium-high heat until it starts to brown. Stir in apricots and crushed red pepper. Cook and stir for 1 minute. Stir in cilantro and honey. Remove from heat; let cool.

2. Meanwhile, in a large bowl combine 1 cup of the flour, the yeast, and salt. Add the ⅔ cup warm water, the 2 eggs, and the oil. Beat with an electric mixer on

SPICY APRICOT AND SAUSAGE BRAID

low to medium for 30 seconds, scraping sides of bowl constantly. Beat on high for 3 minutes. Stir in sausage mixture. Using a wooden spoon, stir in as much of the remaining flour as you can.

3. Turn dough out onto a lightly floured surface. Knead in enough of the remaining flour to make a soft dough that is smooth and elastic (3 to 5 minutes total). Shape dough into a ball. Place in a lightly greased bowl, turning once to grease surface. Cover; let rise in a warm place until double in size (about 1 hour).

4. Punch dough down. Turn dough out onto a lightly floured surface; divide dough into 3 portions. Cover; let rest for 10 minutes. Meanwhile, line a large baking sheet with parchment paper.

5. Gently roll each dough portion into a 16-inch-long rope. Place the ropes 1 inch apart on the prepared baking sheet; braid. Cover.

6. Chill for at least 2 hours or up to 24 hours. Let stand at room temperature for 30 minutes before baking.

7. Preheat oven to 350°F. In a small bowl combine the 1 egg and the 1 teaspoon water; brush over braid. Bake for 20 to 25 minutes or until loaf sounds hollow when lightly tapped. Cool on a wire rack.

PER SLICE *158 cal, 5 g fat, 45 mg chol, 188 mg sodium, 23 g carb, 1 g fiber, 5 g pro.*

Whole Grain Caramelized Onion and Kale Bread

With whole wheat, oats, flax, fruit, kale, pancetta, and Gruyère cheese, this bread is fabulously healthful but worthy of a celebration as well.

PREP 40 minutes RISE 1 hour
CHILL 2 hours STAND 30 minutes
BAKE 25 minutes OVEN 350°F
MAKES 12 slices

3 ounces pancetta, chopped
1 tablespoon butter
1 cup chopped onion (1 large)
½ cup chopped ripe pear
6 clove garlic, minced
2 cups chopped fresh kale
3½ to 4 cups all-purpose flour
1 package active dry yeast
1 teaspoon sea salt
1½ cups warm water (105°F to 115°F)
4 ounces Gruyère cheese, shredded
½ cup whole wheat flour
½ cup ground rolled oats*
½ cup flaxseeds
1 egg
1 teaspoon honey
1 teaspoon water

1. In a large nonstick skillet cook pancetta over medium heat until crisp. Using a slotted spoon, transfer pancetta to a small bowl reserving drippings in skillet. Add butter to drippings in skillet. Add onion, pear, and garlic; cook and stir about 5 minutes or until tender. Stir in kale and pancetta; cook until kale is tender. Remove from heat; cool.
2. In a large bowl combine 1 cup of the all-purpose flour, the yeast, and salt. Add the 1½ cups warm water. Beat with an electric mixer on low to medium for 30 seconds, scraping sides of bowl constantly. Beat on high for 3 minutes. Stir in cooled kale mixture and cheese. Using a wooden spoon, stir in whole wheat flour, ground oats, and flaxseeds. Gradually stir in as much of the remaining all-purpose flour as you can.

3. Turn dough out onto a lightly floured surface. Knead in enough of the remaining all-purpose flour to make a moderately stiff dough that is smooth and elastic (6 to 8 minutes total). Shape dough into a ball. Place in a lightly greased bowl, turning once to grease surface. Cover; let rise in a warm place until double in size (about 1 hour).
4. Punch dough down. Turn dough out onto a lightly floured surface. Cover; let rest for 10 minutes. Line a baking sheet with parchment paper; set aside. Shape dough by gently pulling it into a ball, tucking edges under. Place dough round on prepared baking sheet. Flatten round slightly to about 9 inches in diameter. Cover.
5. Chill for at least 2 hours or up to 24 hours. Let stand at room temperature for 30 minutes before baking.
6. Preheat oven to 350°F. In a small bowl whisk together egg, honey, and the 1 teaspoon water; brush top of dough round with egg mixture. Bake for 25 to 30 minutes or until golden and bread sounds hollow when lightly tapped. Cool on a wire rack.
*Tip: To make ground oats, place ⅔ cup rolled oats in a food processor or blender. Cover and process or blend until ground.
PER SLICE 229 cal, 7 g fat, 27 mg chol, 237 mg sodium, 32 g carb, 3 g fiber, 9 g pro.

Herbed Braidsticks

These gorgeous intertwined breadsticks are almost too beautiful to eat. Almost.

PREP 35 minutes RISE 30 minutes
BAKE 15 minutes OVEN 350°F
MAKES 16 servings

1 to 1¼ cups all-purpose flour
1 package active dry yeast
1 tablespoon snipped fresh rosemary, thyme, and/or oregano
¼ teaspoon coarsely ground black pepper
¾ cup milk
2 tablespoons butter or margarine
1 tablespoon sugar
½ teaspoon salt
1 cup semolina pasta flour*
1 egg white
1 tablespoon water

1. In a large bowl stir together ¾ cup of the all-purpose flour, the yeast, rosemary, thyme, and/or oregano, and pepper. In a small saucepan heat milk, butter, sugar, and salt just until warm (120°F to 130°F) and butter almost melts.
2. Add milk mixture to flour mixture. Beat with an electric mixer on low to medium for 30 seconds, scraping sides of bowl constantly. Beat on high for 3 minutes. Using a wooden spoon, stir in semolina flour. Let stand for 1 minute. Stir in as much of the remaining all-purpose flour as you can.
3. Turn dough out onto a lightly floured surface. Knead in enough of the remaining all-purpose flour to make a stiff dough that is smooth and elastic (8 to 10 minutes total). Shape into a ball. Place in a lightly greased large bowl, turning once to grease surface. Cover; let rise in a warm place until nearly double in size (45 to 60 minutes).
4. Punch down dough. Turn out onto a lightly floured surface. Divide dough in half. Cover; let rest for 10 minutes. Line a baking sheet with foil; grease foil. Roll one dough portion into a 10×9-inch rectangle. Cut lengthwise into 24 strips.
5. For each breadstick, pinch together ends of three strips; braid the dough strips. Pinch the other ends together. Tuck under the thin, pinched ends. Place on the prepared baking sheet. Repeat with remaining dough portion. Cover; let rise in a warm place until nearly double in size (about 30 minutes).
6. Preheat oven to 350°F. In a small bowl beat together egg white and the water. Lightly brush egg white mixture on breadsticks. Bake for 15 to 20 minutes or until golden. Serve warm.
*Tip: Instead of semolina flour, you can use ¾ cup all-purpose flour plus ¼ cup yellow cornmeal.
PER BRAIDSTICK 58 cal, 1 g fat, 0 mg chol, 60 mg sodium, 10 g carb, 0 g fiber, 2 g pro.

WHITE CHOCOLATE-
GINGERBREAD TRIFLE

sweet temptations

SAVE ROOM! Even when you think you can't eat another bite, this selection of fabulous cakes, pies, tarts, and old-fashioned fruit desserts will tempt you to the table again—fork in hand—to end the celebration on a sweet note.

78

85

88

Dutch Apple Cake with Caramel Glaze

Use a variety of apple that will keep its shape when baked into the cake— Granny Smith is a good choice.

PREP 40 minutes BAKE 1 hour
OVEN 325°F MAKES 16 servings

7   apples
3   cups unbleached all-purpose flour
1   teaspoon baking soda
1½   teaspoons ground cinnamon
1   teaspoon salt
½   teaspoon freshly grated nutmeg
3   eggs
1½   cups vegetable oil
1   cup packed brown sugar
1   cup granulated sugar
2½   teaspoons vanilla
1¼   cups chopped pecans
1   recipe Caramel Glaze

1. Preheat oven to 325°F. Butter and flour a 13×9×2-inch baking pan; set aside. Peel apples, quarter, core, and cut each quarter in half lengthwise, then crosswise (16 pieces from each apple).
2. In a medium bowl whisk together the flour, baking soda, cinnamon, salt, and nutmeg; set aside.
3. In a very large mixing bowl whisk eggs to combine. Whisk in oil, sugars, and vanilla until well blended. Gradually whisk in the flour mixture just until well blended. Fold apples and pecans into batter (batter will be thick and just coat apples). Turn into prepared pan, spreading to edges of pan.

4. Bake about 1 hour or until a toothpick inserted in the center of the cake comes out clean. Remove from oven and cool on a wire rack while preparing glaze. Spoon Caramel Glaze over warm cake.
Caramel Glaze: In a medium skillet melt 6 tablespoons unsalted butter. Add ⅓ cup packed dark brown sugar, ⅓ cup packed light brown sugar, ½ cup whipping cream, and a pinch of salt. Cook and stir until blended over medium-low heat for 2 minutes. Increase heat and boil 2 minutes or until dime-size bubbles cover the surface of the glaze. Remove from heat and cool slightly until glaze begins to thicken, about 5 minutes.
PER SERVING *568 cal, 35 g fat, 61 mg chol, 256 mg sodium, 62 g carb, 2 g fiber, 5 g pro.*

Pumpkin Tiramisu Cake

The "tiramisu" flavor in this fancy cake comes from Coffee Syrup that soaks into it and Maple Mascarpone Cream between its layers.

PREP 1 hour STAND 30 minutes
BAKE 15 minutes CHILL 2 hours
OVEN 375°F MAKES 12 servings

3   eggs
¾   cup all-purpose flour
2   teaspoons ground cinnamon
1   teaspoon baking powder
1   teaspoon ground ginger
½   teaspoon salt
½   teaspoon ground nutmeg
1   cup sugar

⅔   cup canned pumpkin
1   teaspoon lemon juice
1   cup finely chopped hazelnuts
     Powdered sugar
1   recipe Coffee Syrup
1   recipe Maple Mascarpone Cream
     Chopped toasted hazelnuts (see note, page 22) (optional)
     Grated bittersweet chocolate (optional)

1. Let eggs stand at room temperature for 30 minutes. Grease a 15×10×1-inch baking pan. Line bottom of pan with waxed paper; grease the paper. Set pan aside. In a small bowl stir together flour, cinnamon, baking powder, ginger, salt, and nutmeg; set aside.
2. Preheat oven to 375°F. In a large mixing bowl beat eggs with an electric mixer on high 5 minutes or until thick and lemon color. Gradually add sugar, beating on medium until fluffy. Stir in pumpkin and lemon juice. Add flour mixture; beat on low just until combined. Pour batter into pan, spreading evenly. Sprinkle with nuts.
3. Bake about 15 minutes or until cake springs back when lightly touched. Immediately loosen edges of cake from pan and turn cake out onto a towel sprinkled with powdered sugar. Remove waxed paper. Cool completely.
4. To assemble, cut cake crosswise into thirds. Place one of the cake layers, nut side up, on a serving plate (if any of the nuts fall off when inverting cake layers, sprinkle them over the cake layers when assembling). Drizzle one-third of the Coffee Syrup over cake layer. Spread evenly with ¾ cup Maple Mascarpone Cream. Repeat layers. Top with remaining cake layer and drizzle with remaining Coffee Syrup. Frost top and sides of cake with remaining Maple Mascarpone Cream.
5. Cover and chill cake for 2 to 24 hours. If desired, garnish the top of cake with additional chopped hazelnuts and grated bittersweet chocolate.
Coffee Syrup: In a small saucepan combine ½ cup sugar, ½ cup water, and 2 tablespoons instant espresso coffee powder. Bring to boiling over medium heat, stirring to dissolve sugar. Boil gently for 1 minute. Remove from heat. Stir in 1 tablespoon amaretto and 1 tablespoon hazelnut liqueur.

Maple Mascarpone Cream: In a large mixing bowl beat 2 cups whipping cream, one 8-ounce container mascarpone cheese, and ¼ cup pure maple syrup with an electric mixer on medium to high until soft peaks form (tips curl).

PER SERVING *467 cal, 32 g fat, 132 mg chol, 173 mg sodium, 42 g carb, 2 g fiber, 9 g pro.*

Chocolate and Vanilla Red Velvet Cake

This Southern classic gets an upscale update with a Mascarpone-Vanilla Bean Filling and Chocolate Ganache.

PREP **45 minutes** BAKE **20 minutes**
STAND **30 minutes** COOL **10 minutes**
OVEN **350°F** MAKES **16 servings**

3	eggs
¾	cup butter
3	cups all-purpose flour
1	tablespoon unsweetened cocoa powder
¾	teaspoon salt
2¼	cups sugar
1	1-ounce bottle red food coloring (2 tablespoons)
1½	teaspoons vanilla
1½	cups buttermilk or sour milk*
1½	teaspoons baking soda
1½	teaspoons vinegar
1	recipe Mascarpone-Vanilla Bean Filling
1	recipe Chocolate Ganache

1. Allow eggs and butter to stand at room temperature for 30 minutes. Meanwhile, grease and lightly flour three 9×9×2-inch square cake pans. Set pans aside. In a medium bowl stir together flour, cocoa powder, and salt; set aside.
2. Preheat oven to 350°F. In a very large bowl beat butter with an electric mixer on medium to high for 30 seconds. Gradually add sugar, about ¼ cup at time, beating on medium until well mixed. Scrape sides of bowl; beat on medium for 2 minutes more. Add eggs, one at a time, beating well after each addition. Beat in red food coloring and vanilla. Alternately add flour mixture and buttermilk, beating on low after each addition just until combined. In a small bowl combine baking soda and vinegar; fold into batter. Spread batter in the prepared pans.

3. Bake for 20 to 25 minutes or until a wooden toothpick inserted near the centers comes out clean. Cool cake layers in pans on wire racks for 10 minutes. Remove cake layers from pans. Cool thoroughly on wire racks.
4. If necessary, with a long serrated knife, level tops of cake layers. Place one cake layer, bottom side up, on serving platter. Spread with half of the Mascarpone-Vanilla Bean Filling. Top with second cake layer, bottom side up. Spread top with the remaining filling. Top with third layer, bottom side up. Spoon Chocolate Ganache over cake top, using a thin spatula to spread on side and top.

Mascarpone-Vanilla Bean Filling: In a small saucepan combine 2 ounces chopped white baking chocolate (with cocoa butter) and 2 tablespoons whipping cream. Cut a vanilla bean in half lengthwise; scrape out seeds. Stir vanilla bean seeds into chocolate mixture. Cook and stir over low heat until chocolate is nearly melted. Remove from heat; stir until smooth. Cool for 15 minutes. In a large bowl beat together ⅓ cup mascarpone cheese or cream cheese, softened, and 3 tablespoons butter, softened, with an electric mixer on medium. Gradually add white chocolate mixture, beating until fluffy. Gradually beat in 2 cups powdered sugar until mixture is a thick spreading consistency.

Chocolate Ganache: In a medium saucepan bring 1 cup whipping cream and 1 tablespoon light-color corn syrup just to boiling over medium-high heat. Remove from heat. Add 2½ cups semisweet or dark chocolate pieces (do not stir). Let stand for 5 minutes. Stir. Let stand for 15 minutes more.

*Tip: To make 1½ cups sour milk, place 4½ teaspoons lemon juice or vinegar in a glass measuring cup. Add enough milk to make 1½ cups total liquid; stir. Let the mixture stand for 5 minutes before using.

PER SERVING *605 cal, 30 g fat, 99 mg chol, 358 mg sodium, 83 g carb, 2 g fiber, 7 g pro.*

CHOCOLATE AND
VANILLA RED VELVET
CAKE

Dulce de Leche Cake

In Spanish, *dulce de leche* means "sweet of milk." It is essentially milk and sugar cooked until it is caramellike.

PREP **1 hour** BAKE **40 minutes**
COOL **10 minutes** CHILL **overnight**
OVEN **350°F** MAKES **12 to 16 servings**

1   2-layer-size white cake mix
¾   cup butter, softened
5   eggs
½   cup water
2   tablespoons finely shredded orange
    peel
1   recipe Dulce de Leche Cream
1   recipe Whipped Cream Frosting
1   recipe Caramelized Sugar Drizzle
    (optional)

1. Preheat oven to 350°F. Grease and flour a 10-inch springform pan.*
2. In a very large bowl beat cake mix, butter, eggs, and the water with an electric mixer on low until combined. Beat on medium for 2 minutes more (batter will be thick). Stir in orange peel. Spread batter in prepared pan.
3. Bake about 40 minutes or until a wooden skewer inserted near the center comes out clean. Cool in pan on a wire rack for 10 minutes (cake may sink slightly during cooling). Loosen cake from side of pan; remove side. Lift cake from pan bottom using a wide metal spatula. Cool cake completely on wire rack.
4. Using a long serrated knife, cut the cake in half horizontally to make two layers. Place one layer, cut side up, on a serving platter. Slide pieces of waxed paper underneath the cake layer on all sides to catch drips. Spread ½ to ¾ cup of the Dulce de Leche Cream on top of layer. Top with the second cake layer, cut side up. Press down lightly. Spread ½ to ¾ cup of the Dulce de Leche Cream over cake. Cover and chill overnight. If necessary, cover and chill any remaining Dulce de Leche Cream.
5. Spread Whipped Cream Frosting over top and sides of cake. Remove waxed paper pieces from under the cake. Just before serving, if desired, drizzle with Caramelized Sugar Drizzle. Serve with any remaining Dulce de Leche Cream.
Dulce de Leche Cream: In a large saucepan combine half of a 14-ounce can sweetened condensed milk and one 13.4-ounce can dulce de leche. Cook over medium heat just until boiling, stirring frequently. Remove from heat. Transfer

DULCE DE LECHE
CAKE

to a bowl. Cover; cool for 5 minutes.

Whipped Cream Frosting: In a large saucepan bring about 1 inch of water to boiling over high heat. Meanwhile, in a 1-cup heatproof glass measuring cup combine 2 tablespoons cold water and 1 teaspoon unflavored gelatin. Let stand for 2 minutes. Place measuring cup in the boiling water in saucepan. Cook and stir about 1 minute or until the gelatin is completely dissolved. Remove measuring cup from saucepan. Cool for 5 minutes. In a chilled large bowl beat 1½ cups whipping cream, 3 tablespoons sugar, and, if desired, 1 tablespoon orange-flavor liqueur with the chilled beaters of an electric mixer on medium while gradually drizzling the gelatin mixture into the cream mixture. Continue beating the cream mixture until stiff peaks form (tips stand straight).

Caramelized Sugar Drizzle: In a large skillet cook ⅓ cup sugar over medium-high heat until sugar starts to melt, shaking skillet occasionally. Do not stir. When sugar starts to melt, reduce heat to low and cook about 5 minutes more or until all of the sugar is melted, stirring as needed with a wooden spoon. Remove from heat. Immediately drizzle over frosted cake.

*Tip: If your springform pan does not have a tight fit, line the outside of the pan with foil.

PER SERVING *582 cal, 33 g fat, 174 mg chol, 475 mg sodium, 64 g carb, 0 g fiber, 9 g pro.*

Classic Fruitcake Loaves

Give a loaf of this fruitcake as a gift and it will not be "regifted"—guaranteed.

PREP 45 minutes BAKE 45 minutes
COOL 20 minutes MARINATE overnight
CHILL 7 days OVEN 325°F
MAKES 2 loaves

1½ cups dried apricots, candied cherries, and/or candied pineapple, coarsely chopped
½ cup candied lemon and/or orange rind, chopped
½ cup chopped pitted dates
½ cup raisins
2 tablespoons chopped crystallized ginger
¾ cup orange juice
½ cup rum
 Nonstick cooking spray
2 cups all-purpose flour
1 teaspoon ground cinnamon
½ teaspoon salt
½ teaspoon baking powder
¼ teaspoon ground allspice
⅛ teaspoon ground cloves
½ cup butter, softened
¼ cup almond paste
1 cup packed brown sugar
3 eggs
¼ cup mild-flavor molasses
1 cup pecan and/or walnut halves, toasted (see tip, page 14)

1. In a large bowl combine apricots, lemon rind, dates, raisins, and crystallized ginger. Add ¼ cup of the orange juice and ¼ cup of the rum. Cover bowl tightly and refrigerate overnight.
2. Preheat oven to 325°F. Line two 8×4×2-inch loaf pans with parchment paper. Lightly coat with cooking spray. In a bowl stir together the flour, cinnamon, salt, baking powder, allspice, and cloves.
3. In a very large mixing bowl beat butter and almond paste with an electric mixer on medium to high for 30 seconds. Add brown sugar. Beat until combined, scraping sides of bowl occasionally. Add eggs, one at a time, beating after each addition. Beat in molasses and remaining ¼ cup of orange juice on low. Stir in nuts. Drain dried fruit mixture well; add liquid to reserved orange juice and rum. Stir fruit and flour mixture into batter. Spoon batter evenly into prepared pans.
4. Bake for 45 to 65 minutes or until a wooden toothpick inserted near the centers comes out clean. Cool in pans on a wire rack for 20 minutes. Remove loaves from pans; cool completely on rack.
5. Brush cooled loaves with some of the reserved rum mixture. Wrap loaves tightly with plastic wrap. Refrigerate loaves for 7 days, brushing each with the remaining rum mixture each day.

PER SERVING *238 cal, 9 g fat, 37 mg chol, 99 mg sodium, 37 g carb, 2 g fiber, 3 g pro.*

Chocolate-Sour Cream Fruitcake

A fruitcake for those who must have chocolate in everything!

PREP 30 minutes BAKE 1 hour
STAND overnight CHILL overnight
OVEN 300°F MAKES 20 servings

2 eggs
¼ cup milk
1½ cups sugar
1 8-ounce carton sour cream
1 teaspoon vanilla
⅓ cup butter, melted
2 cups all-purpose flour
½ cup unsweetened cocoa powder
1 teaspoon baking soda
1 teaspoon salt
¼ teaspoon ground cloves
1½ cups chopped walnuts
1 cup red or green candied cherries
1 cup candied pineapple
1 cup raisins
1 cup dried figs, chopped
 Powdered sugar

1. Preheat oven to 300°F. Grease a 10-inch fluted tube pan; set aside.
2. In a large bowl stir together the eggs, milk, sugar, sour cream, vanilla, and melted butter; set aside. In a medium bowl stir together the flour, cocoa powder, baking soda, salt, and cloves. Add to egg mixture; stir to combine. Stir in nuts and fruit. Spoon into the prepared pan, spreading evenly.
3. Bake 1 hour or until a wooden toothpick inserted near center comes out clean. Cool in pan on a wire rack 10 minutes. Remove cake from pan; cool on rack. Wrap cake tightly with plastic wrap; refrigerate overnight and for up to 1 week. Let stand at room temperature 1 hour before serving. Sprinkle with powdered sugar before serving.

PER SERVING *336 cal, 12 g fat, 34 mg chol, 227 mg sodium, 54 g carb, 2 g fiber, 5 g pro.*

CHOCOLATE-SOUR CREAM FRUITCAKE

Cherry Baby Cakes

These two-bite cakes make a wonderful addition to a dessert buffet.

PREP 40 minutes BAKE 12 minutes
COOL 5 minutes OVEN 350°F
MAKES 30 cupcakes

1⅓ cups all-purpose flour
⅔   cup sugar
2   teaspoons baking powder
¼   teaspoon salt
⅔   cup milk
¼   cup butter, softened
1   egg
1   teaspoon vanilla
⅔   cup cherry marmalade or cherry preserves, large pieces snipped if necessary
60 maraschino cherries with stems, drained
1   recipe Powdered Sugar Icing

1. Preheat oven to 350°F. Line thirty 1¾-inch muffin cups with paper bake cups;* set aside.
2. In a large mixing bowl combine flour, sugar, baking powder, and salt. Add milk, butter, egg, and vanilla. Beat with an electric mixer on low until combined. Beat on medium for 1 minute. Spoon 1 scant teaspoon batter into each muffin cup. Add ½ teaspoon of cherry marmalade and top with ½ teaspoon additional batter.
3. Bake cupcakes about 12 minutes or until a wooden toothpick inserted in centers comes out clean. Cool in pans on a wire rack for 5 minutes. Remove from pans; cool completely on wire rack.
4. Pat maraschino cherries dry with a paper towel. Frost each cupcake with about ½ teaspoon icing. Dip half of each cherry into remaining icing; place on tops of baby cakes.

Powdered Sugar Icing: In a small bowl stir together 2½ cups powdered sugar, 2 tablespoons milk, and ½ teaspoon vanilla. Stir in additional milk, 1 teaspoon at a time, to make icing drizzling consistency.
***Tip:** If you don't have 1¾-inch muffin cups, line sixteen 2½-inch muffin cups with paper bake cups. Prepare batter as directed. Spoon 1 tablespoon batter into each muffin cup. Add 1 teaspoon of marmalade and another tablespoon of batter. (You will use about ⅓ cup marmalade total.) Bake about 15 minutes or until a wooden toothpick inserted in centers comes out clean. Frost with Powdered Sugar Icing. Add a cherry as directed. (You will need 16 cherries.)
PER CUPCAKE *63 cal, 1 g fat, 6 mg chol, 36 mg sodium, 13 g carb, 0 g fiber, 0 g pro.*

Chocolate-Filled Sweet Potato Cupcakes

The filling for these cupcakes couldn't be simpler—just unwrap a chocolate kiss and drop it in the muffin cup.

PREP 25 minutes BAKE 19 minutes
COOL 10 minutes OVEN 350°F
MAKES 24 servings

2   cups all-purpose flour
2   teaspoons pumpkin pie spice
1½   teaspoons baking powder
½   teaspoon baking soda
¼   teaspoon salt
1   cup unsalted butter, softened
1¼   cups granulated sugar
3   eggs
1   pound sweet potatoes, roasted,*
     peeled, and mashed
¼   cup milk
1   teaspoon vanilla
24   milk chocolate or dark chocolate
     kisses, unwrapped
8   ounces milk chocolate, chopped
4   ounces semisweet chocolate,
     chopped
1   cup minus 2 tablespoons unsalted
     butter, softened
½   cup powdered sugar

1. Preheat oven to 350°F. Line twenty-four 2½-inch muffin cups with folded 5×4-inch rectangles of parchment paper or paper bake cups; set aside.
2. In a medium bowl combine the flour, pumpkin pie spice, baking powder, baking soda, and salt; set aside. In a large mixing bowl beat the butter with electric mixer on medium for 30 seconds. Add granulated sugar; beat until light and fluffy, about 2 minutes. With mixer on low, beat in eggs, one at a time, stopping to scrape down sides of bowl between additions. Add the sweet potatoes, milk, and vanilla; beat on low until combined. Add the flour mixture to the sugar-egg mixture; beat on low just until combined.
3. Fill each muffin cup about two-thirds full with batter. Bake for 5 minutes. Carefully remove pan from oven. Gently press kisses, tips up, about halfway into each cup. Bake for 14 minutes more, until tops of cupcakes spring back when touched and chocolate is not visible.

Cool cupcakes in pan for 10 minutes. Remove from pan and cool completely on a wire rack.
4. For frosting, in a medium saucepan over low heat bring 1 inch of water to simmering. Place chopped milk chocolate and semisweet chocolate in a medium mixing bowl. Place the bowl over the saucepan of water. Stir chocolate with a rubber spatula until melted. Remove from heat; cool chocolate for 15 minutes. With electric mixer on low, beat chocolate for 30 seconds. Beat in butter, 1 to 2 tablespoons at a time. Beat in powdered sugar until smooth. Spread frosting on cupcake tops.
*Tip: To roast sweet potatoes, preheat oven to 425°F. Prick unpeeled potatoes all over with a fork. Roast potatoes in a shallow baking pan for 50 minutes or until tender. Cool.
PER SERVING *341 cal, 21 g fat, 68 mg chol, 110 mg sodium, 36 g carb, 1 g fiber, 4 g pro.*

Stout Gingerbread with Lemony Hard Sauce

This old-school gingerbread is the real deal—dark, intense, chewy, spicy, and not overly sweet.

PREP 25 minutes STAND 15 minutes
BAKE 40 minutes COOL 10 minutes
OVEN 350°F MAKES 12 servings

     Nonstick spray for baking
¾   cup stout beer (such as Guinness)
2½   cups all-purpose flour
1   tablespoon ground ginger
2   teaspoons ground cinnamon
1½   teaspoons baking powder
½   teaspoon baking soda
½   teaspoon salt
¼   teaspoon freshly grated nutmeg or
     ⅛ teaspoon ground nutmeg
¼   teaspoon ground cardamom
1   cup butter, softened
1¼   cups packed brown sugar
3   eggs
1   cup mild-flavor molasses
1   tablespoon grated fresh ginger
1   tablespoon powdered sugar
1   recipe Lemony Hard Sauce

1. Preheat oven to 350°F. Generously coat a 10-inch fluted tube pan with nonstick spray for baking. Pour beer into a measuring cup and let stand at room temperature for 15 minutes. In a medium

bowl stir together flour, ground ginger, cinnamon, baking powder, baking soda, salt, nutmeg, and cardamom; set aside.
2. In a large mixing bowl beat butter with an electric mixer on medium to high for 30 seconds. Add brown sugar. Beat until light and fluffy, scraping sides of bowl occasionally. Add eggs, one at a time, beating well after each addition. Stir in molasses and grated ginger. Alternately add flour mixture and beer in three additions, beating on medium just until combined after each addition. Pour batter into the prepared pan.
3. Bake for 40 to 50 minutes or until a wooden toothpick inserted near the center comes out clean. Cool in pan on a wire rack for 10 minutes. Remove cake from pan. Sprinkle with powdered sugar. Serve warm with Lemony Hard Sauce.
Lemony Hard Sauce: In a medium bowl beat ¼ cup butter, softened, with an electric mixer on medium to high until light and fluffy. Beat in ¾ cup powdered sugar, 2 tablespoons lemon or orange liqueur, 2 teaspoons finely shredded lemon or orange peel, and 1 teaspoon vanilla until smooth.
PER SERVING *496 cal, 21 g fat, 104 mg chol, 366 mg sodium, 73 g carb, 1 g fiber, 5 g pro.*

STOUT GINGERBREAD WITH LEMONY HARD SAUCE

Brownie Baked Alaska

Look for dried egg whites in the baking sections of your supermarket.

PREP 30 minutes FREEZE 1 hour
BROIL 1 minute MAKES 9 servings

　　Nonstick spray for baking
1　18.4-ounce package original supreme brownie mix
2　pints premium pistachio ice cream, slightly softened
⅓　cup dried egg whites
⅓　cup warm water
⅓　cup sugar

1. Preheat oven according to brownie package directions. Line an 8×8×2-inch baking pan with foil, extending the foil 2 inches over the edges of the pan. Coat foil generously with spray for baking. Prepare brownie batter according to package directions; spread into prepared pan and bake as directed. Cool in pan on a wire rack. Using the edges of the foil, lift the uncut brownies out of the pan. Trim off uneven edges. Cut brownies into 9 squares. Evenly space brownie squares on a baking sheet.
2. Place a ⅓-cup scoop of ice cream on top of each brownie square. Immediately place baking sheet in the freezer. Freeze for 30 minutes. Tightly wrap baking sheet with plastic wrap; return to freezer. Freeze for at least 30 minutes or up to 2 weeks.

BROWNIE BAKED ALASKA

3. Preheat broiler. For meringue, in a large bowl combine dried egg whites and the warm water. Beat with an electric mixer on medium to high until soft peaks form (tips curl). Gradually add sugar, beating until stiff peaks form (tips stand straight).
4. Remove ice cream-topped brownies from freezer; discard plastic wrap. Working quickly, spread or pipe meringue evenly over each ice cream, swirling decoratively. Broil 4 to 5 inches from heat about 1 minute or until browned. Serve immediately.
PER SERVING 599 cal, 23 g fat, 75 mg chol, 380 mg sodium, 91 g carb, 1 g fiber, 12 g pro.

White Chocolate-Gingerbread Trifle

This recipe combines two English favorites—gingerbread and trifle—in one fabulous dessert.

PREP 50 minutes BAKE 25 minutes
CHILL 2 hours OVEN 350°F
MAKES 10 to 12 servings

2　cups all-purpose flour
1½　teaspoons baking soda
1　tablespoon ground ginger
1　teaspoon ground cinnamon
½　teaspoon salt
1　cup molasses
¾　cup water
½　cup unsalted butter
¼　cup firmly packed brown sugar
2　eggs
4　egg yolks
2　eggs
½　cup sugar
½　cup lemon juice
2　ounces white chocolate, chopped
1　cup whipping cream
1　12-ounce bag cranberries
½　cup water
⅓　to ½ cup sugar
1½　cups sliced strawberries
2　tablespoons slivered candied ginger

1. Preheat oven to 350°F. For the homemade gingerbread, grease a 9×9×2-inch square pan, then line bottom of pan with parchment paper. In a medium bowl sift together the flour, baking soda, ginger, cinnamon, and salt; set aside.

2. In a small saucepan heat molasses, the water, butter, and brown sugar until hot, stirring until butter and brown sugar are melted. In a large bowl whisk the 2 eggs until blended. Slowly whisk in the molasses mixture. Stir in flour mixture. Pour batter in prepared pan. Bake for 25 to 30 minutes, until a skewer inserted near center comes out clean. Cool gingerbread in pan on a wire rack. Remove the gingerbread from the pan. Tear two-thirds of the cake into pieces (about 7 cups). Set aside until ready to assemble trifle.
3. For lemon-white chocolate cream, in a bowl whisk together egg yolks, 2 eggs, sugar, and lemon juice. Transfer to a heavy medium-size saucepan. Cook over medium-low heat, stirring constantly with a wooden spoon until thickened. If mixture becomes lumpy, whisk until smooth. Remove from heat. Whisk in white chocolate until smooth. Strain into a bowl. Cover with plastic wrap directly on surface. Refrigerate until cold.
4. In a large mixing bowl beat the whipping cream until soft peaks form. Remove, cover, and chill ½ cup of the whipped cream to use as topping. Fold remaining whipped cream into the cold lemon-white chocolate cream; refrigerate until ready to assemble trifle.
5. For the cranberry compote, in a medium saucepan combine cranberries, the ½ cup water, and ⅓ to ⅓ cup sugar. Cook over medium heat for 10 minutes, stirring occasionally, until cranberries are soft. Cool completely. Stir in strawberries.
6. To assemble the trifle, spoon half the lemon-white chocolate cream into the bottom of a 7- to 9-inch trifle bowl or other container. Top with pieces of homemade gingerbread. Spoon remaining lemon-white chocolate cream on top of the gingerbread. Top with the cranberry compote. Garnish with the ½ cup reserved whipped cream and slivered candied ginger.
PER SERVING 452 cal, 21 g fat, 205 mg chol, 257 mg sodium, 63 g carb, 3 g fiber, 6 g pro.

Candy Cane Trifles

You can substitute purchased brownies or brownies made from a mix for the homemade brownies.

PREP 40 minutes **BAKE** 25 minutes **OVEN** 350°F **MAKES** 10 servings

- 2   cups all-purpose flour
- 2   cups sugar
- 1   teaspoon baking soda
- ¼   teaspoon salt
- 1   cup butter, cut up
- 1   cup water
- ⅓   cup unsweetened cocoa powder
- 2   eggs
- ½   cup buttermilk
- 1½ teaspoons vanilla
     Nonstick cooking or baking spray
- ¾   cup coarsely crushed candy canes (about 10)
- 3   to 4 cups vanilla ice cream
- ½   cup whipping cream, beaten to stiff peaks
     Mint sprigs

1. Preheat oven to 350°F. Line a 15×10×1-inch baking pan with foil; grease foil. Set aside. In a large mixing bowl stir together flour, sugar, baking soda, and salt; set aside.

2. In a medium saucepan combine butter, the water, and cocoa powder. Bring just to boiling, stirring constantly. Remove from heat. Add cocoa mixture to flour mixture. Beat with electric mixer on medium until combined. Add the eggs, buttermilk, and vanilla. Beat for 1 minute (batter will be thin). Pour batter into prepared pan. Bake for 25 minutes or until a toothpick inserted in center comes out clean. Cool on a wire rack.

3. Coat a 2½-inch round cutter with cooking spray. Cut out 20 brownie circles (clean and recoat cutter as needed). Set aside until ready to assemble trifles.

4. To assemble the trifle, place 1 brownie circle in each of 10 straight-side glasses or tumblers, about 3 inches in diameter. Sprinkle some of the crushed candy on the brownie. Top with ⅓ cup of ice cream. Place another brownie circle on top of the ice cream. Top with whipped cream, additional crushed candy, and a mint sprig.

PER SERVING *519 cal, 24 g fat, 104 mg chol, 306 mg sodium, 72 g carb, 1 g fiber, 5 g pro.*

Mascarpone-Fruitcake Bread Pudding with Hard Sauce

This recipe makes good use of that extra fruitcake you might have received this holiday season.

PREP 30 minutes CHILL 4 hours
BAKE 55 minutes COOL 30 minutes
OVEN 300°F/350°F
MAKES 12 to 15 servings

6   cups 1-inch cubes challah or egg bread
8   ounces mascarpone cheese
¼   cup butter, softened
¾   cup sugar
2   teaspoons vanilla
4   eggs
1½ cups half-and-half or light cream
1   cup milk
4   cups 1-inch cubes Classic Fruitcake Loaves (see recipe, page 77) or other fruitcake
1   recipe Hard Sauce or Sweetened Whipped Cream
    Powdered sugar (optional)

1. Preheat oven to 300°F. Arrange the challah cubes in a large shallow baking pan. Bake cubes about 15 minutes or until dry, tossing once. Cool completely.
2. Grease a 3-quart rectangular baking dish; set aside. In a large mixing bowl beat mascarpone cheese and butter with an electric mixer on medium to high for 30 seconds. Add sugar and vanilla.

MASCARPONE-FRUITCAKE BREAD PUDDING WITH HARD SAUCE

Beat until combined, scraping sides of bowl occasionally. Add eggs, one at a time, beating well after each addition. Gradually add half-and-half and milk, beating on low until combined.
3. Spoon mascarpone mixture into the prepared dish, spreading evenly. Top with half of the challah cubes, all of the fruitcake cubes, and the remaining challah cubes, pressing cubes into the mascarpone mixture. Cover dish with plastic wrap and refrigerate for at least 4 hours or overnight.
4. Preheat oven to 350°F. Bake, uncovered, for 40 to 45 minutes or until set and golden brown. Cool in pan on a wire rack for 30 minutes. Serve warm with Hard Sauce or Sweetened Whipped Cream. If desired, sprinkle bread pudding with powdered sugar.
Hard Sauce: In a medium heavy saucepan cook and stir 1 cup sugar, ½ cup half-and-half or light cream, and ½ cup butter until the butter melts and the mixture is smooth. Remove from heat; stir in ½ teaspoon vanilla. Serve sauce warm.
Sweetened Whipped Cream: In a chilled mixing bowl beat 1 cup whipping cream, 2 tablespoons sugar, and ½ teaspoon vanilla with an electric mixer on medium until soft peaks form (tips curl).
PER SERVING 572 cal, 33 g fat, 171 mg chol, 253 mg sodium, 62 g carb, 2 g fiber, 11 g pro.

Fruit and Almond Country-Style Tart

An almond crust gives this rustic tart a touch of sophistication.

PREP 45 minutes CHILL 4 hours
BAKE 1 hour COOL 30 minutes
OVEN 375°F MAKES 8 servings

1   recipe Almond Pastry
¾   cup almond paste
1   egg white, lightly beaten
½   cup packed brown sugar or granulated sugar
2   cups peeled sliced fresh peaches or frozen sliced peaches, thawed
1   cup fresh red raspberries
½   cup snipped dried apricots
3   tablespoons peach or apricot jam
2   tablespoons sliced almonds
    Milk
    Coarse decorating sugar (optional)

1. Prepare Almond Pastry. On a lightly floured surface roll two-thirds of the pastry from center to edges into a 12-inch circle. Wrap pastry circle around the rolling pin. Unroll into an 11-inch tart pan with a removable bottom; press pastry into fluted sides of pan and trim edges.
2. Preheat oven to 375°F. For filling, in a small bowl crumble almond paste. Stir in egg white and brown sugar. Spread or gently pat filling evenly into the pastry-lined tart pan. In a medium bowl toss together peaches, berries, dried apricots, and jam. Spoon fruit mixture into tart pan. Sprinkle with almonds.
3. Roll remaining pastry until ⅛ inch thick. Cut into ½-inch-wide strips; top tart with pastry strips in a lattice pattern. Trim the pastry strips even with the edge of the tart pan. Press ends of strips against the pan to seal. Lightly brush pastry strips with milk and, if desired, sprinkle with coarse decorating sugar.
4. Bake for 1 hour or until crust is golden. Cool on a wire rack for 30 to 60 minutes. Remove sides from tart pan.
Almond Pastry: In a medium bowl stir together 2 cups all-purpose flour, ½ cup ground almonds, 1 tablespoon sugar, and ½ teaspoon salt. Using a pastry blender, cut in ¾ cup cold butter, cut up, and 3 tablespoons shortening until pieces are pea size. Sprinkle 1 tablespoon ice water over part of the flour mixture; gently toss with a fork. Push moistened pastry to the side of the bowl. Repeat moistening flour mixture, using 1 tablespoon water at a time (4 to 5 tablespoons total), until all the flour mixture is moistened. Gather flour mixture into a ball, kneading gently until it holds together. Flatten dough into a disk. Wrap in plastic wrap and chill for 2 to 24 hours or until dough is easy to handle.
PER SERVING 560 cal, 33 g fat, 46 mg chol, 285 mg sodium, 62 g carb, 5 g fiber, 8 g pro.

Chocolate Revel S'mores Tart

Take a campfire favorite and bring it inside for a holiday celebration.

PREP 25 minutes BAKE 45 minutes
COOL 10 minutes OVEN 325°F
MAKES 12 servings

⅓   cup butter, softened
¾   cup packed brown sugar
¼   teaspoon baking soda
2   eggs
1   teaspoon vanilla

- ½ cup all-purpose flour
- ½ cup quick-cooking oats
- ½ cup graham cracker crumbs
- 1¼ cups milk chocolate pieces
- ½ cup butter, softened
- ⅔ cup granulated sugar
- 1 cup ground almonds
- ⅓ cup all-purpose flour
- 1 egg yolk
- 1 cup tiny marshmallows

1. Preheat oven to 325°F. For crust, in a medium bowl beat the ⅓ cup butter with an electric mixer on medium to high for 30 seconds. Add brown sugar and baking soda. Beat until combined, scraping sides of bowl occasionally. Beat in one of the eggs and the vanilla until combined. Beat in the ½ cup flour. Using a wooden spoon, stir in the oats and graham cracker crumbs. Reserve ½ cup of the crust mixture. Spread remaining crust mixture into the bottom of an ungreased 10-inch tart pan with a removable bottom. Set pan and reserved crust mixture aside.

2. For filling, in a small heavy saucepan heat and stir 1 cup of the chocolate pieces and 2 tablespoons of the ½ cup butter over low heat until just melted and smooth; set aside. In a large bowl beat the remaining butter and the granulated sugar with an electric mixer on medium until combined. Add the melted chocolate, the almonds, the ⅓ cup flour, the remaining egg, and the egg yolk; beat until combined. Stir in ½ cup of the marshmallows. Spread filling evenly over crust in pan.

3. Dot the remaining crust mixture over filling. Bake for 45 minutes or until filling is just set. Sprinkle the remaining ½ cup marshmallows and the ¼ cup milk chocolate pieces over the top. Bake for 5 minutes more. Cool in pan on a wire rack for 10 minutes.

4. Using a small sharp knife, loosen tart from sides of pan. Remove sides of pan. Cool completely on a wire rack.

PER SERVING *483 cal, 26 g fat, 91 mg chol, 190 mg sodium, 57 g carb, 2 g fiber, 7 g pro.*

CHOCOLATE REVEL
S'MORES TART

PRETZEL-CRUSTED
LIME MOUSSE TART
WITH BLACKBERRY
SAUCE

Pretzel-Crusted Lime Mousse Tart with Blackberry Sauce

A pretzel crust contributes a pleasing saltiness to the sweetness in this creamy tart.

PREP 30 minutes BAKE 8 minutes CHILL 30 minutes OVEN 375°F MAKES 10 to 12 servings

- 2 cups pretzels, finely crushed
- 2 tablespoons packed brown sugar
- ¼ cup butter, melted
- 1 14-ounce can sweetened condensed milk
- 1 tablespoon finely shredded lime peel
- ⅔ cup lime juice
- ¼ cup granulated sugar
- 2 drops green food coloring (optional)
- 1½ cups whipping cream
- 1 recipe Blackberry Sauce
  Fresh blackberries

1. Preheat oven to 375°F. In a medium bowl combine crushed pretzels and brown sugar. Add butter; toss to combine. Press pretzel mixture evenly into the bottom and up the sides of a 9-inch fluted tart pan with a removable bottom. Bake for 8 to 10 minutes or until firm. Cool on a wire rack.
2. In another medium bowl combine sweetened condensed milk, lime peel, lime juice, and granulated sugar. If desired, stir in food coloring. Cover and chill 30 minutes or until thickened.
3. In a clean medium bowl beat whipping cream with an electric mixer on medium until soft peaks form (tips curl). Fold whipped cream into lime mixture. Spoon mixture into crust. Chill for at least 6 hours or up to 24 hours or until firm.
4. Serve with Blackberry Sauce. Garnish with blackberries.

Blackberry Sauce: In a medium saucepan combine 3½ cups fresh or frozen blackberries, ¼ cup granulated sugar, ¼ cup lime juice, and 1½ teaspoons cornstarch. Cook and stir over medium heat until thickened and bubbly. Cook and stir for 2 minutes more. Press through a fine-mesh sieve into a small bowl. Discard solids. Cover and chill until serving time or up to 3 days.

PER SERVING *425 cal, 22 g fat, 75 mg chol, 191 mg sodium, 54 g carb, 4 g fiber, 6 g pro.*

Peppermint Panna Cotta with Warm Cocoa Syrup

Panna cotta literally means "cooked cream" in Italian.

PREP 20 minutes STAND 5 minutes CHILL 4 hours MAKES 8 servings

- 1 envelope unflavored gelatin
- ¼ cup cold water
- 2 cups whipping cream
- ½ cup sugar
- 1¼ cups sour cream
- 1 teaspoon vanilla
- 1 teaspoon peppermint extract
- 1 recipe Warm Cocoa Syrup
  Unsweetened Dutch-process cocoa powder (optional)
  Crushed peppermint candies (optional)

1. Place eight 4- to 6-ounce ramekins or 6-ounce custard cups in a shallow pan; set aside.
2. In a small bowl sprinkle gelatin over the cold water. Do not stir. Let stand for 5 minutes.
3. Meanwhile, in a medium saucepan stir together ½ cup of the whipping cream and the sugar. Heat over medium heat until hot but not boiling. Add gelatin; stir until gelatin is dissolved. Remove from heat. Whisk in sour cream until smooth.

Stir in the remaining 1½ cups whipping cream, the vanilla, and peppermint extract. Divide among ramekins. Cover and chill for at least 4 hours or up to 24 hours or until set.
4. To serve, immerse bottom half of each ramekin in hot water for 10 seconds. Using a sharp knife, loosen panna cotta from sides of ramekins. Invert a small shallow bowl or deep dessert plate over each ramekin; turn bowl and ramekin over together. Remove ramekins.
5. Spoon about 2 tablespoons of the Warm Cocoa Syrup around base of each panna cotta. Store leftover syrup in refrigerator. If desired, dust lightly with cocoa powder and/or garnish with crushed peppermint candies.

Warm Cocoa Syrup: In a medium saucepan combine 1½ cups sugar, ¾ cup unsweetened Dutch-process cocoa powder, and ½ teaspoon salt. Stir in 1 cup hot water. Whisk over medium-high heat until boiling; reduce heat. Boil 3 minutes more. Remove from heat; stir in 2 tablespoons light-color corn syrup and 2 teaspoons vanilla. Cool slightly before serving. (Or pour syrup into an airtight container; cover. Chill up to 1 week. To reheat, transfer to a small saucepan; heat and stir over low heat.)

PER SERVING *505 cal, 29 g fat, 98 mg chol, 204 mg sodium, 60 g carb, 3 g fiber, 6 g pro.*

PEPPERMINT PANNA COTTA WITH WARM COCOA SYRUP

Spiced Puffs with Pumpkin Ice Cream and Hot Fudge Sauce

Pumpkin ice cream is often available in the supermarket during the holidays. Substitute it for this version if you like.

PREP 45 minutes BAKE 30 minutes
FREEZE 6 hours OVEN 400°F
MAKES 12 servings

1   cup all-purpose flour
½   teaspoon ground cinnamon
⅛   teaspoon ground cloves
1   cup water
½   cup butter, cut into 8 pieces
⅛   teaspoon salt
4   eggs
½   gallon vanilla ice cream, slightly softened
1   15-ounce can pumpkin
2   tablespoons orange liqueur
4   teaspoons pumpkin pie spice
1   recipe Hot Fudge Sauce
     Powdered sugar

1. For the puffs, preheat oven to 400°F. Lightly grease a large baking sheet or line with parchment paper; set aside. In a small bowl combine flour, cinnamon, and cloves; set aside.
2. In a medium saucepan combine the water, butter, and salt. Bring to boiling. Immediately add flour mixture all at once, stirring vigorously. Cook and stir until mixture pulls away from the sides of the saucepan and forms a ball. Remove from heat; cool for exactly 10 minutes. Add eggs, one at a time, beating well with a wooden spoon after each addition.
3. Drop 12 heaping tablespoons of dough onto prepared baking sheet. Bake for 30 to 35 minutes or until golden and firm. Transfer to a wire rack; cool. Cut each puff in half horizontally.

4. Meanwhile, for pumpkin ice cream, in the bowl of an electric stand mixer or in a very large bowl combine ice cream, pumpkin, liqueur, and pumpkin pie spice. Beat with an electric mixer on medium until combined. Transfer to a freezer container; cover tightly and freeze for at least 4 hours. If necessary, let stand at room temperature for 10 to 15 minutes before scooping. Line a baking sheet with waxed paper or parchment paper. Using a 4-ounce ice cream scoop, scoop ice cream into heaping scoops. (Reserve remaining ice cream for another use.) Place scoops on prepared baking sheet; cover. Freeze for at least 2 hours or up to 24 hours before serving.
5. To serve, place each puff bottom on a dessert plate. Top each with a frozen scoop of the pumpkin ice cream. Spoon about 1 tablespoon of the warm Hot Fudge Sauce over ice cream. Store

SPICED PUFFS WITH
PUMPKIN ICE CREAM
AND HOT FUDGE SAUCE

the remaining Hot Fudge Sauce in refrigerator for another use. Place tops of puffs on ice cream. Dust with powdered sugar. Serve immediately.

Hot Fudge Sauce: In a medium saucepan combine 4 ounces unsweetened chocolate and 3 tablespoons butter. Cook and stir over low heat until melted. Stir in ⅔ cup boiling water. Add 1⅔ cups sugar and ⅓ cup light-color corn syrup. Cook and stir over medium-high heat just until boiling. Adjust heat to maintain a low boil; cook, without stirring, for 9 minutes.

PER SERVING *547 cal, 28 g fat, 148 mg chol, 208 mg sodium, 70 g carb, 4 g fiber, 8 g pro.*

Lime-Coconut Chess Pie

Chess pies—though flavored in various ways—are distinguished by a custardy filling made from eggs, butter, brown sugar, and vanilla.

PREP **30 minutes** BAKE **45 minutes**
COOL **1 hour** CHILL **3 hours**
OVEN **325°F** MAKES **8 servings**

LIME-COCONUT CHESS PIE

1   recipe for Pastry for a Single-Crust Pie
1   cup granulated sugar
½   cup packed brown sugar
2   tablespoons all-purpose flour
5   eggs
⅓   cup unsalted butter, melted
2   teaspoons finely shredded lime peel
2   tablespoons lime juice
½   teaspoon vanilla
¾   cup coconut
     Lime slices (optional)
1   recipe Sweetened Whipped Cream (optional)

1. Preheat oven to 325°F. Prepare Pastry for a Single-Crust Pie. On a lightly floured surface slightly flatten pastry. Roll pastry from center to edges into a 12-inch circle. Wrap pastry circle around the rolling pin; unroll into a 9-inch pie plate. Ease pastry into pie plate without stretching it. Trim pastry to ½ inch beyond edge of pie plate. Fold under extra pastry even with the plate's edge. Crimp edge as desired. Do not prick pastry.
2. For filling, in a large mixing bowl stir together granulated sugar, brown sugar, and flour. Add eggs, one at a time, beating with an electric mixer after each addition until combined. Beat in melted butter, lime peel, lime juice, and vanilla. Sprinkle coconut over bottom of pastry shell. Carefully pour filling over coconut.
3. Bake about 45 minutes or until center appears set when gently shaken. Cool on a wire rack for 1 hour. Cover and chill pie for 3 to 6 hours before serving. If desired, arrange lime slices on top of pie and serve with Sweetened Whipped Cream.

Pastry for a Single-Crust Pie: In a medium bowl stir together 1½ cups all-purpose flour and ½ teaspoon salt. Using a pastry blender, cut in ¼ cup shortening and ¼ cup butter, cut up, or shortening until pieces are pea size. Sprinkle 1 tablespoon ice water over part of the flour mixture; toss gently with a fork. Push moistened pastry to side of bowl. Repeat with additional ice water, 1 tablespoon at a time (¼ to ⅓ cup total), until all of the flour mixture is moistened. Gather mixture into a ball, kneading gently until it holds together.

PER SERVING *554 cal, 34 g fat, 196 mg chol, 133 mg sodium, 57 g carb, 2 g fiber, 7 g pro.*

Sweetened Whipped Cream: In a chilled mixing bowl beat 1 cup whipping cream, 2 tablespoons sugar, and ½ teaspoon vanilla with an electric mixer on medium until soft peaks form (tips curl).

Chocolate Chai Pie

Cinnamon, cardamom, and cloves give this cool and creamy pie the flavors of warm Indian tea.

PREP **1 hour** BAKE **10 minutes**
STAND **1 hour** CHILL **6 hours**
OVEN **350°F** MAKES **10 servings**

1½ cups whipping cream
4   Darjeeling tea bags
2⅔ cups crushed vanilla wafers (about 58 wafers)
¼   cup butter, melted
1   tablespoon granulated sugar
1½ teaspoons vanilla
½   cup butter, softened
2   cups powdered sugar
1½ teaspoons ground cardamom
1½ teaspoons ground cinnamon
¼   teaspoon ground cloves
3   ounces unsweetened chocolate, melted and cooled
1   recipe Candied Orange Whipped Cream
    Chopped candied orange peel (optional)

1. In a small saucepan heat the whipping cream until simmering. Remove from heat; add tea bags. Cover saucepan; let stand 30 minutes. Remove tea bags, squeezing tea bags over the cream mixture to extract as much liquid as you can. Discard tea bags; set cream mixture aside.

2. Preheat oven to 350°F. In a medium bowl combine crushed vanilla wafers, the ¼ cup melted butter, the granulated sugar, and vanilla. Press crumb mixture evenly into the bottom and up the sides of a 9-inch pie plate. Bake for 10 to 12 minutes or until firm. Cool completely on a wire rack.

3. In a large bowl beat the ½ cup butter with an electric mixer on medium to high for 30 seconds. Add powdered sugar, cardamom, cinnamon, and cloves. Beat until combined, scraping sides of bowl occasionally. Add melted chocolate and cream mixture, beating just until combined. Cover and chill for 15 minutes. Beat for 5 minutes or until mixture is slightly thickened and ribbons form.

4. Spoon chocolate mixture into cooled piecrust. Smooth surface. Cover; chill for at least 6 hours or up to 24 hours.

5. To serve, let pie stand at room temperature for 30 minutes. Using a sharp knife, cut pie into thin wedges. Top each slice with some of the Candied Orange Whipped Cream and, if desired, chopped candied orange peel. Serve immediately.

Candied Orange Whipped Cream: In a medium bowl combine 1 cup whipping cream, 2 tablespoons granulated sugar, and 1 teaspoon vanilla; beat with an electric mixer on medium until soft peaks form (tips curl). Gently fold in 2 tablespoons finely chopped candied orange peel. Serve immediately.

PER SERVING *594 cal, 45 g fat, 122 mg chol, 207 mg sodium, 50 g carb, 2 g fiber, 3 g pro.*

Two-Layer Chocolate-Peanut Butter Cream Pie

Sometimes opposites work very well together. The silky whipped-cream topping for this pie is studded with crunchy bits of peanut brittle—yum!

PREP **40 minutes** BAKE **8 minutes**
CHILL **4 hours** OVEN **375°F**
MAKES **8 slices**

2   cups finely crushed peanut butter sandwich cookies (about 16 cookies)
¼   cup butter, melted
¾   cup sugar
3   tablespoons cornstarch
2½ cups half-and-half or light cream
4   egg yolks, lightly beaten
1   tablespoon butter
1½ teaspoons vanilla

⅔   cup semisweet chocolate pieces
⅔   cup peanut butter-flavor pieces
1   recipe Peanut Brittle Whipped Cream

1. Preheat oven to 375°F. In a medium bowl stir together crushed cookies and the melted butter; press onto the bottom and up the sides of a 9-inch pie plate. Bake about 8 minutes or until firm. Cool completely on a wire rack.

2. In a medium saucepan combine sugar and cornstarch. Gradually stir in half-and-half. Cook over medium-high heat until thickened and bubbly, stirring constantly; reduce heat. Cook and stir for 2 minutes more. Remove from heat. Gradually stir about 1 cup of the hot filling into the egg yolks. Add yolk mixture to saucepan. Bring to a gentle boil, stirring constantly; reduce heat. Cook and stir for 2 minutes more. Remove from heat. Stir in the 1 tablespoon butter and the vanilla.

3. Immediately pour half of the hot mixture into a medium bowl; add chocolate pieces. Add peanut butter pieces to the remaining half of the hot mixture. Stir each mixture until melted and smooth. Pour warm chocolate mixture into piecrust; smooth top. Carefully and gently, spoon warm peanut butter mixture over chocolate mixture; smooth top. Gently press a sheet of plastic wrap directly onto the peanut butter filling. Chill for at least 4 hours.

4. Just before serving, spread Peanut Brittle Whipped Cream evenly over pie.

Peanut Brittle Whipped Cream: In a large mixing bowl beat 1 cup whipping cream with an electric mixer on medium to high until soft peaks form (tips curl). Reduce speed to low; beat in 2 tablespoons powdered sugar. Increase speed to medium-high and continue beating until stiff peaks form (tips stand straight). Gently fold in ½ cup coarsely crushed peanut brittle candy.

PER SLICE *753 cal, 47 g fat, 196 mg chol, 282 mg sodium, 78 g carb, 2 g fiber, 9 g pro.*

CHOCOLATE CHAI PIE

Triple Coconut Cream Pie

Fans of coconut, rejoice. You can't pack much more of it into a single dessert than there is in this pie. It's in the crust, the filling, and on top.

PREP **50 minutes** BAKE **38 minutes**
COOL **1 hour** CHILL **3 hours**
MAKES **8 slices** OVEN **325°F**

- 2 cups shortbread cookie crumbs (about 30 cookies)
- ¾ cup sweetened flaked coconut
- 1 teaspoon finely shredded lime peel
- ½ cup butter, melted
- 1 cup sugar
- ⅓ cup cornstarch
- ¼ teaspoon salt
- 3 cups whole milk
- ⅔ cup cream of coconut
- 5 egg yolks
- 1¼ teaspoons coconut extract
- 1 teaspoon vanilla
- 1 recipe Vanilla Meringue
- ¼ cup sweetened flaked coconut

1. Preheat oven to 325°F. In a medium bowl stir together cookie crumbs, the ¾ cup flaked coconut, and the lime peel. Stir in melted butter. Press onto the bottom and up the sides of a 9-inch deep-dish pie plate. Bake for 8 to 10 minutes or until set. Cool completely on a wire rack.
2. In a large saucepan combine sugar, cornstarch, and salt. Gradually stir in milk and cream of coconut. Cook and stir over medium-high heat until thickened and bubbly; reduce heat. Cook and stir for 2 minutes more. Remove from heat. In a small bowl lightly beat egg yolks with a fork. Gradually stir about 1 cup of the hot filling into yolks. Add yolk mixture to saucepan. Bring to a gentle boil, stirring constantly; reduce heat. Cook and stir for 2 minutes more. Remove from heat. Stir in coconut extract and vanilla. Keep filling warm.
3. Prepare Vanilla Meringue. Pour warm filling into cooled piecrust. Spread meringue over warm filling, sealing to edge of crust. Sprinkle with the ¼ cup coconut. Bake for 30 minutes. Cool on a wire rack for 60 minutes. Chill for 3 to 6 hours for before serving; cover for longer storage.

Vanilla Meringue: Allow 4 egg whites to stand at room temperature for 30 minutes. In a mixing bowl combine the whites, 1 teaspoon vanilla, and ½ teaspoon cream of tartar. Beat with an electric mixer on medium about 1 minute or until soft peaks form (tips curl). Gradually add ¼ cup sugar, 1 tablespoon at a time, beating on high about 5 minutes or until mixture forms stiff, glossy peaks (tips stand straight) and sugar dissolves. Immediately spread meringue over hot pie filling, sealing to edge of pastry.

PER SLICE *644 cal, 33 g fat, 177 mg chol, 400 mg sodium, 80 g carb, 1 g fiber, 9 g pro.*

TRIPLE COCONUT CREAM PIE

a cookie for every taste

BAKER'S DOZEN More than any other kind of treat, cookies are synonymous with Christmas. These handheld bites of sweetness—rolled and cut, sliced, shaped, dropped, molded, or made into bars—have come to represent the most personal expression of holiday good wishes.

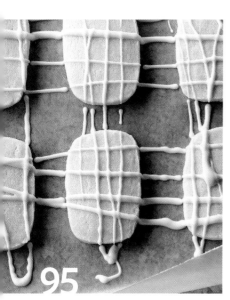

95

106

111

Butter Cookie Cutouts

It's a basic but great recipe for making decorative cookies for the holidays.

PREP 45 minutes CHILL 15 minutes
BAKE 7 minutes per batch
OVEN 375°F MAKES 48 cookies

2½ cups all-purpose flour
¾ cup extra-fine granulated sugar or granulated sugar
¼ teaspoon salt
1 cup butter, cut into 1-inch pieces and softened
2 tablespoons cream cheese, softened
1½ teaspoons vanilla
1 recipe Cream Cheese Icing
Decorative candies or colored decorating sugar (optional)

1. In a large mixing bowl combine flour, extra-fine sugar, and salt. With an electric mixer on medium to low, add butter, 1 piece at a time, beating until mixture is crumbly. Add cream cheese and vanilla. Beat mixture on low just until a ball forms.
2. On a lightly floured surface shape dough into a ball. Divide into 2 pieces. Use your hands to slightly flatten each piece, forming 2 flat round disks. Wrap each in plastic wrap or waxed paper and refrigerate for 15 to 30 minutes or until dough is easy to handle.
3. Preheat oven to 375°F. On a lightly floured surface roll out 1 disk at a time to ⅛ inch thick. Using a 2½- to 4-inch cookie cutter, cut dough into desired shapes. Place 1 inch apart on an ungreased cookie sheets. (Reroll dough scraps.)
4. Bake for 7 or 9 minutes or until edges are firm and bottoms are very lightly browned. Transfer to wire racks and let cool. Frost cookies with a thin layer of Cream Cheese Icing. If you like, decorate cookies with decorative candies or colored decorating sugar.
Cream Cheese Icing: In a large mixing bowl beat one 3-ounce package softened cream cheese, ½ cup softened butter, and ½ teaspoon vanilla with electric mixer until light and fluffy. Gradually add 1½ cups powdered sugar, beating well.
PER COOKIE *108 cal, 7 g fat, 18 mg chol, 60 mg sodium, 11 g carb, 0 g fiber, 1 g pro.*

Santa-Size Gingerbread Cookies

Yes, they're big—but Santa's appetite for cookies knows no limit, especially on Christmas Eve.

PREP 30 minutes CHILL 1 hour
BAKE 15 minutes COOL 10 minutes
OVEN 325°F MAKES 9 cookies

2½ cups all-purpose flour
2½ teaspoons ground ginger
2 teaspoons baking soda
¾ teaspoon ground cinnamon
½ teaspoon salt
⅛ teaspoon freshly grated nutmeg
Dash ground cloves
¾ cup butter, softened
1 cup packed brown sugar
½ cup mild-flavor molasses
1 egg
1 recipe Powdered Sugar Icing

1. In a medium bowl stir together flour, ginger, baking soda, cinnamon, salt, nutmeg, and cloves; set aside.
2. In a large mixing bowl beat butter with an electric mixer on medium to high for 30 seconds. Add brown sugar and molasses. Beat until combined, scraping sides of bowl occasionally. Beat in egg until combined. Gradually beat in flour mixture until combined. Cover and chill dough about 1 hour or until easy to handle.
3. Preheat oven to 325°F. Line 2 cookie sheets with parchment paper. Roll ⅓ cup portions of dough into balls. Place 4 or 5 balls 4 inches apart on each cookie sheet. Flatten balls slightly.
4. Bake for 15 to 18 minutes or until edges of cookies are set. Do not overbake. Cool on cookie sheets for 10 minutes. Transfer cookies to a wire rack and cool completely. Spread cookies with Powdered Sugar Icing. Let stand until icing is set.
Powdered Sugar Icing: In a small bowl stir together 1 cup powdered sugar, ¼ teaspoon vanilla, and 1 tablespoon milk. Stir in additional milk, 1 teaspoon at a time, to make icing spreading consistency.
PER COOKIE *471 cal, 16 g fat, 64 mg chol, 541 mg sodium, 78 g carb, 1 g fiber, 5 g pro.*

Browned Butter and Cardamom Sugar Cookies

Many Scandinavian bakers have their own version of a cookie made with nutty-tasting browned butter. This one incorporates another favored Scandinavian ingredient—cardamom.

PREP 30 minutes
CHILL 30 minutes + 2 hours
BAKE 9 minutes per batch
OVEN 375°F MAKES 48 cookies

1 cup butter
1½ cups sugar
2 eggs
1 teaspoon cream of tartar
1 teaspoon baking soda
1 teaspoon ground cardamom or cinnamon
1 teaspoon vanilla
¼ teaspoon salt
2¾ cups all-purpose flour
¼ cup sugar
¼ to ½ teaspoon ground cardamom or cinnamon

1. In a small heavy saucepan heat and stir butter over medium heat for 10 to 12 minutes or until butter turns the color of light brown sugar. Pour butter into a large bowl; cover and chill for 30 minutes, stirring once.
2. In the large bowl beat the browned butter with an electric mixer on medium to high for 30 seconds. Add the 1½ cups sugar. Beat until combined, scraping bowl occasionally. Beat in eggs, cream of tartar, baking soda, the 1 teaspoon cardamom, vanilla, and salt until combined. Beat in as much of the flour as you can with the mixer. Using a wooden spoon, stir in any remaining flour. Cover and chill about 2 hours or until dough is easy to handle.
3. Preheat oven to 375°F. In a small bowl combine the ¼ cup sugar and the ¼ teaspoon cardamom. Shape dough into 1-inch balls. Roll balls in the sugar mixture to coat. Place 2 inches apart on an ungreased cookie sheet.
4. Bake for 9 to 12 minutes or until edges are lightly browned. Cool on cookie sheet for 1 minute. Transfer to a wire rack; cool.
PER COOKIE *92 cal, 4 g fat, 18 mg chol, 75 mg sodium, 13 g carb, 0 g fiber, 1 g pro.*

SANTA-SIZE
GINGERBREAD
COOKIES

93

WHITE CHOCOLATE
AND CRÈME DE
MENTHE SHORTBREAD

White Chocolate and Crème de Menthe Shortbread

Simple but so pretty, these cookies have the flavor of a favorite department-store chocolate-and-mint candy.

PREP 35 minutes FREEZE 45 minutes
BAKE 10 minutes per batch
OVEN 325°F MAKES 40 cookies

2½ cups all-purpose flour
½ cup sugar
1 cup butter, cut up
1 tablespoon green crème de menthe
6 ounces white chocolate (with cocoa butter), cut up
1 tablespoon shortening
¼ teaspoon mint extract

1. In a large bowl stir together flour and sugar. Using a pastry blender, cut in butter until mixture resembles fine crumbs and starts to cling. Using a fork, stir in crème de menthe. With clean hands, knead until dough forms a ball (mixture may seem crumbly at first, but as you knead the warmth of your hands will bring dough together). Divide dough in half.
2. Shape each half into a 6-inch-long log, turning and flattening each side as you turn. Wrap and freeze for 45 minutes to 1 hour or until firm (if dough gets too firm, let stand at room temperature for 10 minutes before slicing).
3. Preheat oven to 325°F. Cut logs into scant ¼-inch slices. Place slices 2 inches apart on ungreased cookie sheets. Bake for 10 to 12 minutes or until edges are lightly browned. Transfer to wire racks; cool completely.
4. In a small saucepan combine white chocolate and shortening; heat and stir over low heat until melted and smooth. Remove from heat; stir in mint extract. Drizzle over cookies.
PER COOKIE *108 cal, 6 g fat, 13 mg chol, 37 mg sodium, 11 g carb, 0 g fiber, 1 g pro.*

Classic Spice Cookies

The warm and wonderful smell of these cookies baking in the oven is a sure sign that Christmas has arrived.

PREP 30 minutes CHILL 2 hours
BAKE 7 minutes per batch
MAKES 20 large or 44 small cookies
OVEN 375°F

3 cups all-purpose flour
2 teaspoons ground ginger
1 teaspoon baking soda
1 teaspoon ground cinnamon
½ teaspoon salt
¼ teaspoon ground cloves
⅔ cup butter, softened
¾ cup packed brown sugar
½ cup molasses
1 egg
1 recipe Royal Icing
1 recipe Powdered Sugar Icing
  Decorative candies (optional)

1. Stir together flour, ginger, baking soda, cinnamon, salt, and cloves in a medium bowl. Set flour mixture aside.
2. Beat butter in a large bowl with an electric mixer on medium to high for 30 seconds. Add brown sugar and molasses. Beat until combined, scraping sides of bowl occasionally. Beat in egg. Beat in flour mixture on low just until mixture is combined. Divide dough in half. Cover and chill the dough about 2 hours or until dough is easy to handle.
3. Preheat oven to 375°F. Roll each portion of dough to ¼-inch thickness on a well-floured surface. Cut out shapes with a lightly floured 4- to 5-inch person-shape cutter. Place cutouts 2 inches apart on cookie sheets.
4. Bake for 7 to 8 minutes or until edges are light brown. Cool on cookie sheets on wire racks for 1 minute. Transfer cookies to wire racks and cool completely.
5. Decorate cookies with Royal Icing or Powdered Sugar Icing and, if desired, decorative candies.
Royal Icing: In a medium bowl stir together 2 cups powdered sugar and 4 teaspoons meringue powder. Add 3 tablespoons cold water. Beat with an electric mixer on low until combined. Beat on medium to high for 5 to 8 minutes or until icing is very stiff. (If mixture becomes too stiff, add more water, ½ teaspoon at a time, to make icing piping or spreading consistency.) If desired, divide icing into portions and tint each portion with a different paste food coloring. Decorate cookies at once with icing. Keep remaining icing covered when not in use.
Powdered Sugar Icing: In a medium mixing bowl stir together 2 cups powdered sugar, 2 to 3 tablespoons milk, and ½ teaspoon vanilla to make piping or spreading consistency. If desired, divide icing and tint each portion with a different paste food coloring. Decorate cookies at once with icing. Keep icing covered when not in use.
PER LARGE COOKIE *60 cal, 2 g fat, 9 mg chol, 58 mg sodium, 10 g carb, 0 g fiber, 1 g pro.*

CLASSIC SPICE COOKIES

Quick Jam Drops

Substitute dried cherries for the dried cranberries if you like.

PREP 25 minutes
BAKE 10 minutes per batch
OVEN 375°F MAKES 45 cookies

2 cups all-purpose flour
1 teaspoon baking powder
¼ teaspoon salt
¾ cup unsalted butter at room temperature (6 ounces)
¾ cup granulated sugar
1 egg at room temperature
2 tablespoons milk
1½ teaspoons pure vanilla extract
½ cup cranberry relish or orange marmalade
1 cup powdered sugar, sifted
2 tablespoons milk
3 tablespoons dried cranberries, snipped

1. Line 2 cookie sheets with parchment; set aside. Preheat oven to 375°F. In a large bowl whisk together the flour, baking powder, and salt; set aside.
2. In a large mixing bowl beat butter with electric mixer on medium-low until smooth and creamy. Add granulated sugar. Beat for 2 minutes or until well blended. Reduce speed to low. Add egg and beat for 1 minute. Add 2 tablespoons milk and vanilla; beat for 1 minute more.
3. With mixer at lowest speed, steadily add flour mixture, beating only a few seconds after flour is incorporated and a soft dough forms. Beat in relish until evenly incorporated.

4. Using a small (2-teaspoon) cookie scoop, drop dough onto prepared cookie sheets, about 2 inches between mounds. Bake for 10 to 12 minutes or just until slightly firm and golden on bottoms. Transfer cookies to cooling racks. Cool completely.
5. For icing, in a medium bowl combine the powdered sugar and milk. Using a small spatula, stir until smooth for an icing the consistency of heavy cream. If needed, add milk in droplets to reach desired consistency. Stir in snipped cranberries. Line baking sheet with parchment paper. Top each cookie with about ½ teaspoon of icing. Let stand until set.

PER COOKIE *79 cal, 3 g fat, 13 mg chol, 25 mg sodium, 12 g carb, 0 g fiber, 1 g pro.*

Vanilla-Allspice Thumbprints

In this version of thumbprint cookies, the indentation is filled with melted chocolate instead of jam.

PREP 20 minutes CHILL 15 minutes
BAKE 9 minutes per batch
OVEN 350°F MAKES 36 cookies

1¼ cups all-purpose flour
½ teaspoon ground allspice
¼ teaspoon baking powder
¼ teaspoon salt
½ cup unsalted butter (1 stick) at room temperature
¼ cup sugar
1 egg yolk at room temperature
¾ teaspoon pure vanilla extract
½ cup white chocolate baking pieces or semisweet chocolate pieces
¼ teaspoon ground allspice (optional)

1. Preheat oven to 350°F. Line 2 baking sheets with parchment; set aside. In a small bowl whisk together the flour, the ½ teaspoon allspice, baking powder, and salt. Set aside.
2. In a large mixing bowl beat butter with electric mixer on medium for 30 seconds. Add the sugar and beat for 2 minutes or until well blended. Reduce mixer speed to low. Add the egg yolk and beat for 1 minute. Beat in vanilla. Beat in flour mixture, beating only a few seconds after flour is well incorporated into the soft dough.

VANILLA-ALLSPICE THUMBPRINTS

3. Shape rounded teaspoons of dough in balls between palms of hands. Place balls about 2 inches apart on prepared baking sheets. With the handle end of a wooden spoon or a thumb, make indentations in the center of each ball.

4. Bake for 9 to 10 minutes or until cookies are dry and firm to the touch. For even baking, rotate baking sheets top to bottom and front to back after 4 minutes of baking time. Cool cookies on baking sheets on wire racks while preparing filling.

5. For filling, in a small microwave-safe bowl melt chocolate pieces for 45 to 60 seconds on high, stirring until melted. Use a small spoon to fill each indentation with chocolate. Sprinkle with ground allspice if desired. Refrigerate cookies for 15 minutes to set chocolate. Serve cookies at room temperature.

PER COOKIE *63 cal, 4 g fat, 13 mg chol, 24 mg sodium, 7 g carb, 0 g fiber, 1 g pro.*

Chocolate Blooms

Dutch-process cocoa powder has been treated with alkali. It has a mellower, smoother flavor than natural cocoa— and is lighter and redder in color.

PREP **40 minutes**
BAKE **8 minutes per batch**
STAND **2 hours** OVEN **350°F**
MAKES **56 cookies**

½   cup shortening
¼   cup butter, softened
1   cup packed brown sugar
½   teaspoon baking powder
¼   teaspoon salt
1   egg
1   teaspoon vanilla
1½ cups all-purpose flour
¾   cup Dutch-processed cocoa powder
1   cup miniature semisweet chocolate pieces
¾   cup finely chopped almonds (optional)
1   recipe Raspberry Ganache
    Fresh small raspberries (optional)

1. Preheat oven to 350°F. In a large bowl beat shortening and butter with an electric mixer on medium to high for 30 seconds. Add brown sugar, baking powder, and salt; beat until combined. Beat in egg and vanilla; beat until combined.

2. In a small bowl whisk together flour and cocoa powder. Beat as much of the flour mixture into the butter mixture as you can with mixer. Stir in any remaining flour mixture. Stir in chocolate pieces. Shape dough into 1-inch balls. If desired, roll balls in chopped almonds. Place balls 1½ inches apart on an ungreased cookie sheet. Press thumb into the center of each ball to make an indent.

3. Bake for 8 to 10 minutes or until edges are set. Immediately use the rounded side of a 1-teaspoon measure to press down the center of each cookie. Transfer cookies to wire racks to cool.

4. Spoon Raspberry Ganache into center of each cookie. Let stand 2 hours or chill about 15 minutes or until set. If desired, garnish each cookie with a fresh raspberry.

Raspberry Ganache: In a small microwave-safe bowl combine 6 ounces chopped (70% cocoa) dark chocolate, ⅓ cup whipping cream, and, if desired, 1 tablespoon seedless raspberry jam. Heat on high for 1 minute; stir until melted. If desired, add 1 tablespoon raspberry liqueur. Stir until smooth. Let stand until slightly thickened (about 15 minutes).

PER COOKIE *101 cal, 6 g fat, 8 mg chol, 26 mg sodium, 11 g carb, 1 g fiber, 1 g pro.*

DOUBLE VANILLA
MERINGUES

Double Vanilla Meringues

Vanilla in two forms—extract and vanilla bean—flavors these crisp, ethereal cookies.

PREP 20 minutes STAND 30 minutes
BAKE 20 minutes OVEN 300°F
MAKES 16 cookies

3   egg whites
1   vanilla bean, split in half lengthwise
1   cup sugar
½   teaspoon vanilla extract
⅛   teaspoon cream of tarter
⅛   teaspoon salt

1. Allow egg whites to stand at room temperature for 30 minutes. Preheat oven to 300°F. Line a large cookie sheet with parchment paper; set aside. Using the tip of a sharp knife, scrape pulp from vanilla bean. In a small bowl combine vanilla pulp and sugar; set aside. (Reserve bean for another use, such as making vanilla sugar.)
2. For the meringue, in a large bowl combine egg whites, vanilla extract, cream of tartar, and salt. Beat with an electric mixer on medium until soft peaks form (tips curl). Gradually add sugar mixture, about 1 tablespoon at a time, beating on high until stiff peaks form (tips stand straight).
3. Transfer meringue to a pastry bag fitted with a large closed-star tip. To make each cookie, pipe meringue into a 6-inch strip with a curled end onto prepared cookie sheet. Bake about 20 minutes or until tops are very lightly browned and dry. Transfer cookies to wire racks; let cool.
PER COOKIE 53 cal, 0 g fat, 0 mg chol, 29 mg sodium, 13 g carb, 0 g fiber, 1 g pro.

Chocolate Hazelnut Caramel Thumbprint Cookies

Don't worry if you can't get all of the papery skin off of the hazelnuts—just get the loose stuff.

PREP 40 minutes CHILL 1 hour
BAKE 10 minutes per batch
COOL 30 minutes OVEN 350°F
MAKES 36 cookies

½   cup butter, softened
⅔   cup sugar
¼   teaspoon salt
1   egg yolk
2   tablespoons milk
1   teaspoon vanilla
1   cup all-purpose flour
⅓   cup unsweetened Dutch-process cocoa powder
1   egg white, lightly beaten
1   cup finely chopped hazelnuts (filberts)
14   individually wrapped vanilla caramels, unwrapped
3   tablespoons whipping cream
½   cup semisweet chocolate pieces
1   teaspoon shortening
     Toasted hazelnuts*

1. In a medium bowl beat butter with an electric mixer on medium to high for 30 seconds. Add sugar and salt; beat until combined. Beat in egg yolk, milk, and vanilla until combined. In a small bowl stir together flour and cocoa powder; beat into butter mixture until combined. Cover and chill for 1 hour.
2. Preheat oven to 350°F. Grease a cookie sheet; set aside. Shape dough into 1-inch balls. Dip in egg white; roll in hazelnuts. Place 1 inch apart on cookie sheet. Make an indentation with your thumb in the center of each cookie. Bake 10 to 12 minutes or until edges are firm.
3. While cookies bake, prepare caramel filling. In a small saucepan combine caramels and whipping cream. Cook over low heat, stirring frequently, until caramels melt and the mixture is smooth. After removing cookies from the oven, press the center of the cookie again and fill with about 1 teaspoon filling. Transfer cookies to a wire rack; let cool.
4. In a small microwave-safe bowl combine chocolate pieces and shortening. Heat on high for 30 to 45 seconds or until softened; stir until smooth. Place a small mound of chocolate on each cookie. Top with a hazelnut. Let stand until chocolate is set.

Tip: To toast hazelnuts, spread in a single layer in a shallow baking pan. Bake in a 350°F oven for 5 to 10 minutes or until light golden brown, watching carefully and stirring once or twice. To remove the papery skins from hazelnuts, rub them with a clean dish towel.
PER COOKIE 116 cal, 7 g fat, 14 mg chol, 51 mg sodium, 12 g carb, 1 g fiber, 2 g pro.

Italian Amaretti Cookies

Serve these with espresso or cappuccino —or a nice full-bodied coffee.

PREP 30 minutes
BAKE 13 minutes per batch
OVEN 325°F MAKES 48 cookies

1   cup whole blanched or unblanched almonds
½   cup powdered sugar
2   egg whites
1   tablespoon amaretto or ½ teaspoon almond extract
⅛   teaspoon cream of tartar
½   cup granulated sugar
     Whole blanched or unblanched almonds (optional)
     Coarse or regular granulated sugar (optional)

1. Preheat oven to 325°F. Line 2 large cookie sheets with parchment paper or foil. Lightly grease foil, if using. Set aside. In a food processor combine the 1 cup almonds and powdered sugar. Cover and process until finely ground. Set aside.
2. In a large bowl combine egg whites, amaretto, and cream of tartar. Beat with an electric mixer on high until soft peaks form. Gradually beat in the ½ cup granulated sugar, 1 tablespoon at a time, until stiff peaks form. Fold half of the almond mixture into egg white mixture. Fold in remaining almond mixture.
3. Spoon almond mixture into 1-inch mounds 2 inches apart onto the prepared cookie sheets. If desired, place a whole almond on top of each cookie and sprinkle lightly with coarse sugar.
4. Bake for 13 to 15 minutes or until tops are set and lightly browned. Cool on cookie sheets on a wire rack. Peel cookies off parchment paper or foil.
PER COOKIE 32 cal, 2 g fat, 0 mg chol, 3 mg sodium, 4 g carb, 0 g fiber, 1 g pro.

Chocolate and Candied Tangerine Peel Cookies

Substitute candied orange peel for the Candied Tangerine Peel if you like.

PREP 30 minutes STAND 30 minutes
BAKE 10 minutes per batch
OVEN 350°F MAKES 24 cookies

7   ounces bittersweet chocolate, chopped
5   ounces unsweetened chocolate, chopped
½   cup butter
⅓   cup all-purpose flour
¼   teaspoon baking powder
¼   teaspoon salt
1   cup granulated sugar
¾   cup packed brown sugar
4   eggs
¼   teaspoon orange extract
½   cup Candied Tangerine Peel or purchased candied orange peel, finely chopped

1. In a 2-quart saucepan combine bittersweet chocolate, unsweetened chocolate, and butter. Heat and stir over low heat until smooth. Remove from heat. Let stand at room temperature for 10 minutes. In a small bowl stir together flour, baking powder, and salt; set aside.
2. In a large bowl combine granulated sugar, brown sugar, and eggs. Beat with an electric mixer on medium to high for 2 to 3 minutes or until color lightens slightly. Beat in orange extract and melted chocolate mixture until combined. Add flour mixture to chocolate mixture; beat until combined. Stir in finely chopped Candied Tangerine Peel. Cover surface of dough with plastic wrap. Let stand for 20 minutes (dough will thicken as it stands).
3. Preheat oven to 350°F. Line cookie sheets with parchment paper. Drop dough by rounded tablespoons 2 inches apart onto prepared cookie sheets. Bake for 10 to 12 minutes or just until tops are set. Cool on cookie sheets for 1 minute. Transfer to wire racks; cool.
Candied Tangerine Peel: Using a paring knife, cut peels from 3 tangerines into lengthwise quarters, cutting just to the surface of the fruit. Pry back the quartered peel and pull away to remove. Reserve fruit for another use. Using a spoon, scrape away the white pith inside the peel. Cut peel into thin strips. In a 2-quart saucepan combine 1⅓ cups granulated sugar and ⅓ cup water. Cover and bring to boiling. Uncover and add tangerine peel strips. Return to boiling, stirring to dissolve sugar. Reduce heat to medium-low. (Mixture should boil at a moderate, steady rate over entire surface.) Cook, uncovered, about 15 minutes or until peel is almost translucent, stirring occasionally. Using a slotted spoon, remove peel from syrup, allowing syrup to drain. Transfer peel to a wire rack set over waxed paper. Set aside until cool enough to handle but still warm and slightly sticky. Roll in additional granulated sugar to coat. Dry on rack for 1 to 2 hours more. To store, place in an airtight container; cover.

Store in a cool, dry place for up to 1 week or freeze for up to 6 months.
PER COOKIE *194 cal, 11 g fat, 46 mg chol, 70 mg sodium, 26 g carb, 2 g fiber, 3 g pro.*

Blueberry-Walnut Twirls

These spirals are gorgeous on a cookie tray—and they taste wonderful too.

PREP 45 minutes
CHILL 1 hour + 4 hours
BAKE 10 minutes per batch
OVEN 375°F MAKES 42 cookies

1   cup butter, softened
1½   cups sugar
½   teaspoon baking powder
½   teaspoon salt
2   eggs
1   teaspoon vanilla
3½   cups all-purpose flour
½   cup blueberry preserves or jam
1½   teaspoons cornstarch
½   cup very finely chopped toasted walnuts

1. In a large bowl beat butter with an electric mixer on medium to high for 30 seconds. Add sugar, baking powder, and salt. Beat until combined, scraping sides of bowl occasionally. Beat in eggs and vanilla until combined. Beat in as much of the flour as you can with the mixer. Using a wooden spoon, stir in any remaining flour. Divide dough in half. Cover and chill dough about 1 hour or until easy to handle.
2. For filling, in a small saucepan combine preserves and cornstarch; heat and stir over medium heat until thickened and bubbly. Remove from heat. Stir in walnuts. Cover. Set aside to cool.
3. Roll half of the dough between 2 sheets of waxed paper into an 11-inch square. Spread half of the filling over the square, leaving a ½-inch border along the edges. Roll up dough into a spiral. Moisten edges; pinch to seal. Wrap log in waxed paper; twist ends. Repeat with remaining dough and remaining filling. Chill for at least 4 hours or up to 3 days.
4. Preheat oven to 375°F. Line cookie sheets with parchment paper; set aside. Cut logs into ¼-inch slices. Place slices about 1 inch apart on cookie sheets. Bake 10 to 12 minutes or just until firm. Cool on cookie sheets for 2 minutes. Transfer to wire racks to cool completely.
PER COOKIE *128 cal, 6 g fat, 22 mg chol, 68 mg sodium, 18 g carb, 0 g fiber, 2 g pro.*

CHOCOLATE AND CANDIED TANGERINE PEEL COOKIES

MEXICAN CHOCOLATE ICEBOX COOKIES WITH DULCE DE LECHE FILLING

5. Cut each brick lengthwise into 4 slices. (Each piece will have 4 layers in alternating colors.) Stack 4 slices of dough together, alternating colors, to create a checkerboard effect. Trim edges as needed to straighten sides and ends. If necessary, wrap each stack in plastic wrap or waxed paper and chill about 30 minutes or until firm enough to slice.
6. Preheat oven to 350°F. Cut stacks crosswise into ¼-inch slices. Place slices 1 inch apart on an ungreased cookie sheet.
7. Bake for 9 to 11 minutes or just until edges are firm. Cool on cookie sheet for 1 minute. Transfer cookies to a wire rack; cool.

PER COOKIE *84 cal, 4 g fat, 14 mg chol, 72 mg sodium, 11 g carb, 0 g fiber, 1 g pro.*

Mexican Chocolate Icebox Cookies with Dulce de Leche Filling

Be sure to use dulce de leche—not dulce de leche ice cream topping, which is too runny to stay put.

PREP **45 minutes**
CHILL **1 hour + 4 hours**
BAKE **12 minutes per batch**
OVEN **325°F** MAKES **24 cookies**

¾   cup butter, softened
1   cup sugar
¾   cup Dutch-process cocoa powder
½   teaspoon ground cinnamon
¼   teaspoon salt
¼   teaspoon cayenne pepper
1   egg
1½   teaspoons vanilla
1¼   cups all-purpose flour
½   cup jarred or canned dulce de leche

1. In a large bowl beat butter with an electric mixer on medium to high for 30 seconds. Add sugar, cocoa powder, cinnamon, salt, and cayenne pepper. Beat until combined, scraping bowl occasionally. Beat in egg and vanilla until combined. Beat in flour.
2. Divide dough in half; cover and chill 1 hour or until dough is easy to handle.
3. Shape each portion of dough into a 6-inch-long roll about 1¾ inches in diameter. Wrap rolls in plastic wrap or waxed paper and chill about 4 hours or until dough is firm enough to slice.

Chocolate-Mint Checkerboard Cookies

Impress your friends: The checkerboard pattern on these squares only looks fancy and difficult to do.

PREP **50 minutes** CHILL **2 hours**
BAKE **9 minutes per batch**
OVEN **350°F** MAKES **50 cookies**

1   cup butter, softened
1½   cups sugar
1½   teaspoons baking powder
½   teaspoon salt
1   egg
1   teaspoon vanilla
2½   cups all-purpose flour
1   tablespoon unsweetened cocoa powder
1   ounce semisweet chocolate, grated (about ⅓ cup)
½   teaspoon mint extract
    Green paste food coloring

1. In a large mixing bowl beat butter with an electric mixer on medium to high for 30 seconds. Add sugar, baking powder, and salt. Beat until combined, scraping bowl occasionally. Beat in egg and vanilla until combined. Beat in as much of the flour as you can with the mixer. Using a wooden spoon stir in any remaining flour.
2. Divide dough in half. Stir cocoa powder and grated chocolate into one portion of dough. Stir mint extract into the remaining portion of dough; tint dough with green food coloring.
3. Shape each portion of dough into a 7×2×2-inch brick. Wrap each brick in plastic wrap or waxed paper. Chill bricks about 2 hours or until dough is firm enough to slice. Using a long sharp knife, cut each brick lengthwise into four ½-inch slices. (You will have four 7×2-inch pieces from each color of dough.)
4. Stack four pieces of dough together, alternating colors. (You will have two bricks, each with four layers.) Press dough together to seal layers. If necessary, wrap each brick in plastic wrap and chill about 30 minutes or until dough is firm enough to slice.

4. Preheat oven to 325°F. Line a cookie sheet with parchment paper. Cut rolls into ¼-inch-thick slices. Place slices 1 inch apart on prepared cookie sheet.

5. Bake for 12 to 14 minutes or until edges are firm. Cool on cookie sheet for 2 minutes. Transfer cookies to a wire rack; let cool.

6. Spread a rounded tablespoon of dulce de leche on the bottom flat side of each of half the cookies. Top with remaining cookies, flat sides down, pressing together lightly.

PER COOKIE *137 cal, 7 g fat, 25 mg chol, 87 mg sodium, 18 g carb, 1 g fiber, 2 g pro.*

Meyer Lemon- Rosemary Slices

Meyer lemons are a cross between a lemon and an orange. Their flavor is sweeter than a true lemon.

PREP **40 minutes** CHILL **4 hours**
BAKE **8 minutes per batch**
OVEN **350°F** MAKES **80 cookies**

3   cups all-purpose flour
½   teaspoon baking soda
½   teaspoon salt
1½   cups granulated sugar
¾   cup butter, softened
1   egg
2   tablespoons finely shredded Meyer lemon peel or regular lemon peel
¼   cup freshly squeezed Meyer lemon juice or regular lemon juice
2   tablespoons finely snipped fresh rosemary
1   teaspoon lemon extract
½   cup powdered sugar

1. In a medium bowl stir together flour, baking soda, and salt. In a large bowl beat granulated sugar and butter with an electric mixer on medium to high until fluffy, scraping sides of bowl occasionally. Beat in egg, lemon peel, lemon juice, rosemary, and lemon extract. Beat in as much of the flour mixture as you can with the mixer. Using a wooden spoon, stir in any remaining flour mixture.

2. Divide dough into 4 portions. Shape each dough portion into a 6-inch-long log. Wrap each log in waxed paper; twist the ends. Chill for at least 4 hours or up to 3 days.

3. Preheat oven to 350°F. Line cookie sheets with parchment paper; set aside. Cut chilled or frozen logs into ¼-inch slices. Place slices about 1 inch apart on prepared cookie sheets. Bake for 8 to 10 minutes or until edges are lightly browned. Cool on cookie sheets for 2 minutes.

4. Place powdered sugar in a small bowl. Working in batches of 2 or 3 cookies, add warm cookies to the powdered sugar, turning to coat. Transfer to wire racks to cool completely.

PER COOKIES *51 cal, 2 g fat, 7 mg chol, 36 mg sodium, 8 g carb, 0 g fiber, 1 g pro.*

MEYER LEMON- ROSEMARY SLICES

PISTACHIO-VANILLA BEAN COOKIES

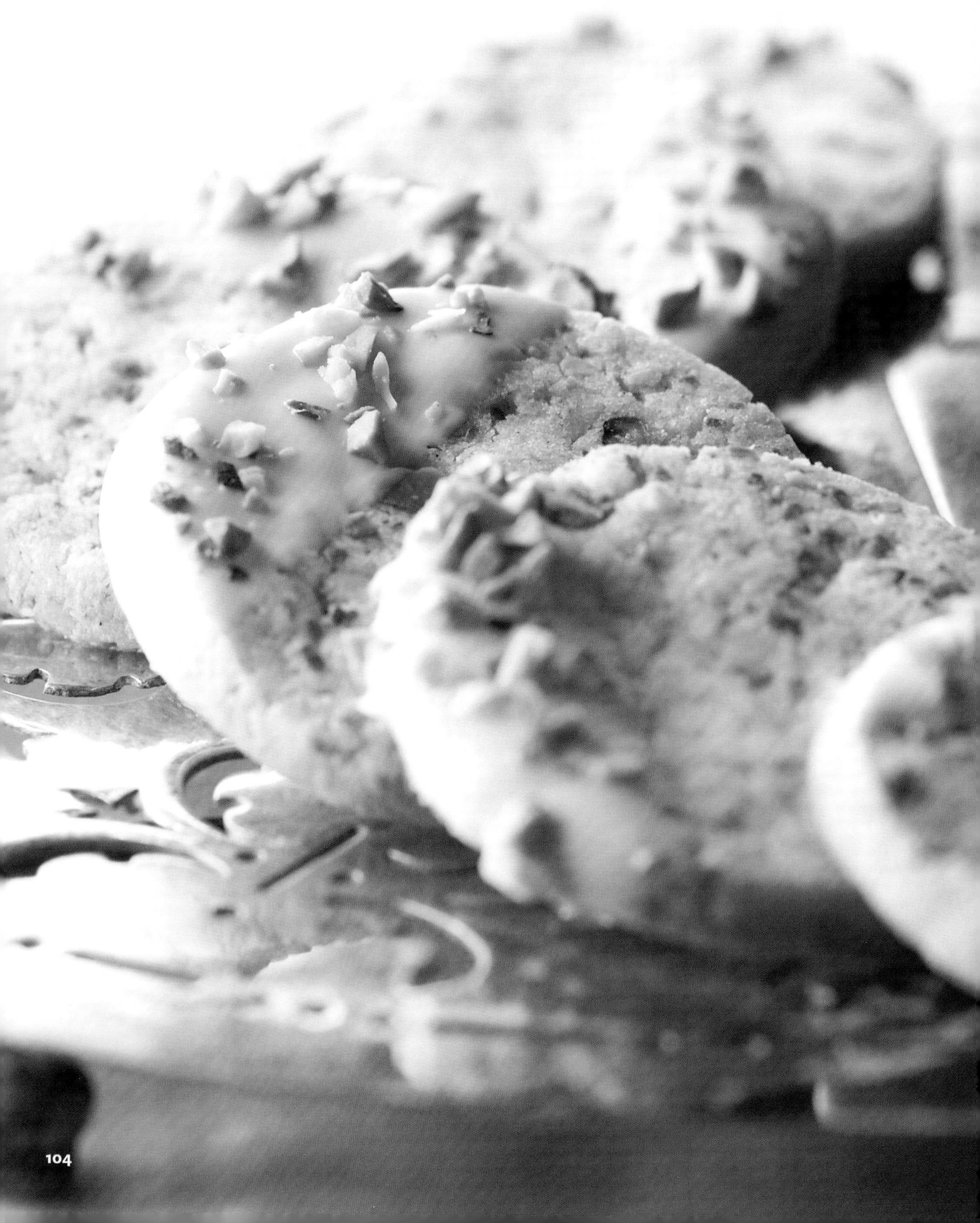

Pistachio-Vanilla Bean Cookies

Be sure that the vanilla bean you use is still soft and pliable. When they dry out, they splinter and crack, making the seeds impossible to scrape out.

PREP 30 minutes CHILL 2 hours
BAKE 10 minutes per batch
OVEN 375°F MAKES 56 cookies

1   cup butter, softened
¾   cup sugar
½   teaspoon vanilla extract
¼   teaspoon salt
1   vanilla bean
2   cups all-purpose flour
1   cup finely chopped salted dry-roasted pistachio nuts
6   ounces white chocolate (with cocoa butter), cut up
2   teaspoons shortening

1. In a large bowl beat butter with an electric mixer on medium to high for 30 seconds. Add sugar, vanilla, and salt. Beat until combined, scraping sides of bowl occasionally. Split vanilla bean in half lengthwise. Using the tip of a knife, scrape seeds from vanilla bean halves into butter mixture. Beat until combined, scraping sides of bowl occasionally. Beat in as much of the flour as you can with the mixer. Using a wooden spoon, stir in any remaining flour. Stir in pistachios.
2. Divide dough in half. Shape each half into a 1½-inch-thick log (about 7 inches long). Wrap each log in waxed paper; twist the ends. Chill for at least 2 hours or up to 2 days.
3. Preheat oven to 375°F. Line cookie sheets with parchment paper; set aside. Cut chilled or frozen logs into ¼-inch slices. Place slices about 1 inch apart on prepared cookie sheets. Bake about 10 minutes or just until firm and browned on the bottoms. Cool on cookie sheets for 1 minute. Transfer to wire racks; cool.
4. In a heavy small saucepan combine white chocolate and shortening; heat and stir over low heat until melted. Dip half of each cookie into melted chocolate mixture; place on a wire rack over waxed paper and let stand until set.
PER COOKIE *88 cal, 6 g fat, 9 mg chol, 46 mg sodium, 8 g carb, 0 g fiber, 1 g pro.*

RASPBERRY-ALMOND PALMIERS

Raspberry-Almond Palmiers

Palmiers—whether a savory pastry or a sweet cookie—are distinguished by their double-swirl shape.

PREP 35 minutes CHILL 2 hours
FREEZE 4 hours BAKE 10 minutes
OVEN 350°F MAKES 72 cookies

½   cup butter, softened
½   cup granulated sugar
½   cup packed brown sugar
½   teaspoon baking powder
½   teaspoon ground cinnamon
¼   teaspoon salt
1   egg
2   tablespoons milk
1   teaspoon vanilla
3   cups all-purpose flour
¾   cup seedless raspberry jam or strawberry preserves
½   cup finely chopped toasted almonds
¼   teaspoon almond extract
     Powdered sugar (optional)

1. In a large mixing bowl beat butter with an electric mixer on medium to high for 30 seconds. Add granulated sugar, brown sugar, baking powder, cinnamon, and salt. Beat until combined, scraping sides of bowl occasionally. Beat in egg, milk, and vanilla until combined. Beat in as much of the flour as you can with the mixer. Using a wooden spoon, stir in any remaining flour. Divide dough in half. Cover and chill about 2 hours or until dough is easy to handle.
2. Meanwhile, for filling, in a small bowl stir together jam, almonds, and almond extract. Cover and chill.
3. On a lightly floured surface roll half of the dough at a time into a 12×8-inch rectangle. Spread half of the filling over each dough half, leaving a ½-inch border on both long edges. Roll the long edges toward each other in scroll fashion to meet in the middle. Lightly brush the seam where the spirals meet with water and gently press together. Wrap each roll in plastic wrap. Freeze about 4 hours or until very firm.
4. Preheat oven to 350°F. Line a cookie sheet with parchment paper. Use a thin-blade knife to cut rolls into ¼-inch-thick slices. Place slices 2 inches apart on the prepared cookie sheet. Bake about 10 minutes or until edges are firm and bottoms are lightly browned. Transfer to a wire rack and let cool. If desired, sprinkle with powdered sugar.
PER COOKIE *56 cal, 2 g fat, 6 mg chol, 22 mg sodium, 9 g carb, 0 g fiber, 1 g pro.*

Peppermint Sandwich Crèmes

Crush the candies in a plastic bag with a rolling pin.

PREP 30 minutes FREEZE 2 hours
BAKE 10 minutes per batch
OVEN 350°F MAKES 35 sandwiches

½   cup butter, softened
1   cup sugar
¼   teaspoon baking soda
¼   teaspoon salt
1   egg
2   teaspoons vanilla
1   teaspoon peppermint extract
1¾ cups all-purpose flour
1   recipe Peppermint-Cream Cheese
    Filling
    Finely crushed peppermint candies
    or sprinkles

1. In a large bowl beat butter with an electric mixer on medium to high for 30 seconds. Add sugar, baking soda, and salt. Beat until combined, scraping bowl occasionally. Beat in egg, vanilla, and peppermint extract until combined. Beat in as much of the flour as you can with the mixer. Using a wooden spoon, stir in any remaining flour.

2. Divide dough into 4 portions. Shape each portion into an 8-inch roll. Wrap each roll in plastic wrap or waxed paper. Freeze for 2 to 3 hours or until dough is firm enough to slice.
3. Preheat oven to 350°F. Unwrap rolls and cut into ⅜-inch slices. Place slices 1 inch apart on an ungreased cookie sheet. Bake for 10 to 12 minutes or just until firm. Transfer cookies to a wire rack to cool.
4. Spread Peppermint-Cream Cheese Filling on bottoms of half of the cookies, spreading to edges. Top with the remaining cookies, bottom sides down. Press lightly until filling comes just slightly over edges. Roll edges of cookies in crushed candies or sprinkles.
Peppermint-Cream Cheese Filling: In a large bowl combine one 3-ounce package softened cream cheese and ¼ cup softened butter. Beat with an electric mixer on medium until smooth. Beat in 1 teaspoon vanilla and ½ teaspoon peppermint extract. Gradually beat in 3 cups powdered sugar. If necessary, beat in enough milk, 1 teaspoon at a time, to make filling spreading consistency.
PER SANDWICH *151 cal, 5 g fat, 19 mg chol, 33 mg sodium, 26 g carb, 0 g fiber, 1 g pro.*

Pineapple-Filled Macaroons

Purchase egg whites in a carton to avoid throwing away three yolks.

PREP 35 minutes STAND 30 minutes
BAKE 10 minutes per batch
OVEN 325°F MAKES 20 cookies

½   cup coarsely chopped macadamia
    nuts (about 3 ounces)
½   cup slivered almonds
2   cups powdered sugar
3   egg whites
½   teaspoon vanilla
¼   teaspoon salt
¼   cup shredded coconut, finely
    chopped
1   recipe Creamy Pineapple Filling

1. Preheat oven to 325°F. Line 2 large cookie sheets with parchment paper; set aside. In a food processor combine macadamia nuts and almonds. Add 1 cup of the powdered sugar. Cover and process until nuts are very finely ground.
2. In a large bowl combine egg whites, vanilla, and salt. Beat with an electric mixer on medium until soft peaks form (tips curl). Add remaining powdered sugar, 1 tablespoon at a time, beating on high just until stiff peaks form (tips stand straight). Sprinkle one-fourth of the nut mixture over egg mixture; gently fold in. Sprinkle and fold in nut mixture, one-fourth at a time, until combined.
3. Spoon macaroon dough into a large decorating bag fitted with a large round tip (about ½ inch). Pipe in 1½-inch flat circles on the prepared cookie sheets. Sprinkle half of the macaroons with coconut. Let stand 30 minutes.
4. Bake for 10 to 15 minutes or just until set. Cool completely on cookie sheets on a wire rack. Peel cookies off parchment paper.
5. Spread about 1 tablespoon of the Creamy Pineapple Filling on flat sides (bottoms) of the cookies without coconut. Top each spread cookie with a coconut-topped cookie, flat side down.
Creamy Pineapple Filling: Drain ½ cup crushed pineapple in a sieve, reserving drained liquid. In a large bowl beat ¼ cup softened butter with an electric mixer on medium until smooth. Add drained pineapple and ½ teaspoon vanilla. Beat until combined. Gradually beat in 3 cups powdered sugar and enough reserved pineapple juice (1 to 2 tablespoons) to make filling spreading consistency.
PER COOKIE *188 cal, 7 g fat, 6 mg chol, 45 mg sodium, 33 g carb, 1 g fiber, 1 g pro.*

PINEAPPLE-FILLED
MACAROONS

Triple-Ginger Crisps

Fresh ginger, ground ginger, and crystallized ginger infuse these crispy cookies with a sense of warmth.

PREP 30 minutes
CHILL 30 minutes + 4 hours
BAKE 8 minutes per batch
OVEN 350°F MAKES 96 cookies

4½ cups all-purpose flour
1 tablespoon ground ginger
1½ teaspoons baking powder
1½ teaspoons ground cinnamon
½ teaspoon baking soda
½ teaspoon salt
¼ teaspoon ground cloves
¼ teaspoon ground nutmeg
1½ cups butter, softened
1¾ cups sugar
2 eggs
½ cup molasses
1 tablespoon grated fresh ginger
2 teaspoons lemon juice
¾ cup finely chopped crystallized ginger

1. In a medium bowl combine flour, ground ginger, baking powder, cinnamon, baking soda, salt, cloves, and nutmeg. Set aside.
2. In a very large bowl beat butter with an electric mixer on medium to high for 30 seconds. Add sugar and beat until fluffy. Add eggs, molasses, fresh ginger, and lemon juice. Beat until well mixed, scraping sides of bowl occasionally. Add flour mixture, stirring until well mixed and smooth. Stir in crystallized ginger.
3. Cover; chill dough about 30 minutes or until easy to work with. Shape dough into three 1½-inch-thick logs (each about 8 inches long). Wrap each log in waxed paper; twist the ends. Chill for at least 4 hours or up to 2 days.
4. Preheat oven to 350°F. Line cookie sheets with parchment paper; set aside. Cut chilled or frozen logs into scant ¼-inch slices. Place slices about 1 inch apart on prepared cookie sheets. Bake for 8 to 10 minutes or just until firm. Cool on cookie sheets for 2 minutes. Transfer to wire racks; cool.

PER COOKIE *72 cal, 3 g fat, 12 mg chol, 48 mg sodium, 11 g carb, 0 g fiber, 1 g pro.*

HOMEMADE
OATMEAL
CREAM PIES

Homemade Oatmeal Cream Pies

Similar to a favorite purchased cookie (but much better), these homey sandwiches make a lovely gift.

PREP **40 minutes** BAKE **8 minutes**
OVEN **350°F** MAKES **13 pies**

¾ cup all-purpose flour
½ teaspoon baking soda
½ teaspoon salt
¼ teaspoon baking powder
½ cup butter, softened
½ cup peanut butter
½ cup granulated sugar
½ cup packed brown sugar
1 egg
1 teaspoon vanilla
1 cup quick-cooking oats
2 teaspoons hot water
¼ teaspoon salt
1 7-ounce jar marshmallow creme
½ cup shortening
⅓ cup powdered sugar

1. Preheat oven to 350°F. Grease a cookie sheet; set aside. In a bowl combine flour, baking soda, salt, and baking powder; set aside. In a mixing bowl beat butter and peanut butter with an electric mixer on medium to high until combined. Beat in granulated sugar and brown sugar until fluffy. Beat in egg and vanilla just until combined. Stir in flour mixture and oats just until combined. Drop dough by rounded teaspoons 2 inches apart onto prepared cookie sheet.
2. Bake for 8 to 10 minutes or until edges are light brown and centers are set. Cool on cookie sheet for 1 minute. Transfer cookies to a wire rack and let cool.
3. Meanwhile, in a mixing bowl combine the hot water and salt. Stir until salt dissolves. Add marshmallow creme, shortening, and powdered sugar. Beat with an electric mixer on medium until combined.
4. Using a star tip, pipe marshmallow mixture onto the flat side of half of the cookies. (Or use an offset spatula to spread marshmallow mixture on cookies.) Top each frosted cookie with another cookie, flat side down. For a gift, arrange the cookies in a foil loaf pan. Cover with plastic wrap.
PER PIE *367 cal, 20 g fat, 35 mg chol, 305 mg sodium, 43 g carb, 1 g fiber, 5 g pro.*

Lemon Drop Sandwiches

These light-as-air lemony bites melt in your mouth.

PREP **45 minutes**
BAKE **1 hour 30 minutes**
OVEN **200°F** MAKES **36 sandwiches**

3 egg whites
½ teaspoon vanilla
¼ teaspoon cream of tartar
⅛ teaspoon salt
¾ cup sugar
1 teaspoon finely shredded lemon peel
1 recipe Lemon Frosting

1. Preheat oven to 200°F. Line cookie sheets with parchment paper; set aside. In a large bowl combine egg whites, vanilla, cream of tartar, and salt. Beat with an electric mixer on medium until soft peaks form (tips curl). Gradually add sugar, 1 tablespoon at a time, beating on high until stiff peaks form (tips stand straight). Gently stir in lemon peel.
2. Spoon meringue mixture into a decorating bag fitted with a ½-inch round tip. Pipe 1½-inch meringues 1 inch apart onto the prepared cookie sheets.
3. Bake for 1½ to 1¾ hours or until meringues appear dry and are firm when lightly touched. Do not open the oven during baking time. Transfer cookies to a wire rack; cool.
4. Before serving, spread about 1 teaspoon of the Lemon Frosting on bottoms of half of the cookies. Top with the remaining cookies, bottom sides down. Serve immediately or let cookies stand at room temperature for up to 2 hours before serving.
Lemon Frosting: In a medium bowl combine ⅓ cup softened butter and 2 teaspoons finely shredded lemon peel. Beat with an electric mixer on medium to high until fluffy. Gradually beat in 2 cups powdered sugar. Beat in 1 tablespoon lemon juice, 1 teaspoon at a time, to make frosting spreading consistency. Makes about 1 cup.
PER SANDWICH *59 cal, 2 g fat, 5 mg chol, 28 mg sodium, 11 g carb, 0 g fiber, 0 g pro.*

LEMON DROP SANDWICHES

Tangy Spice Squares

To get the most juice from fresh lemons, warm in the microwave for 10 seconds, then roll on the counter before juicing.

PREP **10 minutes** BAKE **17 minutes**
OVEN **350°F** MAKES **16 squares**

1   cup all-purpose flour
1   teaspoon cinnamon
½   teaspoon ginger
⅛   teaspoon ground cloves
     Pinch of salt
3   tablespoons sugar
3   tablespoons brown sugar
½   cup cold unsalted butter, cut into
     8 pieces (1 stick)
½   cup sugar
3   tablespoons all-purpose flour
¼   teaspoon baking powder
¼   cup orange juice
¼   cup freshly squeezed lemon juice
     Powdered sugar or coarse sugar
     (optional)

1. Place an oven rack in center of oven. Preheat oven to 350°F. Line an 8×8×2-inch baking pan with foil. Grease foil; set aside.
2. For the crust, in a food processor combine the flour, spices, salt, and sugars. Pulse just until mixed. Add cold butter; pulse several times to break up pieces. Process about 1 minute, just until dough forms moist, popcornlike clumps that hold together when pressed between fingers. Turn dough into pan, pressing evenly. Bake crust for 17 to 20 minutes, until firm and bubbly. Cool on wire rack.
3. Meanwhile, for custard, in a mixing bowl beat the ½ cup sugar, flour, baking powder, orange juice, and lemon juice with electric mixer for 1 minute, scraping sides of bowl as needed. With a spatula, swirl custard a couple of times in bowl; lightly tap bowl against counter to remove any air bubbles. Pour custard into crust, tilting pan to evenly smooth the thin layer.
4. Bake the custard-topped crust about 20 minutes, until golden and set. Cool completely on a wire rack. If desired, dust with sugar. Cut into 2-inch squares. Store in refrigerator or wrap and freeze.
PER SQUARE *131 cal, 6 g fat, 15 mg chol, 17 mg sodium, 19 g carb, 0 g fiber, 1 g pro.*

Five-Spice Pear Pie Bars

Pears are perfectly ripe when they give just slightly to gentle pressure and are aromatic. Avoid hard pears or those with cuts or bruises.

PREP **40 minutes** BAKE **45 minutes**
OVEN **350°F** MAKES **32 bars**

3   cups all-purpose flour
2   tablespoons sugar
½   teaspoon salt
½   cup shortening
½   cup cold butter
2   egg yolks, beaten
⅓   cup milk
1   to 2 tablespoons water
6   cups peeled, cored, and thinly
     sliced ripe pears (about 2¼ pounds)
1   cup sugar
1   cup crushed cornflakes
1   teaspoon five-spice powder
1   egg white, beaten
1   recipe Orange Icing

1. For pastry, in a large bowl combine flour, the 2 tablespoons sugar, and the salt. Using a pastry blender, cut in shortening and butter until pieces are pea size.
2. In a small bowl whisk together egg yolks and milk. Gradually stir egg yolk mixture into flour mixture, tossing with a fork to moisten. Sprinkle the water over the mixture, gently tossing until all of the mixture is moistened. Gather mixture into a ball, kneading gently until it holds together. Divide pastry into 2 portions, making 1 portion slightly larger than the other. Wrap and chill until needed.
3. For filling, in an extra-large bowl combine pears, the 1 cup sugar, the cornflakes, and five-spice powder. Set aside.
4. Preheat oven to 350°F. On a lightly floured surface use your hands to pat the larger portion of pastry onto the bottom of a 15×10×1-inch baking pan. Spoon filling evenly into pastry-lined pan.
5. Roll the remaining pastry portion between 2 sheets of waxed paper to a 15×10-inch rectangle. Carefully peel off top sheet of waxed paper. Invert rectangle, pastry side down, over the filling. Carefully peel off waxed paper. Using damp fingers, press edges of the 2 pastry rectangles together. Cut a few slits in the top pastry; brush lightly with egg white.
6. Bake for 45 to 50 minutes or until pastry is golden, fruit is tender, and filling is bubbly. Cool completely in pan on a wire rack.
7. Drizzle with Orange Icing. Let stand until icing is set. Cut into bars.
Orange Icing: In a medium bowl stir together 1½ cups powdered sugar, 1 teaspoon grated orange peel, ¼ teaspoon vanilla, and enough pear nectar or milk (1 to 2 tablespoons) to make icing a drizzling consistency.
PER BAR *179 cal, 6 g fat, 21 mg chol, 81 mg sodium, 29 g carb, 1 g fiber, 2 g pro.*

FIVE-SPICE PEAR PIE BARS

Four-Nut and Maple Bars

Chocolate-hazelnut spread provides the foundation for the frosting on these nutty bars.

PREP 20 minutes BAKE 25 minutes
OVEN 350°F MAKES 24 bars

2   cups whole wheat flour
1   teaspoon baking powder
1   teaspoon baking soda
2   egg whites
¾   cup pure maple syrup
½   cup canola oil
½   cup fat-free milk
½   cup chopped cashews
½   cup slivered almonds, toasted
½   cup chopped walnuts, toasted
1   cup semisweet chocolate pieces
1   recipe Chocolate-Hazelnut Frosting

⅔   cup pecan halves, chopped cashews, slivered almonds, and/or chopped walnuts, toasted

1. Preheat oven to 350°F. Grease and lightly flour a 13×9×2-inch baking pan; set aside.
2. In large bowl combine flour, baking powder, and baking soda. In another bowl whisk together egg whites, maple syrup, oil, and milk; add to flour mixture. Stir to combine. Stir in ½ cup each cashews, almonds, walnuts, and the 1 cup chocolate pieces. Spread in prepared pan.
3. Bake 25 to 30 minutes or until a toothpick inserted near center comes out clean. Cool on wire rack. Spread with Chocolate-Hazelnut Frosting; sprinkle with pecans, cashews, almonds, and/or walnuts. Cut into bars.

Chocolate-Hazelnut Frosting: In bowl combine ¼ cup chocolate-hazelnut spread, 3 tablespoons fat-free milk, and 1 tablespoon pure maple syrup. Stir in ½ cup unsweetened cocoa powder. Gradually stir in 1 to 1¼ cups powdered sugar to reach spreading consistency.

PER BAR *241 cal, 14 g fat, 0 mg chol, 81 mg sodium, 29 g carb, 3 g fiber, 4 g pro.*

SALTED CHOCOLATE-
CARAMEL CLUSTERS

who wants candy?

VISIONS OF SUGARPLUMS Your kitchen can become the best confectionery in town. Simplify the art and science of candymaking with these foolproof recipes for fudge, cake bites, bark, and crunchy snack mixes. Package them up prettily and no one will believe you made them yourself.

114

118

120

White Fruitcake Fudge

The dried fruit in this smooth and mellow-tasting fudge glows like jewels against the white backdrop.

PREP 30 minutes   COOK 18 minutes
CHILL 1 hour   MAKES 117 pieces

¾   cup chopped walnuts, toasted
¾   cup finely chopped dried apricots
½   cup finely chopped golden raisins or raisins
2   cups sugar
¾   cup sour cream
½   cup butter
12   ounces white baking chocolate, coarsely chopped
1   7-ounce jar marshmallow creme

1. In a medium bowl combine walnuts, apricots, and raisins. Remove ¼ cup to sprinkle on top of fudge. Line a 13×9×2-inch baking pan with foil, extending foil over edges of pan. Butter the foil; set pan aside.
2. Butter sides of a heavy 3-quart saucepan. In saucepan combine sugar, sour cream, and butter. Cook and stir over medium heat until mixture boils. Clip a candy thermometer to side of pan. Reduce heat to medium-low; continue boiling at a moderate, steady rate, stirring occasionally, until thermometer registers 236°F (18 to 20 minutes). Adjust heat as necessary to maintain a steady boil.

3. Remove saucepan from heat. Stir in white chocolate and marshmallow creme. Continue stirring until chocolate is melted and mixture is combined. Stir in fruit and nut mixture. Immediately spread fudge evenly in prepared pan. Top with the reserved ¼ cup fruit and nut mixture. Chill fudge until firm. Use foil to lift fudge out of pan. Cut fudge into squares. Store covered in the refrigerator.
PER PIECE *53 cal, 2 g fat, 3 mg chol, 9 mg sodium, 8 g carb, 0 g fiber, 0 g pro.*

Cinna-Crunch Fudge

A pinch of cayenne pepper adds a little heat to the sweet.

PREP 25 minutes   CHILL 4 hours
MAKES 96 pieces

1   cup chopped cashews
1   14-ounce can sweetened condensed milk
1   ounce semisweet chocolate pieces
1   ounce white baking pieces
1   13-ounce jar chocolate-hazelnut spread
¼   cup strong brewed coffee
½   teaspoon ground cinnamon
¼   teaspoon cayenne pepper
2   tablespoons butter

1. Line a 13×9×2-inch baking pan with foil, extending the foil over the edges of the pan. Butter the foil. Sprinkle bottom of pan evenly with cashews; set aside.
2. In a large microwave-safe bowl heat the condensed milk, chocolate pieces, white pieces, chocolate-hazelnut spread, coffee, cinnamon and cayenne pepper, uncovered, on high for 3 to 4 minutes or until melted and smooth, stirring after every minute. Stir in butter until melted.
3. Gently and quickly spread the fudge mixture over cashews in pan. Let cool to room temperature. Cover and refrigerate at least 4 hours or until firm. When fudge is firm, use foil to lift it out of pan. Cut fudge into pieces. Store tightly covered in the refrigerator.
PER PIECE *71 cal, 4 g fat, 3 mg chol, 14 mg sodium, 9 g carb, 0 g fiber, 1 g pro.*

WHITE FRUITCAKE FUDGE

CINNA-CRUNCH FUDGE

BUTTERSCOTCH-
MARSHMALLOW
CHEWS

Butterscotch-Marshmallow Chews

These are a bit like the chocolate-covered marshmallow cookies of your childhood—but with a crunchy and salty kick from the pretzel base.

PREP **45 minutes** STAND **30 minutes**
MAKES **32 candies**

32 small pretzel rounds or twists
1½ cups butterscotch- or peanut butter-flavor pieces (9 ounces)
1   tablespoon shortening
16 large marshmallows, cut in half crosswise
18 ounces chocolate-flavor candy coating, chopped (3 cups)
3   tablespoons shortening
    White or multicolor sprinkles (jimmies)

1. Place a large wire cooling rack over a sheet of waxed paper. Place pretzels evenly spaced on cooling rack.
2. In a small microwave-safe bowl heat butterscotch pieces and the 1 tablespoon shortening, uncovered, on high for 1 to 2 minutes or until butterscotch pieces melt, stirring every 30 seconds.
3. Place each marshmallow half into melted butterscotch mixture. Using a fork, remove marshmallow from melted butterscotch mixture and let excess drip off. Using the tines of another fork, push the coated marshmallow half onto a pretzel.
4. In a medium microwave-safe bowl heat chocolate candy coating and the 3 tablespoons shortening, uncovered, on high for 1 to 2 minutes or until candy coating melts, stirring every 30 seconds.
5. Spoon about 1 tablespoon melted chocolate mixture over each marshmallow. Let excess drip down sides of marshmallow. Decorate with sprinkles. Let stand about 30 minutes or until coating is set. Store tightly covered in the refrigerator for up to 1 week. Allow to come to room temperature before serving.
PER CANDY *182 cal, 10 g fat, 0 mg chol, 20 mg sodium, 22 g carb, 0 g fiber, 0 g pro.*

Cherry-Almond Truffle Sticks

Marzipan—essentially almond paste with added sugar, like the filling in these chocolate-covered sticks—is a favorite Christmas candy in Northern Europe.

PREP **30 minutes** CHILL **30 minutes**
MAKES **20 sticks**

2   cups powdered sugar
2   tablespoons almond paste
4   teaspoons evaporated milk or milk
1   tablespoon chopped candied red cherries
¼   teaspoon almond extract
¼   teaspoon vanilla
8   ounces semisweet chocolate, chopped
2   teaspoons shortening
    Finely chopped toasted almonds

1. In a food processor combine powdered sugar and almond paste. Cover and process until combined. Add milk, cherries, almond extract, and vanilla. Cover and process until mixture comes together. Remove and knead until smooth.
2. Pinch off 1-inch balls of mixture; shape balls into 2½-inch-long sticks.
3. In a medium saucepan heat chocolate pieces and shortening over low heat until melted and mixture is smooth. Dip sticks into chocolate to coat, allowing excess chocolate to drip off. Set sticks on a sheet of waxed paper. Sprinkle with chopped almonds. Chill until set. Store covered in the refrigerator.
PER STICK *116 cal, 4 g fat, 0 mg chol, 3 mg sodium, 20 g carb, 1 g fiber, 1 g pro.*

CHERRY-ALMOND TRUFFLE STICKS

Cake Bites

You can have your cake—and your candy too—with these candy-coated bites of cake and frosting.

PREP 1 hour 45 minutes
BAKE according to package directions
FREEZE 1 hour
OVEN according to package directions
MAKES 70 cake bites

1   package 2-layer-size cake mix such as chocolate, white, lemon, orange, or red velvet
2   to 4 tablespoons liquid flavor, such as liqueur, strong coffee, juice, or 1 teaspoon almond, rum, or peppermint extract (optional)
1   teaspoon pumpkin pie spice, apple pie spice, or cinnamon (optional)
1   16-ounce can frosting (choose a flavor to go with the cake mix and flavorings, if used)
2   pounds vanilla- or chocolate-flavor candy coating, melted
    Decorative sprinkles, coarse sugar, crushed peppermint, or other hard candies, or finely chopped nuts (optional)

1. Prepare the cake mix according to package directions. If desired, substitute a liquid flavor for part of the liquid used to make the mix and stir in a spice. Use any suggested pan size and bake according to package directions. Cool in pan on wire rack.
2. Remove from pan and crumble into a very large mixing bowl. Add the can of frosting. Beat with an electric mixer until combined (mixture will be soft). Using a melon baller or small (1-tablespoon) cookie scoop, shape into 1-inch balls. Place balls on waxed paper-lined trays or baking pans; freeze at least 1 hour or until firm.
3. Working with one-third of the balls at a time, using a fork or crafts (lollipop) stick, dip each ball into candy coating to cover completely. Place on waxed paper. Sprinkle with a topping, if desired. Let stand until set.

PER CAKE BITE *140 cal, 7 g fat, 9 mg chol, 66 mg sodium, 19 g carb, 0 g fiber, 1 g pro.*

Salted Chocolate-Caramel Clusters

Adding a sprinkle of coarse salt to the top of each piece of candy balances the sweetness and adds a pleasing crunch.

PREP 20 minutes STAND 1 hour
MAKES 20 clusters

1   8-ounce package pecan halves, toasted
1   14-ounce package vanilla caramels, unwrapped
1   tablespoon milk
1   12-ounce package dark chocolate pieces
2   ounces white chocolate, chopped (⅓ cup) (optional)
1   teaspoon shortening (optional)
    Coarse sea salt or Fleur de Sel (optional)

1. Line a baking sheet or tray with foil or parchment paper; grease the foil or parchment. For each, arrange 5 pecan halves in a single-layer cluster.
2. In a small heavy saucepan combine vanilla caramels and milk. Heat and stir over medium-low heat until caramels melt and mixture is smooth. Spoon some of the caramel mixture over each cluster of pecans. Let stand about 30 minutes or until firm.
3. In a medium heavy saucepan heat and stir the dark chocolate pieces over low heat until chocolate melts and is smooth. Remove ¼ cup of the melted chocolate; set aside. Spoon some of the remaining melted chocolate over each cluster, gently spreading to the edges. Let clusters stand about 30 minutes or until firm (if necessary, place trays in refrigerator for 5 to 10 minutes until firm).
4. Meanwhile, if desired, in a small microwave-safe bowl combine white chocolate and shortening. Heat, uncovered, on high for about 1 minute or until chocolate melts and is smooth, stirring every 30 seconds. Spread some of the white chocolate over the top of each cluster. Pour reserved melted chocolate into a small resealable plastic bag. Snip off a very small piece from one corner. Use bag to drizzle chocolate over the top of each cluster. If desired, sprinkle each cluster with coarse sea salt. Let stand until all chocolate is set.

PER CLUSTER *255 cal, 16 g fat, 1 mg chol, 53 mg sodium, 26 g carb, 2 g fiber, 3 g pro.*

Bing Candy

If you are nostalgic for the red-and-white-wrapped namesake of this recipe, you will certainly enjoy this chocolate-and-cherry confection.

PREP 35 minutes
CHILL 1 hour 20 minutes
MAKES 120 pieces

1   12-ounce package semisweet chocolate pieces
¾   cup creamy peanut butter
2   cups finely chopped pecans, toasted, or finely chopped roasted peanuts
1½   cups sugar
12   marshmallows
½   cup butter
1   5-ounce can evaporated milk
1   10-ounce package cherry- or peanut butter-flavor pieces

1. Line a 13×9×2-inch baking pan with heavy foil, allowing foil to extend over sides of pan; grease and set aside.
2. In a medium saucepan combine chocolate pieces and peanut butter; heat and stir over low heat until melted. Stir in nuts. Spread half of the mixture (about 1¼ cups) in prepared pan. Transfer to refrigerator. Let remaining chocolate mixture stand at room temperature.
3. In another medium saucepan combine sugar, marshmallows, butter, and evaporated milk. Cook and stir over medium heat until mixture comes to a boil; cook 5 minutes more, stirring constantly. Remove from heat. Stir in cherry pieces until melted. Cool 10 minutes. Carefully spread over chocolate layer in pan. Chill 20 minutes.
4. Carefully spread on remaining chocolate mixture.* Cover and chill at least 1 hour. Lift from pan using foil. Cut into small pieces. Store in an airtight container in the refrigerator.
* If too firm to spread, place in a microwave-safe bowl and heat on medium for 30 seconds.

PER PIECE *69 cal, 5 g fat, 3 mg chol, 15 mg sodium, 7 g carb, 0 g fiber, 1 g pro.*

Dark Chocolate Candy Bark

PREP 15 minutes   CHILL 30 minutes
MAKES 36 pieces

6   ounces chocolate-flavor candy coating, chopped (1 cup)
6   ounces dark chocolate, chopped (1 cup)
1   tablespoon shortening
2   cups chopped assorted chocolate candy bars, such as chocolate-coated caramel-topped nougat bars with peanuts, chocolate-covered English toffee, chocolate-covered peanut butter cups, or malted milk balls
½   cup salted peanuts, chopped

1. Line a large baking sheet with heavy foil; grease foil. Set aside. In a large microwave-safe bowl combine candy coating, chocolate, and shortening. Heat, uncovered, on high for 1½ to 2 minutes or until chocolate melts, stirring every 30 seconds.
2. Stir 1 cup of the assorted chopped candy bars and the peanuts into melted chocolate mixture. Pour mixture onto prepared baking sheet. Spread mixture into an even layer about ¼ inch thick. Sprinkle with the remaining 1 cup chopped candy bars; lightly press pieces into chocolate.
3. Chill about 30 minutes or until firm. Use foil to lift candy out of pan. With a sharp knife, cut candy into pieces.
PER PIECE *112 cal, 6 g fat, 2 mg chol, 29 mg sodium, 12 g carb, 1 g fiber, 2 g pro.*

White Chocolate Candy Bark: Prepare as directed, except substitute vanilla-flavor candy coating for the chocolate-flavor candy coating; chopped white baking chocolate for the dark chocolate; and chopped, toasted slivered almonds for the salted peanuts.

Cranberry-Orange Caramel Corn

PREP 25 minutes   BAKE 30 minutes
OVEN 275°F   MAKES 10 servings

12   cups popped popcorn
1   cup dried cranberries
½   cup whole almonds
½   cup butter
½   cup packed brown sugar
¼   cup light-color corn syrup
2   tablespoons orange juice
2   teaspoons vanilla
½   teaspoon baking soda

1. Preheat oven to 275°F. In a very large bowl combine the popped popcorn, dried cranberries, and almonds; set aside.
2. In a 2-quart saucepan cook and stir the butter, brown sugar, and corn syrup over medium heat until butter melts. Stir in the orange juice. Bring to boiling over medium heat. Boil at a moderate, steady rate for 2 minutes. Remove from heat. Stir in vanilla and baking soda (mixture will foam up).
3. Pour the syrup mixture over the popcorn mixture; stir to coat well. Transfer to a 15×10×1-inch baking pan or a shallow roasting pan. Bake for 30 minutes, stirring twice. Transfer caramel corn to a large sheet of greased heavy foil and let cool. Store caramel corn in covered container.
PER SERVING *130 cal, 7 g fat, 12 mg chol, 68 mg sodium, 17 g carb, 1 g fiber, 1 g pro.*

Pistachio-Cinnamon Brittle

PREP 10 minutes   MAKES 20 pieces

½   cup sugar
½   cup light-color corn syrup
1   cup salted dry-roasted pistachio nuts and/or cashews
1   tablespoon butter
½   teaspoon baking soda
½   teaspoon ground cinnamon
½   teaspoon vanilla

1. Line a small baking sheet with foil. Butter foil; set baking sheet aside. In a 4-cup microwave-safe glass measure or small bowl combine sugar and corn syrup. Heat, uncovered, on high for 3 minutes, stirring twice.
2. Stir in nuts and butter. Heat, uncovered, on high for 2 to 3 minutes more or just until mixture turns light golden, stirring after 1 minute and then every 30 seconds. (The mixture continues to cook and becomes more golden when removed from the microwave.)
3. Quickly stir in baking soda, cinnamon, and vanilla, stirring constantly. Immediately pour mixture onto prepared baking sheet, spreading it as thin as possible. Cool completely. To serve, break into irregular pieces.
PER PIECE *74 cal, 4 g fat, 2 mg chol, 64 mg sodium, 10 g carb, 1 g fiber, 1 g pro.*

Black-and-White Pretzels

PREP 45 minutes   STAND 1 hour
MAKES 5½ cups coated pretzels

6   ounces chocolate-flavor candy coating, chopped (1 cup)
4   cups small pretzel twists (6 ounces)
¼   cup white sprinkles (jimmies)
6   ounces vanilla-flavor candy coating, chopped (1 cup)
¼   cup chocolate-flavor sprinkles (jimmies)

1. Line a large baking sheet pan with waxed paper. In a microwave-safe bowl heat chocolate candy coating, uncovered, on high for 2 minutes or until candy coating melts, stirring every 30 seconds.
2. Dip one side of each pretzel twist into melted chocolate candy coating. Let excess drip off. Place coated pretzels on prepared baking sheet. Decorate coated portion of pretzel with white sprinkles. Let stand about 30 minutes or until coating is set.
3. In a microwave-safe bowl heat vanilla candy coating, uncovered, on high for 2 minutes or until candy coating melts, stirring every 30 seconds.
4. Holding onto the chocolate-coated side of each pretzel, dip the uncoated side into melted vanilla candy coating. Let excess drip off. Place coated pretzels on prepared baking sheet. Decorate vanilla-coated portion of pretzel with chocolate sprinkles. Let stand about 30 minutes or until coating is set.
PER ½ CUP *280 cal, 13 g fat, 0 mg chol, 340 mg sodium, 39 g carb, 0 g fiber, 2 g pro.*

CRANBERRY-ORANGE CARAMEL CORN

BLACK-AND-WHITE
PRETZELS

CHEDDAR AND RED
PEPPER WAFERS

gifts to give

MADE BY HAND When you're looking for something special to give this season, look no farther than your very own kitchen. Pour your heart into the pleasure of making a superlative sweet or savory surprise—personalized and made with love.

124

127

128

SO-EASY
APPLE BUTTER

CANDIED FRUIT
SAUCE

So-Easy Apple Butter

If you have the time, bake a loaf of yeast bread to give as well. A slice, toasted, is delicious slathered with apple butter.

PREP 30 minutes COOK 5 hours (high)
MAKES 4 half-pint jars (4 servings per jar)

4   pounds cooking apples, peeled, cored, and sliced (about 12 cups)
2   cups sugar
⅓   cup water
2   tablespoons vinegar
2   teaspoons ground cinnamon
¼   teaspoon ground cloves
⅛   teaspoon ground allspice
⅛   teaspoon ground nutmeg

1. Place apple slices in a 3½- or 4-quart slow cooker. Stir in sugar, the water, vinegar, cinnamon, cloves, allspice, and nutmeg.
2. Cover and cook on high-heat setting for 5 to 6 hours. Stir and cool.
3. Ladle apple butter into 4 half-pint canning jars or airtight containers, leaving a ½-inch headspace. Seal and label. Store in the refrigerator for up to 3 weeks.
PER 2 TABLESPOONS 71 cal, 0 g fat, 0 mg chol, 1 mg sodium, 18 g carb, 1 g fiber, 1 g pro.

Candied Fruit Sauce

Measure the dried apricots first, then cut into slivers.

PREP 10 minutes COOK 10 minutes
MAKES 5 half-pint jars (10 servings per jar)

1   cup dried apricots, cut into thin slivers
⅔   cup dried tart cherries
2   cups sugar
1   cup water
½   cup dark-color corn syrup
¼   cup brandy or orange juice
2   tablespoons butter

1. In a large saucepan combine apricots, cherries, sugar, the water, and corn syrup. Bring to boiling over medium heat, stirring to dissolve sugar; reduce heat. Simmer, uncovered, for 10 minutes. Remove from heat; stir in brandy and butter.
2. Ladle into 5 half-pint canning jars, leaving a ½-inch headspace. Seal and label. Store in the refrigerator for up to 2 weeks.
PER 2 TABLESPOONS 147 cal, 1 g fat, 3 mg chol, 22 mg sodium, 34 g carb, 1 g fiber, 0 g pro.

Orange-Butter Sauce

This is delicious spread on warm pancakes, biscuits, or waffles.

PREP 5 minutes COOK 15 minutes
MAKES 5 half-pint jars (10 servings per jar)

2   cups orange marmalade
1½ cups orange juice
6   tablespoons butter

1. In a large saucepan combine orange marmalade and orange juice. Bring to boiling, stirring frequently. Reduce heat and simmer, uncovered, for 15 minutes or until reduced to 2 cups, stirring occasionally. Remove from heat. Stir in butter.
2. Ladle into 5 half-pint canning jars, leaving a ½-inch headspace. Seal and label. Store in the refrigerator for up to 2 weeks.
PER 2 TABLESPOONS 118 cal, 3 g fat, 9 mg chol, 43 mg sodium, 23 g carb, 0 g fiber, 0 g pro.

Almond Pastry Fingers

This rich pastry tastes like it was made in a European-bakery—but it takes just minutes to make. Package it in white bakery boxes, available at craft stores.

PREP 30 minutes   BAKE 20 minutes
COOL 4 hours   OVEN 400°F
MAKES 48 servings

1   17.3-ounce package (2 sheets) frozen puff pastry sheets, thawed
1   12.5-ounce can almond pastry and dessert filling
1½ cups white baking pieces
⅔   cup slivered almonds, toasted and finely chopped
Powdered sugar

1. Preheat oven to 400°F. Line a very large cookie sheet with parchment paper; set aside. Unfold pastry sheets onto a work surface. Cut each sheet lengthwise into 2 rectangles (4 rectangles total). Generously prick pastry rectangles all over with the tines of a fork.
2. Spread each pastry rectangle with one-fourth of the almond filling (about ¼ cup), spreading to within ¾ inch of the edges. Top each with one-fourth of the white baking pieces and one-fourth of the almonds. Brush edges of rectangles with water. Fold each rectangle in half lengthwise; gently press edges with fork to seal. Place rectangles 2 inches apart on the prepared cookie sheet.
3. Bake for 20 to 25 minutes or until golden brown. Transfer rectangles to wire racks; let cool for at least 4 hours. Generously sprinkle with powdered sugar. Cut each rectangle crosswise into 12 strips.

PER SERVING *119 cal, 7 g fat, 0 mg chol, 57 mg sodium, 13 g carb, 1 g fiber, 1 g pro.*

Coconut Cake Balls

The cake-bite craze hits full tilt with these coconut, cream cheese, and cake-filled confections.

PREP **1 hour**
BAKE **according to package directions**
STAND **30 minutes** FREEZE **1 hour**
MAKES **80 cake balls**

1 package 2-layer-size reduced-sugar or regular cake mix
1 14-ounce can unsweetened light coconut milk
1 8-ounce package reduced-fat cream cheese (Neufchâtel), softened
1 cup shredded coconut
1 pound semisweet or dark chocolate or white baking chocolate
2 tablespoons shortening
⅓ cup shredded coconut, toasted if desired (see tip, page 14)

1. Prepare the cake mix according to package directions, except substitute 1 cup of the coconut milk for 1 cup of the liquid in the cake and decrease the oil by 2 tablespoons. Use any suggested pan size and bake according to package directions. Cool in pan on a wire rack. Line trays or baking pans with waxed paper; set aside.

2. In a very large mixing bowl beat cream cheese with an electric mixer until smooth. Gradually beat in remaining coconut milk until smooth. Stir in the 1 cup coconut. Remove cake from pan and crumble into the cream cheese mixture. Beat until combined. Using a small cookie scoop, drop mixture into 1-inch mounds onto prepared pans; freeze for 30 minutes. Roll mounds into balls. Freeze for 30 to 60 minutes more or until balls are firm.

3. In a medium saucepan heat chocolate and shortening over medium-low heat until melted and smooth, stirring occasionally. Remove from heat. Working in batches, dip balls into melted chocolate; allow excess to drip off and place balls on clean waxed paper-lined trays or baking pans. Immediately sprinkle tops of balls with coconut before chocolate is set. Let stand until chocolate is set. If chocolate in saucepan begins to set up, reheat over low heat. To store, layer cake balls between waxed paper in an airtight container. Cover and seal.

PER CAKE BALL *81 cal, 5 g fat, 10 mg chol, 66 mg sodium, 10 g carb, 1 g fiber, 1 g pro.*

Cupcakes in a Jar

The decorated jar is a festive way to deliver a cupcake, but it also protects the cupcake from being squished.

START TO FINISH 30 minutes
MAKES 12 cupcakes

1   cup (2 sticks) butter, softened
4   cups powdered sugar
¼   cup milk
1   teaspoon vanilla
12   unfrosted red velvet cupcakes (made from your favorite recipe or mix)

1. In a large mixing bowl beat butter with an electric mixer on medium to high for 30 seconds. Add 2 cups of the powdered sugar, the milk, and vanilla. Beat until smooth. Add remaining powdered sugar and beat until combined. Beat on high for 2 minutes. Place frosting in a pastry bag fitted with a large star tip or in a resealable plastic bag with one corner cut; set aside.
2. Remove paper bake cups from cupcakes if using. Cut cupcakes in half horizontally. Place bottom half of cupcakes, cut sides up, in half-pint canning jars. Pipe frosting on top of each. Add cupcake tops, cut sides down. Pipe frosting on top of each. Add lids to jars and decorate as desired.
PER CUPCAKE *482 cal, 22 g fat, 80 mg chol, 338 mg sodium, 70 g carb, 0 g fiber, 3 g pro.*

Italian Pasta Treats

Here's a completely different way to enjoy pasta—fried until it's crispy, then tossed with nuts, cheese, and seasonings.

START TO FINISH 45 minutes
MAKES 14 servings

12   ounces assorted dried bite-size pasta, such as bow ties, corkscrews, and/or wagon wheels
     Vegetable oil for deep-fat frying
1½   cups whole almonds, toasted (see tip, page 14)
3   tablespoons pine nuts, toasted (see tip, page 14)
3   tablespoons butter, melted
4   teaspoons balsamic vinegar
⅓   cup grated Romano cheese
½   teaspoon garlic salt

½   teaspoon dried Italian seasoning, crushed
½   teaspoon crushed red pepper

1. Cook pasta according to package directions; drain. Rinse with cold water; drain again. Pat pasta dry with paper towels.
2. In a heavy, deep 3-quart saucepan or fryer heat oil to 365°F. Using a spoon, carefully add cooked pasta, about ½ cup at a time, to hot oil. Fry for 30 to 60 seconds or until golden brown, stirring occasionally. Using a slotted spoon, carefully remove fried pasta from hot oil; drain on paper towels. Repeat with remaining pasta. When cool, separate any pasta that stuck together during frying.
3. In a large bowl combine fried pasta, almonds, and pine nuts. Drizzle with melted butter and vinegar; toss gently to coat. In a small bowl combine cheese, garlic salt, Italian seasoning, and crushed red pepper. Sprinkle cheese mixture over pasta mixture; toss gently to coat. Place pasta treats in box; close box.
PER SERVING *256 cal, 16 g fat, 9 mg chol, 77 mg sodium, 22 g carb, 3 g fiber, 7 g pro.*

Maple Cookie Sticks

These twice-baked cookies are similar to biscotti. They're crisp and crunchy and perfect for dipping into a cup of coffee.

PREP 30 minutes BAKE 37 minutes
COOL 1 hour OVEN 375°F/325°F
MAKES 52 cookie sticks

½   cup butter, softened
½   cup shortening
1   cup packed brown sugar
½   cup pure maple syrup
½   teaspoon baking soda
½   teaspoon salt
2   eggs
1   teaspoon maple flavoring
1   teaspoon vanilla
2   cups all-purpose flour
¾   cup finely ground pecans
1   cup miniature white baking pieces or regular white baking pieces
     Chopped pecans (optional)

1. Preheat oven to 375°F. Line a 13×9×2-inch baking pan with foil, extending the foil over edges of pan. Set aside.

2. In a large bowl beat combine butter and shortening. Beat with an electric mixer on medium to high for 30 seconds. Add brown sugar, maple syrup, baking soda, and salt. Beat until combined, scraping sides of bowl occasionally. Beat in the eggs, maple flavoring, and vanilla until combined. Beat in as much of the flour as you can with the mixer. Stir in any remaining flour and the ground pecans. Stir in white baking pieces. Press dough evenly into prepared pan. If desired, sprinkle with additional chopped pecans.
3. Bake for 25 to 28 minutes or until golden brown and center is set. Cool in pan on a wire rack for 1 hour.
4. Preheat oven to 325°F. Using the edges of the foil, gently lift cookies out of pan and place on a cutting board, leaving cookies on foil. Cut cookies crosswise into 4½×½-inch slices. Place slices, cut sides down, about 1 inch apart on an ungreased cookie sheet.
5. Bake about 12 minutes or until cut edges are crisp. Carefully transfer cookies to wire rack (cookies will be tender); cool completely.
PER COOKIE STICK *113 cal, 6 g fat, 13 mg chol, 57 mg sodium, 13 g carb, 0 g fiber, 1 g pro.*

MAPLE COOKIE STICKS

Chocolate-Dipped Almond Thins

If you're using a food processor to chop the nuts, let them cool completely before you put them in the processor bowl.

PREP 25 minutes STAND 30 minutes
BAKE 6 minutes per batch
OVEN 375°F MAKES 26 cookies

2 egg whites
½ cup very finely chopped toasted almonds and/or pecans
3 tablespoons butter, melted
½ teaspoon vanilla
½ cup sugar
½ cup flour
4 ounces semisweet or dark chocolate, melted

1. In a medium bowl let egg whites stand at room temperature for 30 minutes.
2. Preheat oven to 375°F. Line large cookie sheets with foil or parchment paper. If using foil, lightly grease the foil; set aside. In a small bowl combine almonds, butter, and vanilla; set aside.
3. Beat egg whites with an electric mixer on medium until soft peaks form (tips curl). Gradually add sugar, beating on high until stiff peaks form (tips stand straight). Fold in about half of the flour. Gently stir in almond mixture. Fold in the remaining flour until thoroughly combined.
4. For each cookie, drop 1 level tablespoon of the batter onto prepared cookie sheets, leaving 2 inches between mounds. Using the back of a spoon, spread each mound into a 2-inch circle. If necessary, coat the back of the spoon with nonstick cooking spray to prevent sticking.
5. Bake for 6 to 8 minutes or until cookies are just golden brown around edges and centers are set. Cool cookies completely on cookie sheets; lift cookies off parchment paper or foil and place on wire racks.
6. Dip each cookie halfway into melted chocolate. Use a thin metal spatula to scrape chocolate to a thin, even layer on the cookie. Place cookie on a waxed paper-lined cookie sheet and let stand until chocolate is set (if necessary, place cookies in the refrigerator to set the chocolate). Store in the refrigerator for up to 3 days.

PER COOKIE *69 cal, 4 g fat, 4 mg chol, 14 mg sodium, 9 g carb, 1 g fiber, 1 g pro.*

Pistachio-White Chocolate Pretzels

These supersimple chocolate-coated pretzel sticks are the essence of the salty-sweet treat.

START TO FINISH 20 minutes
MAKES 16 pretzels

4 ounces white baking chocolate (with cocoa butter), semisweet baking chocolate, or dark chocolate
½ cup finely chopped roasted pistachio nuts or toasted pecans
16 honey-wheat pretzel sticks
1 tablespoon snipped dried tart cherries

1. In a small saucepan heat chocolate over low heat until melted and smooth, stirring frequently. Spread pistachio nuts on a sheet of waxed paper.
2. Dip each pretzel into melted chocolate, covering about two-thirds of the pretzel. Let excess chocolate drip off. Roll dipped pretzels in pistachios to coat. Press a few cherry pieces into the chocolate on each pretzel. Place pretzels on a clean sheet of waxed paper; let stand until chocolate is set.

PER PRETZEL *79 cal, 4 g fat, 1 mg chol, 75 mg sodium, 8 g carb, 1 g fiber, 2 g pro.*

PISTACHIO-WHITE CHOCOLATE PRETZELS

Citrus Biscotti

Give these crispy cookies to the health-conscious people on your list. They're low in fat and fortified with oat bran.

PREP 30 minutes   BAKE 36 minutes
COOL 1 hour   OVEN 375°F/325°F
MAKES 28 biscotti

¼   cup butter, softened
½   cup sugar
1   teaspoon baking powder
¼   teaspoon baking soda
⅛   teaspoon salt
½   cup refrigerated or frozen egg product, thawed, or 2 eggs
½   cup oat bran
1   teaspoon finely shredded orange peel
1   teaspoon finely shredded lemon peel
1   teaspoon finely shredded lime peel
1¾ cups flour

1. Preheat oven to 375°F. Line a large cookie sheet with parchment paper; set aside. In a large mixing bowl beat butter with an electric mixer on medium for 30 seconds. Add sugar, baking powder, baking soda, and salt, beating until well combined. Beat in eggs. Beat in oat bran, orange peel, lemon peel, and lime peel. Beat in as much of the flour as you can with the mixer. Using a wooden spoon, stir in the remaining flour.

2. Divide dough in half. If necessary, cover and chill dough for 1 hour or until easy to handle. Shape each portion into an 8-inch-long log. Place logs 3 inches apart on prepared cookie sheet; flatten the logs slightly until 2 inches wide. Bake for 18 to 20 minutes or until firm and a wooden toothpick inserted near center of each log comes out clean. Cool on cookie sheet on wire rack for 1 hour.

3. Preheat oven to 325°F. Using a serrated knife, cut each log diagonally into ½-inch-thick slices. Arrange slices, cut sides down, on cookie sheet. Bake for 10 minutes; turn slices. Bake for 8 to 10 minutes more or until dry and crisp. Transfer to a wire rack; cool completely.

PER BISCOTTI *63 cal, 2 g fat, 4 mg chol, 55 mg sodium, 11 g carb, 0 g fiber, 2 g pro.*

CITRUS BISCOTTI

Cheddar and Red Pepper Wafers

A spike of crushed red pepper gives these rich cheese-and-sesame crackers a little bit of heat.

PREP 45 minutes
BAKE 8 minutes per batch
OVEN 350°F MAKES 120 wafers

2   cups all-purpose flour
1   cup sesame seeds, toasted
2   cups finely shredded sharp cheddar cheese (8 ounces)
1   tablespoon packed brown sugar
½   to 1 teaspoon red pepper flakes
¼   teaspoon salt
¼   teaspoon baking powder
½   cup butter, melted
1   egg

1. Preheat oven to 350°F. In a large mixing bowl combine flour, sesame seeds, cheddar cheese, brown sugar, red pepper flakes, salt, and baking powder. Add butter and egg and mix until blended.
2. For each wafer, shape 1 teaspoon dough into a small ball; place on parchment- or nonstick-foil-lined baking sheet and flatten to 1½-inch circle. Bake 8 to 10 minutes or until edges and bottoms are lightly browned. Cool on baking sheets 2 minutes; transfer crackers to wire racks to cool completely. Divide crackers into gift packages. Refrigerate to store.
PER WAFER *30 cal, 2 g fat, 6 mg chol, 24 mg sodium, 2 g carb, 0 g fiber, 1 g pro.*

Cinnamon Nuts

The flavor of freshly ground nutmeg is far superior to preground in a jar. Stored in a cool, dry place, whole nutmeg lasts almost indefinitely.

PREP 20 minutes BAKE 40 minutes
MAKES 6 cups OVEN 300°F

1   egg white
1   tablespoon water
1   teaspoon vanilla
1½   pounds walnut halves and/or pecan halves
1   cup sugar
2   tablespoons ground cinnamon
1   teaspoon freshly grated nutmeg or ½ teaspoon ground nutmeg

1. Preheat oven to 300°F. Grease a 15×10×1-inch baking pan; set aside. In an extra-large bowl beat together egg white, the water, and vanilla with a fork. Add nuts, tossing to coat.
2. In a small bowl combine sugar, cinnamon, and nutmeg. Sprinkle sugar mixture over nut mixture, tossing to coat. Spread nuts evenly in the prepared baking pan.
3. Bake about 40 minutes or until nuts are toasted and crisp, stirring once halfway through baking time. Spread nuts evenly on waxed paper; cool. If necessary, break into pieces.
PER ¼ CUP *221 cal, 19 g fat, 0 mg chol, 3 mg sodium, 13 g carb, 2 g fiber, 4 g pro.*

CHEDDAR AND RED PEPPER WAFERS

Apple Pie Spiced Hot Tea Mix

Holiday-theme mugs are widely available and inexpensive during this season. Pick up a few and use them to prettily package this spiced tea mix for giving.

START TO FINISH **15 minutes**
MAKES **4 spice bags (4 servings per bag)**

12 2½- to 3-inch sticks cinnamon
⅓ cup crystallized ginger
1 tablespoon whole allspice
1 tablespoon whole cloves
16 white and/or green tea bags
2 cups crisp dried apple chips* or dried apples

1. For spice bags, cut four 7- to 8-inch squares of double-thick 100%-cotton cheesecloth. Divide cinnamon sticks, crystallized ginger, allspice, and cloves among cheesecloth squares. Tie closed with clean kitchen string. Divide tea bags, apple chips, and spice bags among 4 decorative containers. For each gift, give 1 spice bag, 1 container of apple chips and tea bags, and the serving directions.

2. To serve each gift, in a medium saucepan, combine spice bag and 4 cups water. Bring to boiling; reduce heat. Cover and simmer for 20 minutes. Remove saucepan from heat. Add apple chips and tea bags to spiced water mixture. Let tea steep for 5 minutes. Remove and discard tea and spice bags. ***Tip:** Look for apple chips with no added oils or sugar.

PER SERVING *16 cal, 0 g fat, 0 mg chol, 14 mg sodium, 4 g carb, 0 g fiber, 0 g pro.*

BRACIOLE-STYLE
FLANK STEAK

new year's celebration

RING IT IN! Gather a few friends for a dine-in New Year's celebration with sophisticated fare that is surprisingly easy to make. Delicious options include crispy-fried risotto balls, creamy crab dip, short-rib ragu, chocolate-peppermint tart, and a triple-layer coconut cake. With a beginning like this, it's bound to be a very good year.

134

135

143

Fried Mushroom Risotto Balls

The risotto for these crisp-coated rice balls can be made up to 24 hours ahead.

PREP **45 minutes** CHILL **3 hours**
COOK **2 minutes per batch**
OVEN **200°F** MAKES **40 servings**

2   tablespoons vegetable or olive oil
2   tablespoons butter
4   ounces fresh cremini and/or button mushrooms, chopped
½   cup chopped onion (1 medium)
2   cloves garlic, minced
1   cup uncooked arborio rice
2   14.5-ounce cans reduced-sodium chicken broth
½   cup finely shredded Parmesan or Asiago cheese (2 ounces)
½   cup snipped fresh parsley
⅛   teaspoon black pepper
1   cup vegetable oil
2   eggs, lightly beaten
1   cup seasoned fine dry bread crumbs

1. Lightly grease a 15×10×1-inch baking pan; set aside. In a large saucepan heat 2 tablespoons oil and 1 tablespoon of the butter over medium heat. Add mushrooms, onion, and garlic. Cook until onion is tender and liquid is evaporated, stirring occasionally. Add rice; cook and stir for 2 to 3 minutes or until rice starts to brown.
2. Meanwhile, in a medium saucepan bring broth to boiling; reduce heat and simmer. Slowly add 1 cup of the broth to rice mixture, stirring constantly. Continue to cook and stir over medium heat until liquid is absorbed. Add an additional ½ cup of the broth to rice mixture, stirring constantly. Continue to cook and stir until liquid is absorbed. Add the remaining broth, ½ cup at a time, stirring constantly until liquid is absorbed (about 15 minutes.) Stir in the remaining 1 tablespoon butter, cheese, parsley, and pepper.
3. Pour rice mixture into the prepared pan, spreading evenly. Cover and chill about 1 hour or until completely chilled. Using lightly greased or wet hands, shape mixture into 1-inch balls. Return balls to the baking pan. Cover and chill about 2 hours or until balls are completely chilled.

4. In a large skillet heat 1 cup oil over medium-high heat. Roll rice balls in beaten eggs, then in bread crumbs to coat.
5. Cook rice balls, about 10 at a time, in hot oil for 2 to 3 minutes or until golden brown, carefully turning once. Using a slotted spoon, remove rice balls and drain on paper towels. Keep warm in a 200°F oven while cooking the remaining rice balls.

PER SERVING *95 cal, 7 g fat, 13 mg chol, 144 mg sodium, 6 g carb, 0 g fiber, 2 g pro.*

Saucy Spiced Apricot Meatballs

A slow cooker easily stands in for a chafing dish to keep these sweet and spicy meatballs warm for the duration of the party without drying out.

PREP **25 minutes** BAKE **15 minutes**
OVEN **350°F** MAKES **12 servings**

½   cup soft bread crumbs
2   tablespoons fat-free milk
1   egg white
¼   cup finely chopped onion
¼   cup finely snipped dried apricots
½   teaspoon salt
1   garlic, minced
¼   teaspoon ground ancho chile pepper or chili powder
6   ounces lean ground pork
6   ounces uncooked ground turkey breast
1   recipe Spiced Apricot Sauce

1. Preheat oven to 350°F. Line a 15×10×1-inch baking pan with foil; lightly grease foil. Set aside. In a medium bowl combine bread crumbs and milk. Let stand for 5 minutes. Stir in egg white, onion, dried apricots, salt, garlic, and ground chile pepper. Add ground pork and ground turkey; mix well.
2. Shape meat mixture into 24 meatballs. Place meatballs in the prepared baking pan. Bake for 15 to 20 minutes or until meatballs are cooked through (165°F). If necessary, drain meatballs on paper towels. Place meatballs in a 1½-quart slow cooker. Add Spiced Apricot Sauce; toss gently to coat. Turn cooker to warm setting or low-heat setting; keep warm for up to 2 hours. Serve meatballs with short skewers or toothpicks.
Spiced Apricot Sauce: In a small saucepan combine 1 cup apricot nectar, 2 teaspoons cornstarch, ½ teaspoon ground ancho chile pepper or chili

powder, ¼ teaspoon salt, and ¼ teaspoon ground nutmeg. Cook and stir over medium heat until thickened and bubbly. Cook and stir for 1 minute more.

PER 2 MEATBALLS *89 cal, 3 g fat, 16 mg chol, 203 mg sodium, 9 g carb, 1 g fiber, 7 g pro.*

Roasted Corn and Crab Dip

Canned crabmeat varies widely in price depending on where it comes from on the crab. Claw crabmeat, the least expensive, is perfectly fine for this dip.

PREP **25 minutes** BAKE **20 minutes**
ROAST **20 minutes** OVEN **425°F/375°F**
MAKES **10 to 12 servings**

     Nonstick cooking spray
1   cup frozen whole kernel corn, thawed
1   cup chopped red sweet pepper
2   teaspoons olive oil
1   cup cooked crabmeat or one 6-ounce can crabmeat, drained, flaked, and cartilage removed
1   cup shredded Monterey Jack cheese with jalapeño chile peppers (4 ounces)
⅓   cup mayonnaise
¼   cup sour cream
¼   cup sliced green onions (2)
¼   teaspoon freshly ground black pepper
     Broken tostada shells, toasted baguette-style French bread slices, and/or crackers

1. Preheat oven to 425°F. Lightly coat a 1-quart quiche dish or shallow baking dish with cooking spray; set aside. In a shallow baking pan combine corn and sweet pepper. Drizzle with olive oil; toss to coat. Roast, uncovered, about 20 minutes or until vegetables start to brown, stirring occasionally. Remove from oven and let cool. Reduce oven temperature to 375°F.
2. Meanwhile, in a medium bowl stir together crabmeat, cheese, mayonnaise, sour cream, green onions, and black pepper. Stir in roasted vegetables. Transfer mixture to prepared dish.
3. Bake about 20 minutes or until bubbly around edges. Serve with toasted broken tostada shells.

PER SERVING *151 cal, 12 g fat, 29 mg chol, 180 mg sodium, 5 g carb, 1 g fiber, 7 g pro.*

ROASTED CORN AND
CRAB DIP

PINEAPPLE-GINGER
PUNCH

Christmas Cider

If you want the hot cider to be clear, use an apple cider or juice that is shelf-stable, not the type that is refrigerated.

PREP 10 minutes COOK 20 minutes
MAKES 16 servings

3   cups water
4   black chai tea bags*
8   cups apple cider or apple juice
     (64 ounces)
2   cups low-calorie cranberry juice
½   cup orange juice
4   3-inch-long sticks cinnamon
3   whole cloves
     Cinnamon sticks and/or fresh
     cranberries (optional)

1. In a medium saucepan bring the water to boiling. Remove from heat. Add tea bags. Cover and let steep for 5 minutes. Discard tea bags.
2. In a 6- to 8-quart Dutch oven combine apple cider, cranberry juice, orange juice, the 4 cinnamon sticks, cloves, and the steeped tea. Bring to boiling; reduce heat. Cover and simmer for 20 minutes. Discard cinnamon sticks and cloves. Serve warm. If desired, garnish with additional cinnamon sticks and/or cranberries.

*Tip: To keep the cider from looking cloudy, be sure to purchase chai tea bags that do not contain milk solids.
PER SERVING *68 cal, 0 g fat, 0 mg chol, 6 mg sodium, 17 g carb, 0 g fiber, 0 g pro.*

Pineapple-Ginger Punch

This soda pop-free punch made with ginger syrup, pineapple juice, and club soda is refreshing and alcohol-free.

PREP 20 minutes COOL 1 hour
CHILL 2 hours MAKES 8 servings

1   cup water
½   cup sugar
⅔   cup thinly sliced unpeeled fresh
     ginger (about 4 ounces)
2½   cups unsweetened pineapple juice,
     chilled
3   tablespoons lemon juice
3   tablespoons lime juice
1   1-liter bottle club soda, chilled
     Ice cubes
     Lime slices and/or pineapple
     wedges

1. In a small saucepan combine the water, sugar, and ginger. Bring to boiling, stirring until sugar is dissolved; reduce heat. Simmer, uncovered, for 10 minutes. Cool ginger mixture to room temperature. Strain ginger mixture through a fine-mesh sieve into a bowl. Cover with plastic wrap; chill for at least 2 hours.
2. In a large punch bowl or pitcher combine the chilled ginger mixture, pineapple juice, lemon juice, and lime juice. Stir in club soda. Add ice cubes and lime slices and/or pineapple wedges.
PER SERVING *102 cal, 0 g fat, 0 mg chol, 30 mg sodium, 26 g carb, 1 g fiber, 1 g pro.*

Fruit-Filled Pork Tenderloin

Butterfly and stuff the tenderloins several hours ahead of time, then cover and refrigerate until roasting time.

PREP 35 minutes ROAST 25 minutes
STAND 40 minutes OVEN 425°F
MAKES 8 servings

½ cup ruby port wine or pomegranate juice
¾ cup golden raisins
¾ cup dried cranberries
⅔ cup dried apricots, quartered
¼ teaspoon apple pie spice
2 14- to 18-ounce pork tenderloins
½ teaspoon salt
¼ teaspoon black pepper

1. For stuffing, in a small saucepan bring port just to boiling. Remove from heat. Stir in raisins, dried cranberries, dried apricots, and apple pie spice. Cover and let stand for 15 minutes. Transfer mixture to a food processor. Cover and process for 10 to 15 seconds or until coarsely ground.
2. Make a lengthwise cut down the center of each tenderloin, cutting almost to but not through the other side. Spread open. Place each tenderloin between 2 pieces of plastic wrap. Using the flat side of a meat mallet, pound meat lightly from center to edges until slightly less than ½ inch thick. Remove plastic wrap.
3. Divide fruit filling between meat portions, spreading to within ½ inch of edges. Starting from a long side, roll up each portion into a spiral. Tie at 2-inch intervals with 100%-cotton kitchen string. Sprinkle rolls with salt and pepper.
4. Preheat oven to 425°F. Meanwhile, remove plastic wrap. Place tenderloins on a rack in a shallow roasting pan; let stand at room temperature for 15 minutes. Roast for 25 to 35 minutes or until juices run clear and an instant-read thermometer inserted into meat registers 145°F. Remove from oven. Cover loosely with foil; let stand for 10 minutes before slicing.
5. Remove and discard string. Cut tenderloins into ½-inch-thick slices.
PER SERVING 241 cal, 2 g fat, 64 mg chol, 199 mg sodium, 30 g carb, 2 g fiber, 22 g pro.

Holiday Corn Bread Stuffing

Can't decide between corn bread stuffing or traditional yeast-bread stuffing? This recipe has both.

PREP 20 minutes BAKE 45 minutes
OVEN 350°F MAKES 20 servings

½ pound unsalted butter (2 sticks)
1 onion, chopped
6 celery stalks, chopped (¼ cup chopped celery leaves reserved)
1 challah, brioche, or other soft egg bread, cut into 1-inch cubes (about 12 cups)
1 recipe Salt and Pepper Skillet Corn Bread
2 tablespoons chopped fresh sage
2 tablespoons chopped fresh marjoram
1 teaspoon sea salt
1 teaspoon dried crumbled sage
½ teaspoon freshly ground black pepper
2 cups low-sodium chicken broth
4 eggs

1. Preheat oven to 350°F. In a very large deep ovenproof skillet* melt butter over medium heat. Add the onion and celery; cook about 5 minutes, stirring occasionally, until onion is soft and golden.
2. Remove from heat. Add bread cubes, corn bread, reserved celery leaves, fresh sage, marjoram, salt, dried sage, and pepper to onion mixture; stir to combine. Add broth and eggs; stir to combine and moisten bread.
3. Bake dressing, uncovered, for 45 minutes to 1 hour or until golden brown on top. If dressing begins to brown too quickly, cover it with foil and continue to bake. Serve warm.
Salt and Pepper Skillet Corn Bread: Preheat oven to 425°F. Coat a 9- or 10-inch cast-iron skillet with 2 tablespoons bacon grease or olive oil. Heat the skillet in the oven while mixing batter. In a large bowl stir to combine 1½ cups yellow cornmeal, ½ cup all-purpose flour, ¼ cup sugar, 2 teaspoons baking powder, 1 teaspoon sea salt, 1 teaspoon black pepper, and ½ teaspoon baking soda. Stir in 2 cups well-shaken buttermilk, 2 large lightly beaten eggs, and 2 tablespoons melted unsalted butter just until combined. Batter should be lumpy; do not overmix. Pour batter into hot skillet. Bake about 25 minutes, until the top is golden brown and a wooden skewer inserted in center comes out clean. Turn corn bread out of skillet, cut into wedges, and serve warm. Or cool slightly to crumble to make Holiday Corn Bread Stuffing.
*Tip: If the skillet is not large enough to mix all the dressing ingredients, after cooking the onion and celery, use a large bowl for mixing. Either return some of the unbaked dressing to the skillet to bake or divide dressing between two 13×9×2-inch baking pans or 3-quart baking dishes. For two pans, cut baking time by about half. Center of dressing should register 165°F on an instant-read thermometer.
PER SERVING 275 cal, 15 g fat, 109 mg chol, 373 mg sodium, 28 g carb, 2 g fiber, 6 g pro.

Short Rib Ragu with Polenta Croutons

The polenta croutons are made from cubes of firm chilled polenta that are brushed with olive oil and baked on top of the casserole until crisp.

PREP 45 minutes
BAKE 3 hours 15 minutes
COOL 30 minutes CHILL 8 hours
OVEN 325°F/375°F MAKES 8 servings

3 pounds boneless beef short ribs
   Salt
   Black pepper
2 to 3 tablespoons olive oil

FRUIT-FILLED PORK TENDERLOIN

**SHORT RIB RAGU WITH
POLENTA CROUTONS**

2   onions, thinly sliced
6   garlic, minced
3   carrots, halved lengthwise and
    sliced (1½ cups)
1   cup coarsely chopped celery
    (2 stalks)
1   14.5-ounce can reduced-sodium
    beef broth
1½ cups dry red wine, such as Merlot
    or Cabernet Sauvignon
1   6-ounce can tomato paste
4   sprigs fresh thyme
1   8-ounce package cremini
    mushrooms, quartered (thickly
    slice larger caps)
1   recipe Firm Polenta
1   tablespoon snipped fresh parsley
    or basil (optional)

1. Preheat oven to 325°F. Sprinkle ribs
with salt and pepper. In a 6- to 8-quart
oven-going Dutch oven heat 1 tablespoon
of the olive oil over medium heat.
Brown ribs, half at a time if necessary,
in the hot oil, turning to brown all sides;
remove ribs and set aside. In the same

Dutch oven cook onions and garlic for
2 minutes, adding another 1 tablespoon
of the oil if needed. Add carrots and
celery; cook about 5 minutes more or
until vegetables are tender.
2. Return ribs to Dutch oven with the
vegetables. Stir in broth, wine, tomato
paste, and thyme sprigs. Bring to
boiling. Cover; bake for 1½ hours. Stir in
mushrooms. Bake, uncovered, for 45 to
60 minutes more or until ribs are tender
and sauce is slightly thickened. Cool
for 30 minutes. Discard thyme sprigs.
Season to taste with additional salt and
pepper.
3. Transfer rib mixture to a large airtight
container; cover. Chill for at least
8 hours or up to 3 days.
4. Preheat oven to 375°F. Lightly grease
a 3-quart rectangular baking dish; set
aside. Using a spoon, remove any fat
from surface of the sauce. Spoon ribs
and sauce into prepared baking dish.
If desired, cut short ribs into smaller
portions. Run a thin metal spatula
around the edges of the Firm Polenta in

the loaf pan. Remove polenta loaf from
pan and cut into 1-inch cubes. Arrange
cubes evenly over the ribs and sauce in
the baking dish. Brush the cubes with
the remaining 1 tablespoon olive oil.
5. Bake, uncovered, about 1 hour or until
ribs and sauce are heated through and
polenta is lightly browned. If desired,
sprinkle with parsley.
Firm Polenta: In a medium saucepan
bring 2½ cups water to boiling. In
a medium bowl stir together 1 cup
coarse-ground cornmeal, 1 cup cold
water, and 1 teaspoon salt. Slowly add
cornmeal mixture to the boiling water,
stirring constantly. Cook and stir until
mixture returns to boiling. Reduce
heat to medium-low. Cook for 25 to
30 minutes or until mixture is thick,
stirring frequently and adjusting heat as
needed to maintain a slow boil. Pour into
an 8×4×2-inch loaf pan. Cover; chill for at
least 8 hours or up to 3 days.
PER SERVING *593 cal, 41 g fat, 86 mg
chol, 716 mg sodium, 26 g carb, 3 g fiber,
22 g pro.*

Braciole-Style Flank Steak

Make your favorite marinara or use good-quality jarred sauce for this recipe.

PREP 45 minutes ROAST 20 minutes
STAND 15 minutes
BAKE 1 hour 30 minutes
OVEN 425°F/350°F MAKES 4 servings

- 3 yellow sweet peppers
- 1 tablespoon olive oil
- ⅓ cup diced pancetta
- ¾ cup finely chopped onion (1 medium)
- 3 cloves garlic, minced
- 1½ 10-ounce packages frozen chopped spinach, thawed, well drained, and pressed dry
- ¼ cup coarsely grated Pecorino Romano cheese
- ¼ cup dried currants
- 2 tablespoons pine nuts, toasted
- ¾ teaspoon salt
- ½ teaspoon black pepper
- 2 1½-pound beef flank steaks
- 3 tablespoons olive oil
- 1½ cups marinara sauce
- ½ cup dry red wine

1. Preheat oven to 425°F. Line a baking sheet with foil; set aside. Cut sweet peppers in half lengthwise; remove stems, seeds, and membranes. Place pepper halves, cut sides down, on prepared baking sheet. Roast for 20 to 25 minutes or until charred and very tender. Bring foil up around peppers and fold edges to enclose. Let stand about 15 minutes or until cool enough to handle. Using a sharp knife, loosen edges of the skins; gently pull off the skins in strips and discard. Cut peppers into strips; set aside.
2. In a medium saucepan heat 1½ teaspoons of the olive oil over medium-high heat. Add pancetta; cook until browned, stirring frequently. Add onion and garlic; cook and stir over medium heat for 3 minutes. Remove from heat. Add spinach, cheese, currants, pine nuts, ¼ teaspoon of the salt, and ¼ teaspoon of the black pepper.
3. Place flank steak between two pieces of plastic wrap. Using the flat side of a meat mallet, pound lightly until ½ inch thick. Remove top piece of plastic wrap. Sprinkle steak with remaining salt and black pepper.
4. Arrange sweet pepper strips lengthwise down the center of the flank steak, leaving 3 to 4 inches uncovered on both sides. Spoon spinach mixture evenly over the pepper strips.
5. Starting with a long side, use bottom plastic wrap to guide flank steak over and around filling, making a long roll. Tie roll at 1½-inch intervals with 100%-cotton kitchen string. Tuck in the ends of the roll; using a long piece of string, tie roll lengthwise.
6. Preheat oven to 350°F. In a roasting pan or braising pan heat the 3 tablespoons olive oil over medium-high heat. Add meat roll; cook until browned on all sides, turning frequently.
7. In a small saucepan combine marinara sauce and wine. Cook over low heat just until boiling. Pour sauce mixture over meat roll in roasting pan. Cover tightly. Bake about 1½ hours or until meat is fork-tender.
8. Remove meat from skillet; remove strings and cut meat into 1-inch slices. If desired, cook down the remaining sauce in the roasting pan to thicken.

PER SERVING 611 cal, 30 g fat, 70 mg chol, 1,238 mg sodium, 33 g carb, 5 g fiber, 45 g pro.

Farro Salad with Roasted Veggies

Farro is a whole grain that is related to wheat. Look for it in health food markets or specialty grocery stores.

PREP 20 minutes COOK 20 minutes
ROAST 47 minutes OVEN 400°F
MAKES 10 to 12 servings

- 1 17.6-ounce package farro (3 cups)
- ¼ cup olive oil
- 1 head cauliflower, chopped (4 cups)
- 1 pint cherry tomatoes
- 1 bunch fresh basil, chopped (1½ cups)
- ¼ teaspoon crushed red pepper
   Salt and black pepper

1. Preheat oven to 400°F. In a large saucepan bring 6 cups of salted water to boiling. Add farro; reduce heat. Cover and simmer 20 minutes or until tender; drain. Toss farro with 2 tablespoons of the olive oil; set aside to cool.
2. In a shallow baking pan toss cauliflower with 1 tablespoon of the olive oil. Roast, uncovered, for 35 minutes or until lightly browned and crisp. Add cauliflower and any pan juices to farro.
3. Add cherry tomatoes to baking pan. Roast, uncovered, 12 minutes or until the tomatoes blister and the skins begin to burst. Add tomatoes and any pan juices to farro.
4. Add basil and crushed red pepper to farro and toss to combine. Season to taste with salt and pepper. Serve at room temperature or cover and chill up to 24 hours.

PER SERVING 200 cal, 16 g fat, 6 mg chol, 474 mg sodium, 11 g carb, 3 g fiber, 4 g pro.

Spinach, Pear, and Shaved Parmesan Salad

Add the olive oil in a slow, steady stream as you whisk to emulsify and thicken the dressing.

START TO FINISH 20 minutes
MAKES 8 servings

- 8 cups fresh baby spinach
- 2 Bosc pears, quartered lengthwise, cored, and thinly sliced
- 2 ounces Parmesan or Parmigiano-Reggiano cheese, shaved
- 2 tablespoons balsamic vinegar
- 1 tablespoon whole-grain mustard
- 1 teaspoon sugar
- 1 teaspoon salt
- ¼ teaspoon freshly ground black pepper
- ½ cup extra virgin olive oil

1. Combine spinach, pears, and cheese. For dressing whisk together vinegar, mustard, sugar, salt, and pepper. Whisk in oil. Drizzle on salad and pass remaining.

PER SERVING 200 cal, 16 g fat, 6 mg chol, 474 mg sodium, 11 g carb, 3 g fiber, 4 g pro.

FARRO SALAD WITH ROASTED VEGGIES

SPINACH, PEAR, AND
SHAVED PARMESAN
SALAD

WILD RICE, BARLEY,
AND DRIED CHERRY
PILAF

PECAN-TOPPED APPLES
AND CARROTS

Pecan-Topped Apples and Carrots

Fuji, McIntosh, and Winesap apples are good choices for making this vegetable-and-fruit side dish.

PREP **20 minutes** COOK **9 minutes**
MAKES **8 servings**

4   carrots, peeled and cut into bite-size strips
4   teaspoons butter
4   red-skin cooking apples, quartered, cored, and thinly sliced
2   teaspoons grated fresh ginger
¼   teaspoon salt
2   tablespoons white wine vinegar
¼   cup finely chopped pecans, toasted (see tip, page 14)
2   tablespoons snipped fresh parsley

1. In a large skillet cook carrots, covered, in a small amount of boiling water for 5 minutes. Drain off liquid.
2. Add butter to carrots in skillet. Add apples, ginger, and salt. Cook, uncovered, over medium heat for 4 to 6 minutes or until carrots and apples are just tender, stirring occasionally. Add vinegar and toss to coat. Transfer to a serving dish. In a small bowl stir together pecans and parsley. Sprinkle over carrots and apples.
PER SERVING *102 cal, 5 g fat, 5 mg chol, 109 mg sodium, 16 g carb, 3 g fiber, 1 g pro.*

Wild Rice, Barley, and Dried Cherry Pilaf

Be sure to use regular, not quick-cooking, barley for this recipe. The long cooking time would turn quick barley to mush.

PREP **10 minutes** COOK **10 minutes**
BAKE **1 hour** OVEN **325°F**
MAKES **6 to 8 servings**

¾   cup uncooked wild rice
2   14.5-ounce cans chicken broth
¾   cup regular barley
½   cup snipped dried cherries, apricots, and/or dried cranberries
¾   teaspoon dried marjoram or dried oregano, crushed
2   tablespoons butter
⅓   cup coarsely chopped pecans, toasted
    Salt and black pepper

1. Preheat oven to 325°F. Place rice in a pan of warm water, stir, and remove particles that float to the top. Drain and rinse again.
2. In a saucepan combine rice and chicken broth. Bring to boiling; reduce heat. Cover and simmer for 10 minutes. Remove from heat. Stir in barley, cherries, marjoram, and butter. Spoon into a 1½-quart casserole.
3. Bake, covered, for 60 to 65 minutes or until rice and barley are tender and liquid is absorbed, stirring once. Fluff rice mixture with a fork; stir in pecans. Season to taste with salt and pepper.
PER SERVING *279 cal, 9 g fat, 12 mg chol, 658 mg sodium, 44 g carb, 7 g fiber, 8 g pro.*

Clam Chowder with Parmigiano-Reggiano Cheese

For a casual New Year's supper with friends, serve some crusty rolls and a crisp green salad with this rich soup.

PREP **25 minutes** COOK **45 minutes**
MAKES **8 to 10 servings**

1½ pints shucked clams or three 6.5-ounce cans minced clams
6   slices bacon, halved crosswise
1½ cups chopped onions (3 medium)
¾   cup finely chopped celery (3 stalks)
½   cup dry white wine
3   cups chopped, peeled potatoes (3 large)
2   teaspoons instant chicken bouillon granules
1½ teaspoons snipped fresh thyme
¼   teaspoon black pepper
¼   teaspoon crushed red pepper
3   cups milk
1½ cups whipping cream
3   tablespoons all-purpose flour
¾   cup shredded Parmigiano-Reggiano cheese or Parmesan cheese (3 ounces)
    Snipped fresh parsley (optional)
    Shredded Parmigiano-Reggiano cheese or Parmesan cheese (optional)

1. If using, chop fresh clams, reserving juice; set clams aside. Strain clam juice to remove bits of shell. (Or drain canned clams, reserving the juice.) If necessary, add enough water to the reserved clam juice to make 1½ cups total liquid; set aside.

2. In a 4-quart Dutch oven cook bacon until crisp. Remove bacon, reserving 2 tablespoons drippings in pan. Drain bacon on paper towels; crumble bacon and set aside. Add onions and celery to bacon drippings; cook and stir over medium heat until tender.
3. Stir in wine; bring to boiling. Boil gently, uncovered, for 2 to 3 minutes. Stir the reserved clam juice, potatoes, bouillon granules, thyme, black pepper, and crushed red pepper into Dutch oven. Bring to boiling; reduce heat. Simmer, covered, about 15 minutes or until potatoes are tender. With the back of a fork, mash potatoes slightly against side of pan.
4. In a medium bowl stir together milk, whipping cream, and flour; add to potato mixture. Bring to a simmer; cook and stir until slightly thickened. Stir in clams and the ¾ cup cheese. Reduce heat. Cook and stir for 1 to 2 minutes more or until heated through and cheese is melted. Sprinkle each serving with crumbled bacon and, if desired, parsley and additional cheese.
PER SERVING *438 cal, 27 g fat, 113 mg chol, 583 mg sodium, 24 g carb, 2 g fiber, 22 g pro.*

CLAM CHOWDER WITH PARMIGIANO-REGGIANO CHEESE

Bacon-Cracked Pepper Biscuits

You can buy cracked pepper—or turn your grinder to the coarsest setting.

PREP 15 minutes   BAKE 10 minutes
OVEN 450°F   MAKES 12 biscuits

3   cups all-purpose flour
1   tablespoon baking powder
1   tablespoon sugar
1   teaspoon cracked black pepper
¾   teaspoon cream of tartar
½   teaspoon salt
¾   cup butter or ½ cup butter and
      ¼ cup shortening
1¼   cups buttermilk or sour milk* or
      1 cup milk
¼   cup bacon, crisp-cooked and
      crumbled (4 slices)
¼   cup shredded cheddar or white
      cheddar cheese (1 ounce)
      (optional)
1   strip bacon, crisp-cooked and
      crumbled (optional)

1. Preheat oven to 450°F. In a large bowl combine flour, baking powder, sugar, pepper, cream of tartar, and salt. Using a pastry blender, cut in butter until mixture resembles coarse crumbs. Make a well in the center of the flour mixture. Add buttermilk and the ¼ cup bacon all at once. Using a fork, stir just until mixture is moistened.
2. Turn dough out onto a lightly floured surface. Knead dough by folding and gently pressing for 4 to 6 strokes or just until dough is nearly smooth. Pat or lightly roll dough until ¾ inch thick. Cut dough with a floured 2½-inch biscuit cutter; reroll scraps as necessary. Dip cutter into flour between cuts. Place dough circles 1 inch apart on an ungreased baking sheet.
3. If desired, sprinkle biscuits with cheese and the 1 strip crumbled bacon. Bake for 10 to 14 minutes or until golden. Serve warm.
*Tip: To make 1¼ cups sour milk, place 4 teaspoons lemon juice or vinegar in a glass measuring cup. Add enough milk to make 1¼ cups total liquid; stir. Let stand for 5 minutes before using.
PER BISCUIT *246 cal, 13 g fat, 34 mg chol, 359 mg sodium, 27 g carb, 1 g fiber, 5 g pro.*

Peppermint Cream Tart

This peppermint tart is perfect for entertaining; it can be made up to 48 hours ahead.

PREP 35 minutes   BAKE 8 minutes
COOL 30 minutes   CHILL 4 hours
OVEN 350°F   MAKES 10 slices

2   cups crushed chocolate wafer
      cookies (about 38)
⅓   cup butter, melted
1   cup sugar
3   tablespoons cornstarch
2¼   cups whole milk
½   cup butter, cut up
¼   teaspoon salt
½   teaspoon vanilla
½   teaspoon peppermint extract
½   cup coarsely crushed peppermint
      candies
1   recipe Peppermint Whipped Cream
      Crushed peppermint candies
      (optional)

1. Preheat oven to 350°F. In a medium bowl stir together crushed cookies and the melted butter; press onto the bottom and up the sides of a 10-inch fluted tart pan with a removable bottom. Bake for 8 to 10 minutes or until set. Cool completely on a wire rack.
2. In a medium saucepan combine the sugar and cornstarch. Stir in milk, the cut-up butter, and salt. Cook and stir over medium heat until thickened and bubbly; reduce heat. Cook and stir for 2 minutes more. Remove from heat. Stir in vanilla and peppermint extract. Stir in the ½ cup crushed peppermint candies just until combined.
3. Pour filling into cooled crust. Cool on a wire rack for 30 minutes. Place tart on a platter. Cover; chill for 4 to 24 hours.
4. Using a small sharp knife, gently loosen edge of tart from sides of pan; remove sides from pan. Cut tart into wedges. Serve with Peppermint Whipped Cream and, if desired, additional crushed peppermint candies. Cover and store leftover tart in the refrigerator; serve within 48 hours.
Peppermint Whipped Cream: In a medium mixing bowl combine 1 cup whipping cream, 2 tablespoons powdered sugar, and ¼ teaspoon peppermint extract. Beat with an electric mixer on medium to high until stiff peaks form (tips stand straight).
PER SLICE *485 cal, 29 g fat, 80 mg chol, 335 mg sodium, 53 g carb, 1 g fiber, 4 g pro.*

Triple-Layer Coconut Cake with Lime Cream

To make fresh coconut curls, separate coconut meat from the shell in large pieces. Use a vegetable peeler to thinly slice the coconut. Bake in a single layer for 3 to 5 minutes in a 350°F oven or until slices start to brown.

PREP 45 minutes   STAND 30 minutes
BAKE 15 minutes   OVEN 350°F
COOL 10 minutes   MAKES 12 servings

4   eggs
2   cups all-purpose flour
2   teaspoons baking powder
½   teaspoon salt
2   cups sugar
1   cup unsweetened coconut milk or
      milk
¼   cup butter
2   teaspoons vanilla
½   teaspoon coconut extract
      (optional)
¾   cup flaked coconut, toasted
1   recipe Lime Cream or two 10-ounce
      jars purchased lime, lemon, or
      orange curd
1   recipe Creamy Rich Frosting
      Fresh coconut curls

1. Allow eggs to stand at room temperature for 30 minutes. Meanwhile, preheat oven to 350°F. Grease and lightly flour two 9×1½-inch round cake pans; set aside. In a small bowl stir together flour, baking powder, and salt; set aside.

BACON-CRACKED PEPPER BISCUITS

2. In a large bowl beat eggs with an electric mixer on high about 4 minutes or until thick and lemon colored. Gradually add sugar, beating on medium for 4 to 5 minutes or until light and fluffy. Add flour mixture; beat on low to medium just until combined.

3. In a small saucepan combine coconut milk and butter. Cook and stir over medium heat until butter is melted. Stir in vanilla and, if desired, coconut extract. Add warm milk mixture to egg mixture; beat until combined. Stir in coconut. Divide batter into thirds. Pour one-third (about 2 cups) batter into each of the 2 prepared pans, spreading evenly. Chill remaining one-third batter.

4. Bake for 15 to 18 minutes or until a toothpick inserted in centers comes out clean. Cool in pans on wire racks for 10 minutes. Remove from pans; cool completely on racks.

5. Wash and dry one of the pans. Repeat baking with the remaining one-third batter. (Cover the first layers while you bake remaining layer to keep moist.)

6. To assemble, spread 2 layers with the Lime Cream. Stack layers, cream sides up, on a serving plate. Place remaining cake layer on top. Frost top and sides of cake with Creamy Rich Frosting. Garnish with coconut curls.

Lime Cream: In a medium saucepan stir together 1 cup sugar and 2 tablespoons cornstarch. Stir in 1 tablespoon finely shredded lime peel, 6 tablespoons lime juice, and 6 tablespoons whipping cream. Cook and stir over medium heat until thickened and bubbly. Stir half of the lime mixture into 6 beaten egg yolks. Return egg yolk mixture to saucepan. Cook, stirring constantly, over medium heat until mixture comes to a gentle boil. Cook and stir for 2 minutes more. Remove from heat. Add ½ cup butter, cut up, stirring until melted. If desired, stir in 1 or 2 drops green food coloring. Remove from heat. Cover surface with plastic wrap. Chill for at least 1 hour.

Creamy Rich Frosting: In a large bowl beat 1½ cups powdered sugar, one 8-ounce carton sour cream, 1 cup whipping cream, 1 teaspoon vanilla, and, if desired, ½ teaspoon finely shredded lime, lemon, or orange peel with an electric mixer on medium until frosting is thickened and soft peaks form (tips curl).

PER SERVING *708 cal, 37 g fat, 253 mg chol, 316 mg sodium, 89 g carb, 2 g fiber, 8 g pro.*

TRIPLE-LAYER
COCONUT CAKE WITH
LIME CREAM

PEPPERMINT
CREAM TART

MILK CHOCOLATE
TOFFEE BARS

just a few friends

COMPANY'S COMING Open your door to holiday house guests with complete confidence. These quick-to-fix dishes—soups, sandwiches, salads, breads, and sweets—will please even the pickiest eaters. They allow you to feed your guests with grace and style so you can relax and enjoy the pleasure of their company.

146

147

151

POTLUCK
CHOUCROUTE
GARNI

Creamy Chicken Noodle Soup

A small amount of cream cheese gives this slow-cooker soup its creaminess.

PREP 25 minutes COOK 6 hours (low) or 3 hours + 20 minutes (high)
MAKES 8 servings

1   32-ounce container reduced-sodium chicken broth
3   cups water
2½ cups chopped cooked chicken (about 12 ounces)
1½ cups sliced carrots (3 medium)
1½ cups sliced celery (3 stalks)
1½ cups mushrooms, sliced (4 ounces)
¼   cup chopped onion
1½ teaspoons dried thyme, crushed
¾   teaspoon garlic pepper
3   ounces reduced-fat cream cheese (Neufchâtel), cut up
2   cups dried egg noodles

1. In a 5- to 6-quart slow cooker combine chicken broth, the water, chicken, carrots, celery, mushrooms, onion, thyme, and garlic pepper.
2. Cover and cook on low-heat setting for 6 to 8 hours or on high-heat setting for 3 to 4 hours.
3. If using low-heat setting, turn cooker to high-heat setting. Stir in cream cheese. Stir in uncooked noodles. Cover and cook for 20 to 30 minutes more or just until noodles are tender.
PER SERVING *170 cal, 6 g fat, 54 mg chol, 401 mg sodium, 11 g carb, 2 g fiber, 17 g pro.*

Potluck Choucroute Garni

Serve this Alsatian specialty with white wine, beer, or sparkling cider.

PREP 45 minutes
BAKE 1 hour 5 minutes OVEN 350°F
MAKES 12 servings

1   tablespoon olive oil or vegetable oil
1   red onion, cut into very thin wedges
4   cloves garlic, minced
1   12-ounce bottle ale or beer
1½ cups apple juice, apple cider, or chicken broth
3   tablespoons cornstarch
3   tablespoons coarse-grain brown mustard
1   tablespoon caraway seeds
1   tablespoon snipped fresh rosemary
½   teaspoon cracked black pepper

Chicken and Sweet Potato-Stuffed Manicotti

Orange-flesh sweet potatoes—commonly called yams—are the best choice for this stuffed pasta dish.

PREP 40 minutes
COOK 30 minutes BAKE 45 minutes
OVEN 350°F MAKES 6 servings

1½ pounds sweet potatoes
¼   cup half-and-half, light cream, or whipping cream
2   tablespoons butter
2   tablespoons chopped fresh ginger
6   cloves garlic, sliced
½   teaspoon salt
¼   teaspoon black pepper
1½ cups chopped cooked chicken
12 dried manicotti shells
1   10-ounce carton savory garlic cream cheese for cooking
¼   cup milk
¼   cup grated Pecorino Romano cheese or Parmesan cheese
1   tablespoon snipped fresh chives or chopped green onion

1. Preheat oven to 350°F. For filling, in a large saucepan cook sweet potatoes, covered, in enough boiling water to cover about 30 minutes or until tender; drain. Cool slightly; peel. Return sweet potatoes to saucepan. Mash with a potato masher.
2. Meanwhile, in a small saucepan combine half-and-half, butter, ginger, and garlic; bring to boiling. Remove from heat. Cover and let stand for 15 minutes. Strain through a fine-mesh sieve; discard solids. Stir half-and-half mixture, salt, and pepper into mashed sweet potatoes. Stir in chicken; cover and set aside.
3. Cook manicotti according to package directions. Rinse with cold water; drain well. Lightly grease a 3-quart rectangular baking dish; set aside.
4. Using a small spoon, stuff each manicotti with a scant ⅓ cup of the filling. Place in the prepared dish. In a small bowl combine cream cheese for cooking and milk; spoon over manicotti. Sprinkle with cheese. Cover with foil.
5. Bake, covered, about 45 minutes or until heated through. Sprinkle with chives.
PER SERVING *420 cal, 14 g fat, 70 mg chol, 713 mg sodium, 53 g carb, 4 g fiber, 22 g pro.*

12 ounces fingerling potatoes or tiny new potatoes, quartered

3 carrots, sliced

2 7.5-ounce packages cooked smoked boneless pork chops, cut into bite-size pieces

1 pound cooked smoked kielbasa, halved lengthwise and bias-sliced into 1-inch pieces

2 cooking apples, such as Granny Smith or Jonagold, cored and cut into chunks

1 14-ounce can sauerkraut, rinsed and squeezed dry
Coarse-grain brown mustard (optional)

1. Preheat oven to 350°F. In a medium saucepan heat oil over medium heat. Add onion and garlic and cook about 4 minutes or until tender. Stir in ale. In a medium bowl stir together apple juice, cornstarch, the 3 tablespoons mustard, the caraway seeds, rosemary, and pepper; stir into onion-ale mixture. Cook and stir until thickened and bubbly. Cool for 10 minutes.

2. Meanwhile, in a large saucepan cook potatoes and carrots, covered, in a large amount of boiling lightly salted water about 10 minutes or until slightly tender but still firm. Drain; set aside.

3. In a 3-quart rectangular baking dish layer pork chops, kielbasa, potato-carrot mixture, apples, and sauerkraut. Spoon apple juice-onion mixture evenly over sauerkraut.

4. Bake, covered, for 65 to 70 minutes or until potatoes are tender and center is hot. If desired, serve with additional mustard.

PER SERVING *289 cal, 15 g fat, 49 mg chol, 654 mg sodium, 23 g carb, 3 g fiber, 14 g pro.*

Antipasto Italian Panini

When the crowd is small and casual, these toasty grilled sandwiches make a lovely supper. Wrap them in parchment or waxed paper to serve if you like.

PREP **20 minutes** GRILL **12 minutes** MAKES **4 servings**

1 9- to 10-inch focaccia (about 1 pound)

2 tablespoons butter, softened

¼ cup olive tapenade and/or pesto

4 ounces sliced provolone cheese

3 ounces sliced salami

3 ounces sliced coppocola

4 pepperoncini

6 fresh basil leaves

1. Cut focaccia in half horizontally. If necessary, trim off the top and bottom of the focaccia halves to make each half about ¾ inch thick. Butter the outside of the focaccia halves. Spread insides of focaccia halves with tapenade. Place half of the provolone on 1 of the focaccia halves. Top with salami, coppocola, pepperoncini, and basil leaves. Top with remaining provolone and remaining focaccia half.

2. Arrange medium-hot coals around the outside edge of a charcoal grill. Test for medium heat in the center of the grill. Place sandwich on a grill rack in the center of the grill. Place a baking sheet on top of the sandwich and weight it with two bricks. Cover and grill 12 to 16 minutes, turning once, or until bread is golden brown and cheese melts. (For a gas grill, preheat grill. Reduce heat to medium. Adjust for indirect grilling. Place sandwich on a grill rack away from heat. Grill as above.) To serve, cut in wedges.

PER SERVING *604 cal, 35 g fat, 78 mg chol, 1,912 mg sodium, 51 g carb, 3 g fiber, 25 g pro.*

ANTIPASTO ITALIAN PANINI

Brandy-Soaked Currant, Thyme, and Parmesan Scones

If you don't have a food processor, in a large bowl use a pastry blender to cut the butter into the flour mixture until the mixture resembles coarse crumbs.

PREP 25 minutes STAND 15 minutes
CHILL 30 minutes BAKE 20 minutes
OVEN 375°F MAKES 8 scones

½   cup dried currants
¼   cup brandy or apple juice
1¾ cups all-purpose flour
¾   cup finely shredded Parmigiano-Reggiano cheese (3 ounces)
1   tablespoon baking powder
1   tablespoon sugar
1   tablespoon finely snipped fresh thyme
1   teaspoon freshly ground black pepper
½   teaspoon salt
¼   cup cold butter, cut into small pieces
⅔   cup whipping cream
1   egg
1   tablespoon water

1. Line a baking sheet with parchment paper; set aside.
2. In a small saucepan combine currants and brandy. Heat over medium heat just until warm. Remove from heat. Cover and let stand for 15 minutes. Drain.

3. In a food processor combine flour, ½ cup of the cheese, the baking powder, sugar, thyme, pepper, and salt; cover and pulse with several on/off turns to combine. Sprinkle butter pieces over flour mixture; cover and pulse with several on/off turns until mixture resembles coarse crumbs. Add drained currants; cover and pulse with several on/off turns to combine. With the motor running, slowly add whipping cream through the feed tube, processing just until combined.
4. Turn out dough onto a lightly floured surface. Quickly knead dough by folding and gently pressing for 10 to 12 strokes or just until dough holds together. Pat or lightly roll the dough to an 8-inch circle, about ¾ inch thick. In a small bowl whisk together egg and the water; brush over dough circle. Sprinkle with the remaining ¼ cup cheese. Using a pizza cutter or floured sharp knife, cut dough circle into 8 wedges. Cover and chill for 30 minutes.
5. Preheat oven to 375°F. Bake about 20 minutes or until golden. Serve warm.
PER SCONE *311 cal, 16 g fat, 75 mg chol, 467 mg sodium, 31 g carb, 1 g fiber, 7 g pro.*

Roasted Broccoli and Tomatoes

Roasting the broccoli gives it a wonderfully crisp exterior. The tomatoes roast just long enough to soften and turn juicy.

PREP 20 minutes ROAST 15 minutes
OVEN 450°F MAKES 6 servings

6   cups broccoli florets (12 ounces)
¼   cup coarsely chopped shallots
2   tablespoons olive oil
2   teaspoons snipped fresh thyme
¼   teaspoon salt
¼   teaspoon black pepper
2   cups cherry or grape tomatoes, halved
2   cloves garlic, minced
¼   cup shaved Asiago cheese (1 ounce)

1. Preheat oven to 450°F. Lightly grease a 15×10×1-inch baking pan. In the prepared pan combine broccoli and shallots. In a small bowl combine oil, thyme, salt, and pepper. Drizzle oil mixture over broccoli and shallots; toss gently to coat.

2. Roast, uncovered, for 10 minutes, stirring once. Stir in tomatoes and garlic. Roast, uncovered, for 5 to 10 minutes more or until broccoli is crisp-tender and tomatoes are soft. Sprinkle each serving with cheese.
PER SERVING *107 cal, 6 g fat, 5 mg chol, 183 mg sodium, 10 g carb, 3 g fiber, 5 g pro.*

Bruschetta Biscuits with Feta

Serve these Mediterranean-inspired biscuits alongside bowls of your favorite minestrone or Italian wedding soup.

PREP 30 minutes BAKE 15 minutes
OVEN 425°F MAKES 9 servings

¾   cup milk
⅓   cup olive oil
1   cup fresh baby spinach leaves, chopped
¼   cup fresh basil leaves, chopped
¼   cup dried tomatoes (not oil packed), chopped
¼   cup pitted kalamata olives, chopped
2   cups all-purpose flour
2   teaspoons baking powder
½   teaspoon salt
3   tablespoons crumbled feta cheese
1   tablespoon pine nuts

1. Preheat oven to 425°F. Line a baking sheet with parchment paper. In a bowl combine milk, oil, spinach, basil, tomatoes, and olives. In a large bowl combine flour, baking powder, and salt. Make a well in center of flour mixture. Add milk mixture all at once; with a fork, stir until moistened.
2. Gently knead dough on a lightly floured surface until dough holds together. Pat into an 8×8-inch square. Cut into 9 squares.
3. Place biscuits 1 inch apart on prepared baking sheet. Brush lightly with milk. Sprinkle with feta cheese and pine nuts. Bake 15 minutes or until golden. Cool slightly before serving.
PER SERVING *210 cal, 11 g fat, 5 mg chol, 332 mg sodium, 24 g carb, 1 g fiber, 5 g pro.*

BRANDY-SOAKED CURRANT, THYME, AND PARMESAN SCONES

BRUSCHETTA BISCUITS
WITH FETA

Wilted Spinach Salad with Pears and Cranberries

Blue cheese and dried cranberries dress up a classic wilted spinach salad for the holidays.

START TO FINISH **35 minutes**
MAKES **6 servings**

2 medium pears, cored and thinly sliced
2 tablespoons lemon juice
12 cups packaged fresh baby spinach or torn spinach (12 ounces)
¾ cup thinly sliced red onion
   Dash ground black pepper (optional)

4 slices bacon
   Vegetable oil (optional)
½ cup dried cranberries
⅓ cup red wine vinegar
1 tablespoon sugar
½ teaspoon dry mustard
   Gorgonzola cheese, crumbled (optional)
   Dried cranberries (optional)

1. Place pears in a bowl; drizzle with lemon juice. Fill bowl with enough water to cover pears. Place a small plate over pears to submerge pears; set aside. In a large bowl combine spinach and red onion. If desired, sprinkle with pepper; set aside.
2. For dressing, in a Dutch oven cook bacon until crisp. Remove bacon, reserving ¼ cup drippings in Dutch oven. (If necessary, add enough oil to equal ¼ cup.) Crumble bacon; set aside. Stir the ½ cup cranberries, the vinegar, sugar, and mustard into drippings in Dutch oven. Bring to boiling; remove from heat. Add spinach mixture. Toss mixture in skillet for 30 to 60 seconds or just until spinach is wilted.
3. Transfer spinach mixture to a large bowl. Add bacon; toss to combine. Divide spinach mixture among 6 salad plates; drain pears and arrange on top of spinach mixture. If desired, sprinkle with Gorgonzola cheese and additional cranberries.
PER SERVING *214 cal, 11 g fat, 14 mg chol, 225 mg sodium, 25 g carb, 5 g fiber, 5 g pro.*

Milk Chocolate-Toffee Bars

These bars are simple to make but, thanks to pecans and toffee, seem like special-occasion treats.

PREP 25 minutes BAKE 25 minutes
STAND 5 minutes OVEN 350°F
MAKES 36 bars

2   cups all-purpose flour
1   cup packed brown sugar
½   teaspoon ground cinnamon
1   cup butter, softened
1   teaspoon vanilla
¾   cup chopped pecans
1   cup milk chocolate pieces
½   cup toffee pieces

1. Preheat oven to 350°F. Line a 13×9×2-inch baking pan with foil, extending foil over the edges of the pan. Grease foil; set pan aside.
2. In a large mixing bowl stir together flour, brown sugar, and cinnamon. Add butter and vanilla. Beat with an electric mixer on low until mixture resembles coarse crumbs. Stir in pecans and ½ cup of the milk chocolate pieces. Press mixture evenly into the bottom of the prepared pan.
3. Bake for 25 to 30 minutes or until golden brown. Sprinkle bars with the remaining ½ cup milk chocolate pieces; let stand on a wire rack for 5 minutes to soften. Using a table knife, swirl the chocolate pieces and spread a thin layer of chocolate over the bars. Immediately sprinkle with the toffee pieces. Cool completely in pan on a wire rack. Use foil to lift uncut bars out of pan. Cut into bars.

PER BAR *151 cal, 9 g fat, 17 mg chol, 55 mg sodium, 16 g carb, 1 g fiber, 1 g pro.*

Triple-Citrus Pound Cake

Buttery and moist, this shapely cake is infused with the flavors of grapefruit, lime, and orange.

PREP 20 minutes BAKE 40 minutes
COOL 10 minutes OVEN 350°F
MAKES 16 servings

½   cup milk
2   teaspoons finely shredded grapefruit peel
2   teaspoons finely shredded lime peel
2   teaspoons finely shredded orange peel
1   tablespoon grapefruit juice
1½   cups sugar
1¼   cups butter, softened
3   eggs
1   teaspoon vanilla
2¼   cups all-purpose flour
¾   teaspoon baking powder
½   teaspoon baking soda
¼   teaspoon salt
2   tablespoons butter, melted
1   to 2 tablespoons orange juice
¾   cup powdered sugar
     Finely shredded grapefruit peel, lime peel, and/or orange peel (optional)

1. Preheat oven to 350°F. Grease and flour a 10-inch fluted tube pan; set aside.
2. In a small bowl combine milk, the 2 teaspoons grapefruit peel, the 2 teaspoons lime peel, the 2 teaspoons orange peel, and the grapefruit juice. Mix well.
3. In a large bowl combine sugar and the 1¼ cups butter. Beat with an electric mixer on medium until light and fluffy.
Add eggs, one at a time, beating well after each addition. Stir in vanilla.
4. In a medium bowl combine flour, baking powder, baking soda, and salt. Alternately add flour mixture and milk mixture to butter mixture, beating just until moistened after each addition.
5. Spread batter into prepared pan. Bake for 40 to 45 minutes or until a toothpick inserted near the center of the cake comes out clean. Cool in pan on a wire rack for 10 minutes. Remove cake from pan; cool completely on wire rack.
6. To serve, in a small bowl combine the 2 tablespoons melted butter and 1 tablespoon of the orange juice. Add powdered sugar; beat until smooth. If necessary, add enough of the remaining 1 tablespoon orange juice to make drizzling consistency. Drizzle over cake. If desired, sprinkle with additional grated peel.

PER SERVING *319 cal, 17 g fat, 82 mg chol, 228 mg sodium, 39 g carb, 1 g fiber, 3 g pro.*

TRIPLE-CITRUS POUND CAKE

holiday menus

GO-TO GUIDES Think of these menus as kits—little packets that provide everything you need to shine at holiday festivities that revolve around food (and what holiday gathering doesn't?). With these carefully chosen menus, there's no need to worry about what goes with what. Just choose the right menu for the occasion and you're good to go.

menu 1

A Day in the Snow

After an afternoon of sledding and building snowpeople, this hearty fare will warm cold toes and fill empty tummies.

Honey-Mulled Apple Cider, page 39

Creamy Chicken Noodle Soup, page 146

Bacon and Dried Tomato Scones, page 64

Wilted Spinach Salad with Pears and Cranberries, page 150

Roasted Broccoli and Tomatoes, page 148

Chocolate Revel S'mores Tart, page 82

menu 2

Deck the Halls

Decorate the house for the holidays, then settle in and admire your handiwork while enjoying this simple, easy-to-fix supper.

Turkey Breast Stuffed with Sausage, Fennel, and Figs, page 10

Bacon-Topped Green Bean Casserole, page 18

Easy Pommes Anna-Style Casserole, 21

Spinach, Pear, and Shaved Parmesan Salad, page 138

Triple-Citrus Pound Cake, page 151

menu 3

St. Nick's PJ Breakfast

Open gifts on Christmas morning, then enjoy this yummy breakfast in your bunny slippers and robe.

Lemon Breakfast Parfaits, page 54

Sugared Bacon-Wrapped Sausages, page 46

Greek-Style Frittata, page 42

Cranberry-Buttermilk Muffins, page 48

Orange-Honey Sweet Rolls, 66

Iced Caramel-Cream Coffee, 55

menu 4

Holiday Sing-Along

Gather around the piano with a few friends and fuel the music with this sampling of savory nibbles.

Saucy Spiced Apricot Meatballs, page 134

Creamy Fennel and Leek Dip, page 36

Mini Gruyère Puffs, page 32

Antipasto Platter with Tomato Chutney, page 35

Marinated Feta, page 36

Christmas Cider, page 135

menu 5

Big-Screen Tailgating

Take in the big game with friends in the comfort of your own home, fortified by this festive finger food.

menu 6

Cookies to Share

Show your neighbors, teachers, mail carrier—and others who make your life better—how much you appreciate them.